Live the
LIGHT

Five Weeks to a Life that Shines

Live the
LIGHT

Five Weeks to a Life that Shines

LARRY DAVIES

Live the LIGHT: Five Weeks to a Life that Shines
Copyright ©2007 Larry Davies. All rights reserved.

Published by ABM Enterprises, Inc.
t/a The Amelia Bulletin Monitor
Amelia Court House, Virginia

Editor: Sandra Davis Mick
Cover and Interior Design: Davis Mick Design, Lynchburg, Va.
Cover Photo (lighthouse): Philip Gatward/Alamy

Requests for information, including reprint requests:
Sowing Seeds Ministry
Timberlake United Methodist Church
21649 Timberlake Road
Lynchburg, VA 24502
www.SowingSeedsofFaith.com

ISBN-13: 978-0-9656688-4-2
ISBN-10: 0-9656688-4-3

ACKNOWLEDGMENTS

I am thankful ...

For my church. *Live the LIGHT: Five Weeks to a Life that Shines,* may bear my name as author, but this book is more about God's impact on the church I serve. The "Live the LIGHT" concept was a team project created by the people of Timberlake United Methodist Church, who gave their hearts, minds and souls to God. Their enthusiasm and encouragement are inspiring. For them I am eternally grateful and to them, especially, I proudly dedicate this book.

For my staff, past and present, who dreamed up an inspired vision for our church that eventually became the title of this book. Every Wednesday we share ideas, learn new ways to serve, and seek God's will for our ministry. They have provided more encouragement, creativity, leadership and hard work than any pastor has a right to expect.

For our many church leaders and volunteers who devote countless hours of labor — away from their jobs and families — to carry out our numerous church ministries and projects. The number of volunteers we depend on is staggering. Thanks to their efforts, Timberlake UMC makes a real difference in the lives of people in our community and around the world.

For those who have inspired me. For the churches that nurtured me, the many people who encouraged me. They made a difference in my life and I am keenly aware of their significance. I pray that, in this book, I will pass on a little of what they so generously gave to me.

For Sandra Davis Mick, who spent countless hours turning my words and ramblings into a coherent book. Sandra's gifts and creativity are simply amazing. Her hard work and dedication to this project will help many learn to "Live the LIGHT" and make a greater commitment to God.

For my family, who inspire me and put up with me. My son, Stephen, now works as an Activities Director in a nursing home and yes, he still writes and performs rap. My daughter, Lisa, works for a local attorney and is preparing to attend graduate school. My sister, Kathy, lives in Virginia Beach with her husband, Greg, and their two sons, Joe and Bob. They are active members of the church where I grew up. My mother, Martha, also lives in Virginia Beach. She is an active Bible study teacher and volunteers at CBN.

For my wife, Mell, who continues to be an incredible light in my life. She's been my rock through most of my years as pastor. As a gifted elementary school teacher, she has influenced thousands of young children to do more than they ever believed possible. At church, she has sung in the choir, played the piano, led small groups and helped clean up after our many fellowship meals. At the end of a hard day, I can think of no greater delight than to be with her.

For God. How can I say thank you strongly enough? God's love and grace are amazing and His guidance and Spirit changed my life. God has given me the opportunity to witness miracle after miracle, many of which you will read about in this book. Even in the midst of tragedies, I have found Him working among the victims, providing comfort and hope. Jesus said, *"I am the light of the world. If you follow me, you won't be stumbling through the darkness because you will have the light that leads to life."* (John 8:12) My prayer is that the pages of this book will guide you to God's amazing light.

CONTENTS

WEEK THREE: GROW

WEEK FOUR: HELP OTHERS

WEEK FIVE: TO LIVE LIKE CHRIST

LIVING THE LIGHT: NOW WHAT? / 251

REFERENCES / 259

FOREWORD

It's the pictures that I remember most. I was standing in a hospital in Sri Lanka, surrounded by people in need — young mothers bringing their children to the doctor for a checkup, an old woman who lost all of her belongings and was now living in a tent. When the tsunami struck, she was praying in a nearby temple. She believed the sturdy building — which fared much better than most in the surrounding area — saved her life.

In broken English, Bindu, my hired driver and interpreter for the day explained: "She has left only ... with her ... only clothes ... not more." The woman's face showed wrinkles. Her eyes showed sadness. She possessed a strength I couldn't help but notice. Still, I remember the pictures most.

On this day, a month after the tsunami, I had already seen entire neighborhoods flattened, children left without homes and without parents. I saw panicked Sri Lankans run for cover upon hearing rumors that another monster wave was coming. I saw crews exhuming the bodies of tourists who had been buried on that terrible day — December 26, 2004 — so they could be sent back to their home countries. Still, I keep thinking of the pictures.

The pictures were made of crayon and drawn by tiny hands. They had a big impact on me, as I stood and studied them. The children were told to draw them as a way of reliving — and getting beyond — the tragedy. Their primary color was blue. It covered so much of each page. Their pictures showed the water — and the destruction and death underneath. There were cars, people, trees at awkward angles, and homes in ruins. But the one that stood out among them really wasn't a picture at all. It was one sentence, written in green, by a child named Hansani. It read: "Tsunami is the most unfortunate moment happen in my life."

When I read that one sentence, I felt the tears well up. I had seen so much. But the scene I imagined — a child, with a child's honesty, filling a page with a simple statement about a brutal tragedy — was enough to break me. I'll never forget that moment or that trip. That journey changed my life.

It was there, in Sri Lanka, that I got to know the Reverend Larry Davies. Larry and his church, Timberlake United Methodist, had always been active in our home community. But this trip was something entirely different. Larry traveled with the Reverend Ron Davidson of Gleaning for the World, the Reverend Ray Buchanan of Stop Hunger Now, and me, to see how his church could help people literally half a world away. We all leaned on each other, marveled at the damage, and made a difference. When we returned to Lynchburg, we established the "Heart of Virginia Tsunami Lifeline." By sending enough money to buy 33 new fishing boats and nets, the Tsunami Lifeline put the fishermen in the village of Kalmunai, Sri Lanka, back to work.

Other projects followed, like the Hurricane Lifeline, to help the Gulf Coast recover from the Katrina disaster. Working with Larry, I've grown to have the utmost respect and admiration for him. He is a tireless worker, a wise and godly man, and a great friend.

I was overjoyed at the idea of being one of the first to read his new book. I'm happy to tell you that, much like its author, it's one of a kind. In the coming pages, you'll be led closer to God through a series of lessons on life and on the Bible. The lessons come mostly from Larry's real-life experiences. Some are so funny you'll laugh out loud, as I did many times. Others are so touching, you'll feel you know the people he's talking about — and care for them as much as he.

Len Stevens
Anchor/Reporter, ABC-13 News
Lynchburg, Virginia

LIVE THE LIGHT

Five Weeks to a Life that Shines

INTRODUCTION

*Jesus said: "You are the light of the world — like a city on a mountain,
glowing in the night for all to see. Don't hide your light under a basket!
Instead, put it on a stand and let it shine for all. In the same way,
let your good deeds shine out for all to see,
so that everyone will praise your heavenly Father."*
Matthew 5:14-16

A few years ago, I delivered a children's message I called "Christ and the Lighthouse." The kids were asked to imagine themselves on a ship, lost offshore in a fierce squall. To make the story more realistic, we added special effects and, in my best storyteller voice, I began:

"It is a dark and stormy night (*the room becomes dark*) … Lightning flashes (*various lights begin blinking*) … The wind is howling (*sounds of a storm fill the room*) … The ship is tossed about (*everyone sways from side to side*) …" And here is the best part: "Huge waves crash overhead (*I started squirting the children with a spray bottle*) …"

Can you picture what's happening? Children are squealing and laughing. There's total chaos in the room as the "storm" continues to rage and the children shout: "We're drowning! Help! Who will save us?"

Then God gives us a miracle. Still in my best storyteller voice, I shout: "Look! … Up ahead! What's that?" (*In the far corner of the room a light begins to shine.*) "It's a light … from a lighthouse! We're saved! We were lost and now we are found!"

Wow! What a great lesson. After all, could anything offer more hope and direction to a ship caught in the grip of a fierce storm than the bright, steady beam of light from a lighthouse? What could possibly provide more comfort than that reassuring glow — a light to guide you safely home?

1

But, as recent headlines attest, ships are not the only ones that need a lighthouse:

It is a dark and stormy night … (*Violence continues in the Middle East.*)
Lightning flashes … (*AIDS after 25 years: 65 million infected.*)
The wind is howling … (*Teenagers face terrorist charges.*)
The ship is tossed about … (*Divorce rates at all-time high.*)
Huge waves crash overhead … (*Destruction long after Katrina.*)

Can you picture what's happening? People are crying and dying. There's total chaos in the world as storms continue to rage. People shout: "We're drowning! Help! Who will save us?"

Then God gives us a miracle. Still in my best storyteller voice, I shout to anyone who will listen: "Look! … Up ahead! What's that?" (*In a far corner of the world, a light begins to shine.*) "It's a light … from a lighthouse! We're saved! We were lost and now we are found!"

Wow! What a great promise! After all, what could possibly provide more comfort than the reassuring glow of a lighthouse — God's lighthouse?

- "*Lord, you have brought light to my life; my God, you light up my darkness.*" (*Psalm 18:28*) Like a lighthouse, God offers the light of direction to lead us out of the darkness.

- "*The Lord is my "light" and my salvation — so why should I be afraid?*" (*Psalm 27:1*) Like a lighthouse, God offers the light of salvation to rescue us from the storms of life.

- "*Jesus said, 'I am the light of the world. If you follow me, you won't be stumbling through the darkness, because you will have the light that leads to life.'*" (*John 8:12*) Like a lighthouse, God offers us a strong steady light to follow that leads to life.

Have you been experiencing a few dark and stormy nights, complete with lightning flashes and howling winds? Do you often feel like a helpless ship, tossed about with huge waves crashing over your head? Maybe now is the time to turn toward the eternal light: "Look! …Up ahead! What's that?" (*In the quiet corner of your soul, a light begins to shine.*) "It's a light … from The Lighthouse!"

"We're saved! We were lost and now we are found!" What could possibly provide more comfort than the reassuring glow of The Lighthouse — the One who promises to guide you safely home?

If you are going through storms ... If you are searching for purpose ... If you are seeking a new ministry ... If you want to deepen your relationship with God ... I pray this book will be a lighthouse for you — a light to guide you safely home.

Nice statement; but what does it really mean to be a lighthouse?

Our church staff recently grappled with this very question as we worked to agree on a vision and goals that could unite and excite us. I only planned to spend one meeting on the whole thing, thinking we already knew this stuff. We just needed to write it down and get to work.

I was so wrong. We were struggling and arguing throughout the meeting. Why? I soon realized we were disagreeing for the best of reasons. Our church has so many wonderful mission and ministry opportunities, we found it difficult to focus on only a few areas. Maybe our struggle symbolizes your struggle.

Our church logo depicts a lighthouse and, enclosed within its protective glow, is our mission statement: "A Light to Guide You Safely Home." For our vision, we were looking for something simple that would explain our mission statement in a fresh way.

One staff member suggested, "If we're going to be 'a light to guide you safely home,' we must learn how to actually live the light."

Live the light? That's it! "Live the LIGHT."

Our staff continued working to expand on just exactly what we meant. A simple sentence and diagram was the result. *"Live the LIGHT."* For us, "LIGHT" means:

L   Love our Lord as we
I   Invite,
G   Grow and
H   Help others
T   To live like Christ.

With this new vision statement in place, we added short explanations:

Love our Lord as we ... *The Lord is our cornerstone.*
Invite ... *Intentionally include others within God's love.*

Grow and … *Deepen our relationship with Jesus Christ.*
Help others … *Respond to our community and world.*
To live like Christ … *We model Christ's example.*

Jesus said: *"You are the light of the world — like a city on a mountain, glowing in the night for all to see. Don't hide your light under a basket! Instead, put it on a stand and let it shine for all. In the same way, let your good deeds shine out for all to see, so that everyone will praise your heavenly Father."* (Matthew 5:14-16)

As you embark on this five-week journey, I pray that you and your church will be inspired to "Live the LIGHT." Each week will focus on one element of the LIGHT. Within the five weeks, daily readings provide a progression to guide you:

- **Monday:** We Need Light
- **Tuesday:** Opportunities to Shine
- **Wednesday:** Becoming God's Lighthouse
- **Thursday:** An Attitude that Shines
- **Friday:** Simplify
- **Saturday:** Start Shining
- **Sunday:** Live the Light

At the end of each day, in "Share the LIGHT," you will find questions to help you or your small group deepen your understanding of the day's message. Space is also provided for a few short notes.

My favorite section following each daily reading is "Live the LIGHT: The Lighthouse in Action." This section is made up of three important parts:

- An idea that worked for our church.
- A question to help your develop your own action ideas.
- Comments from real people trying to "Live the LIGHT."

Why do I place so much emphasis on the lighthouse? Years ago, I became a lighthouse. But before you think I've lost my mind, let me explain. The Lighthouse Movement is a coalition of Christians representing churches around the world. Our goal is to pray for and care for our neighbors while looking for opportunities to sensitively share our beliefs.

One of the founders of this movement wrote, "I am convinced that if we Christians can mobilize and equip our people to get out of the church walls and into their neighborhoods, schools and offices and establish Lighthouses for their neighbors, we can witness an amazing movement of God."

Jesus said to the people: *"I am the light of the world. If you follow me, you won't be stumbling through the darkness because you will have the light that leads to life." (John 8:12)* In other words, we are called to *be light* while remembering that *Jesus is the source of light.* What better modern symbol than the Lighthouse?

The Lighthouse Movement is based on a simple idea: Choose three to four people in your neighborhood, school or workplace. Then:

1. **Pray.** Regularly pray for them by name and ask God to use you as an influence.
2. **Care.** Look for opportunities to demonstrate God's love with simple acts of caring.
3. **Share.** Trust God to provide an opportunity to sensitively share your faith.

Just before facing the cross, Jesus said to his disciples: *"Yes, I am the vine; you are the branches. Those who remain in me and I in them will produce much fruit." (John 15:5)* In other words, Jesus is the lighthouse; you are the light. If you stay connected to the source of your light, the lighthouse in you will shine brightly and guide many lost ships and lost souls safely home.

After hearing this, I wondered: Who has been a light for me? Who has been influential in my life? Sometimes we overlook the obvious — the light of those we see every day.

Of course, it begins with family: My wife, Mell, loves me even when I'm not very loveable. And, as a gifted schoolteacher, she subtly offers Godly influence to her first graders. Stephen and Lisa, my grown children, allowed me to learn and grow as dad. My sister and mother still provide an atmosphere of love and support. What about you? How has family been a light for you?

"Come, people of Israel, let us walk in the light of the Lord!" (Isaiah 2:5)

There are the "lights" who appear suddenly and burn brightest when we need them most. What would we do without them? Whose light has burned brightest for you? In my life there have been several:

- A boss who believed in me and taught the meaning of the statement, "you can do anything if you try."
- An author and motivational speaker who strengthened my commitment to serving Christ.
- An unknown missionary who warned me: "Larry, keep your nose buried in God's Word."
- An elderly lady who opened her home and heart while I was a struggling seminary student.
- A neighbor who stayed awake all night and helped me through a devastating divorce.

"You are the light of the world — like a city on a mountain, glowing in the night for all to see. Don't hide your light under a basket! Instead, put it on a stand and let it shine for all." (Matthew 5:14)

For years, Frances Hardy has been just such a light. Our assistant pastor, Charlie Johnson, sent this e-mail after visiting her in the hospital:

"I left work at 5:30 and met Frances at the hospital. She told me about the beginnings of our church. She told me of her experiences with God and how she touched lives. She told me about the Sunday school class she taught. When I glanced at my watch, it was 7:30. She told me how much she loved the church. Now, it wasn't all spiritual stuff. She also told me about her driving reputation, the little old ladies in her Sunday school class, playing bridge and more. She told me about the loss of her husband and son. When I left it was after 9:30. I told her that if she could bless others like she did me, she wasn't through by a long shot. I spent the evening with a special 86-year-old woman and got so much more than I could have expected."

You, too, can be a light from God's lighthouse. Actually, you have always been a light. The real questions are:

- How close are you to the Source?
- How bright is your light burning?

A friend, Drayton Hawthorn, recently wrote describing some tense moments he experienced while waiting for his wife's surgery. "It was ten o'clock at night and she was outside looking at the stars! I thought it was settled and done. Robin's surgery was a few short days away and, although the doctors assured her this was a routine procedure, she was still looking as if they were going to amputate something!

"As her husband, I assumed my duty was to hide concern while showing a strong front. Like most men, I substituted statistics and reason for assurance and thought it was enough. Now she was worrying again. I walked toward her ready to offer more of my male logic.

"That's when the miracle happened.

"Everything I planned to say vanished. Unknown words came from my lips, as I silently wrapped my arms around her waist and kissed her cheek. 'God loves you. Everything will be all right. You will see a shooting star as my promise that you will be OK.' In an instant the most spectacular shooting star we ever saw blazed across the sky from horizon to horizon. A surprised and delighted, 'Ooh!' came from Robin! For a long moment neither of us spoke. What could we say?

"Moments before, I was an insensitive, scolding husband walking towards a fearful, anxious wife. Somehow, God miraculously intervened and changed us both into vessels of His gracious love."

Usually, our influence as a lighthouse is seen through a steady, consistent beam of light. People know and remember us by our day-to-day actions among our family and friends. We might be a family member continuously offering love and acceptance, a boss supplying encouragement when needed most, or we could be the friend who telephones when others are at a low point.

But, occasionally, there are life-changing moments when God's extraordinary light suddenly shines into the darkest need and the only word that adequately describes what happens next is *miracle*. Drayton and Robin witnessed a miracle. Here is another:

What started, as a normal day at a local high school became a tragedy for a young 16-year-old boy full of enthusiasm and friendly mischief. During tennis practice he suddenly dropped to the ground, clutching his chest. Within minutes this vivacious young man was gone.

Lighthouses quickly appeared from all over the county. School officials opened up the high school auditorium and encouraged the students to gather. A minister's wife got word to fellow pastors. The students themselves began to gather in small groups, sharing condolences, memories and tears.

But, just as we were starting to leave, Russell, a father of one of the students stood and said: "Before we go, I think we should pray. Let's form a circle and hold hands. I'll start and the rest of you join with me."

Hundreds of crying parents, students, pastors and school officials formed a large circle, bowed their heads and earnestly began to pray. For a few moments, we could all feel the Holy Spirit of God in our circle of mourners: Russell was a lighthouse of God amidst the grief.

As lighthouses, you and I are given the opportunity to be rays of hope in the midst of darkness.

Drayton Hawthorne went on to write: "Being an instrument of God's will at times may not be voluntary or even expected. I always believed God would use me as a prophet only if I asked and was spiritually clean.

"Sometimes, this is undeniably true, but not in my case. God abruptly interrupted my mission and lovingly substituted His own. I wanted to comfort Robin with common sense and almost interrupted a miraculous moment of faith. No matter the reason for why it happens, when God, uses you for whatever purpose, you will feel blessed because of it.

"Thinking of the wonderful moment Robin and I shared with God is very emotional for me. Several times in telling our shooting star story, Robin would need to finish because I became too 'choked up' So, once more, I will let her finish."

Robin smiled and then said: "After we stood there a few moments, just soaking in what happened, I turned to Drayton and whispered, 'Do it again!'"

As you begin this five week journey to "Live the LIGHT," I pray you will find inspiration to make your life really shine. God has a mission and a purpose for you. You are an instrument of His will. When you discover and fully utilize that purpose, you will feel especially blessed — so much so, that you may find yourself excitedly whispering to God, "Do it again!"

During the next five weeks, do your best to stick to the plan and not miss a single daily reading. Don't read ahead, but rather, spend extra time reflecting on each day's message. As always, we place our primary emphasis on prayer, our fundamental link with God. In this way, God's Holy

Spirit will have the best possible opportunity to brighten your light.

Together with my church family at Timberlake United Methodist in Lynchburg, Virginia, I strive to be "a light to guide you safely home!" *Please know that our church is praying for you.* Like you, we must daily seek God's guidance to help us live the LIGHT. What a privilege ... and a challenge! No wonder we put so much emphasis on prayer.

God bless you on this journey.

Larry

WEEK ONE

LOVE THE LORD

MONDAY—We Need Light

The cure to spiritual blindness is found in the Light.

Oh, the joys of those who do not remain afloat in the darkness,
or stand around with sinners, or join in with scoffers.
But they delight in doing everything the Lord wants
Psalm 1:1-2

As we gathered, the teacher instructed each of us to choose a partner. "One of you will be blindfolded and the other will be a guide," he added. Everything went black as I slipped on the blindfold and allowed my partner to nudge me forward and lead me by the hand. A once-familiar classroom was suddenly a maze of desks and chairs to bump into or trip over. No longer self-reliant, I was utterly dependent on my guide for directions and safety. But the worst was yet to come.

Leaving the classroom, we staggered down the hall. My other senses, once ignored, began to provide clues as to where we were. Laughter and talking meant other students were nearby. We must be in the hall. Ouch! That must be a door. The hard surface under my feet indicated a sidewalk. Automobile sounds fading in and out, suggested we were near a road.

A road? Wait a minute. We're on a road — with cars! Isn't that ... dangerous?!

"You are now stepping off the curb and onto the highway," said the teacher. Suddenly, my body lurched out of balance as the ground under my feet dropped eight inches. Imagine eight tiny inches with the power to disrupt everything that was secure in my life. Knowing exactly where I was never seemed to matter before, but now details were crucial. How could I take the next step if I didn't know where that step might lead?

"Stop and listen," commanded the teacher. I heard the familiar sound of an automobile engine, only this time it was getting louder. Alarms in my brain screamed loudly, "You idiot, run. A car is heading straight toward you!" But the sound went safely by, only to be quickly followed by a similar sound from the opposite direction. Again, the voice inside me screamed, "Run!" But again, nothing happened. We removed the blindfolds, rubbed our eyes, and found ourselves standing in the middle of a busy highway with cars whizzing by.

I never before grasped the fear and helplessness that accompanies blindness. This was a terrifying lesson for me.

Is this what God means by spiritual blindness? At first, you think you can manage okay as other senses provide clues; but suddenly something shifts and you are thrown off balance. Alarms in your brain scream out as you sense approaching danger. Your spiritual eyesight now becomes crucial but you seem to be blindfolded. How can you take the next step in life if you cannot see where to place your feet?

Spiritual blindness produces feelings of helplessness and fear. But Psalm One offers hope for the blind:

> Oh, the joys of those who do not follow the advice of the wicked, or stand around with sinners, or join in with scoffers. But they delight in doing everything the Lord wants; day and night they think about his law. They are like trees planted along the riverbank, bearing fruit each season without fail. Their leaves never wither, and in all they do, they prosper. But this is not true of the wicked. They are like worthless chaff, scattered by the wind. They will be condemned at the time of judgment. Sinners will have no place among the godly. For the Lord watches over the path of the godly, but the path of the wicked leads to destruction. (Psalm 1)

Let's break this down. God offers light to the blind. "Oh, *the joys of those who do not follow the advice of the wicked ... they delight in doing everything the Lord wants.*" This is not a lighthearted promise of joy as in eating ice cream. This indescribable joy can only come from God. How do we obtain it? We begin to open our spiritual eyes and carefully watch where we place our feet. Don't search for shortcuts. Rather, begin to look seriously at the reality of our spiritual blindness and the benefits of relying on God's light.

There are two opposing principles within Psalm One. First is the promise: *"They are like trees planted along the riverbank, bearing fruit each season without fail. Their leaves never wither, and in all they do, they prosper."* In other words, the storms still exist but God gives strength to withstand and continue bearing fruit.

Second is the warning: *"But this is not true of the wicked. They are like worthless chaff, scattered by the wind. They will be condemned at the time of judgment."* Most of us would not quickly claim to be spiritual trees, but none of us wants to be chaff either. So, what do we do? How can we improve our eyesight?

The experience of being blindfolded and a careful reading of Psalm One yield four valuable lessons:

1. Appreciate what you already possess—the abilities God has given you. *Oh the joys of those ...*
2. Learn to develop other senses. Strengthen Godly relationships. *They are like trees — bearing fruit ...*
3. Avoid crowded highways. Let go of damaging relationships. *Do not follow the advice of the wicked ...*
4. Know and trust your guide. Learn Who is your real Guide. *The Lord watches over your path ...*

Psalm One ends with a promise and a warning: *"For the Lord watches over the path of the godly, but the path of the wicked leads to destruction."* Are you struggling with spiritual blindness? Has your equilibrium been knocked around? Are you sensing approaching danger? Maybe it's time for a new Light — from a lighthouse Who knows exactly where you need to go and can be depended upon to light your way to safety. What are you waiting for? Open your eyes and pray for God's light to guide your journey. It sure beats an oncoming car.

SEE THE LIGHT

Before we can fully love our Lord, we must first recognize our spiritual blindness and seek out the light of God's Lighthouse.

SHARE THE LIGHT

1. Choose a partner. Take turns blindfolding each other and being led around a room, through a building, and then outside. How did the experience make you feel?
2. What does it mean to be spiritually blind?
3. How could Psalm One help you improve your spiritual eyesight?
4. How can you strengthen the Godly relationships you have and create more?
5. Letting go of damaging relationships may be the hardest step of all. How can you replace them with Godly relationships?
6. What can you do right now to find a spiritual guide?
7. How can you share this information and your newfound insights with others and help them avoid spiritual blindness?

Notes:

LIVE THE LIGHT: The Lighthouse in Action

When people join Timberlake United Methodist Church, we ask them to join us in making four commitments that we believe help us avoid spiritual blindness and become brighter lights for God.

1. **Attend** weekly worship services faithfully when able. This seems simple but good worship gives you something that will help make the rest of the week worthwhile.
2. **Grow** in your faith by participating in at least one small group each year. This is where you talk about your needs and concerns. You form a new family with those in your small group. Godly friendships begin and ministry forms.
3. **Serve** in a ministry setting at least once each year. This is your opportunity to give something back to others. Whether you teach children in Sunday school or join a group to repair the house of a poor neighbor in your community.
4. **Give.** This is more than just a financial commitment. Giving is an attitude that reflects how you spend your money, your time, your talents and, ultimately, your life. Giving is a discipline that, in addition to blessing others, also richly blesses you.

Your Action Ideas:
You've read what a church can expect of you. What should you expect from a church?

1. _____

2. _____

3. _____

"I walked into a church to see a play my son was in. I had not [been] for years. I had given up on Christianity. Something melted inside my heart. I felt an aching sense that I was missing something which could fill the spiritual hole inside me. The pull of that service kept tugging on me and I kept going back. The church has been responsible for nurturing my spiritual growth through [worship], Bible Studies, workshops, prayer, the list goes on. Why is the church important to me? Without it, I would still be lost." —Eveline

TUESDAY—Opportunities to Shine

There are snakes all around us.

You prepare a table for me in the presence of my enemies.
You anoint my head with oil.
Psalm 23:5

You know the feeling. Snow is melting, the sun is shining ... spring is here at last! Are you ready? Spring may be about sunshine and beauty, but for me it just means more chores and yard work. There are sticks and debris from winter snowstorms to pick up and grass to mow.

One spring day, instead of moaning and groaning about the yard work, I took a break and strolled around the yard to admire the view of the freshly cut lawn. Then, a sudden movement caught my eye. Slithering up the steps toward the entrance to our house was the longest black snake I've ever seen.

"Now what do I do?" The snake wasn't poisonous but I certainly didn't want to annoy him. *(Was it a him? Do you really think I checked?!)* Maybe if I wait he will slink off to hassle someone else. But no — this snake was obviously after something on the other side of our door. I never saw a snake so persistent. At one point, while slithering up the door frame, his head was over the top of the frame while his tail almost touched the bottom. He was at least twenty feet long! *(OK, would you believe seven feet?)* I definitely had a predicament on my hands.

Quietly and menacingly the snake draped his body over the top of the doorway and waited. Seconds later, my wife Mell appeared at the door. "Please don't open that door, Honey!" I yelled. She stared at me quizzically, glanced up, saw the snake, screamed and ran off.

With the aid of a neighbor, I quickly and carefully moved the snake and uttered a sincere prayer of thanks. It was frightening to see that huge beast draped over our doorway. Suppose my wife actually walked out the door and the snake dropped over her shoulders? *(I don't even want to think about it.)* What if he had gotten into the house? *(We would have moved! Just kidding.)*

I write this because life can seem pretty humdrum at times, full of daily chores. Then a sudden movement catches your eye and, out of nowhere, comes a "slithering snake" of dilemmas. You wait hoping he'll slink off and hassle someone else. But no, this snake is more aggressive. He's perched over the doorway waiting for an unsuspecting soul to pass underneath. For example:

- You get a call from the doctor's office; they want to see you right away.
- A sleepy driver runs a stop light — directly in front of your moving car.
- The school office reports your child was absent for the last three days.
- The manager calls you into his office to explain the meaning of downsizing and how it affects your job.
- Our nation is at war. Terrorism can strike anytime, anywhere.

Do you remember this portion of Psalm 23? *"You prepare a table before me in the presence of my enemies. You anoint my head with oil."* The passage seems to be talking about food, but that wouldn't make much sense in a Psalm about sheep and shepherds. Some interpreters think David is really writing about snakes. Yes, you read correctly: Snakes!

In mountainous regions, a "table" describes a flat section of land. Before entering a new "table," a good shepherd inspects the ground for holes — potential hiding places for poisonous brown snakes. Then he "prepares the table" by pouring thick oil in each snake hole. The oil makes it difficult for the snake to come out of the hole. The shepherd then "anoints" the sheep's noses and mouths with the same oil, making them too slippery to bite.

Good shepherds who lovingly care for their sheep do that. What a relief!

We don't like to admit it, but snakes do exist and they will occasionally attempt a bite. God, our loving shepherd, inspects the "tables" before us, providing safety. And when an occasional snake does break through, we are anointed with the oil of comfort, protecting us from the poisonous bite.

Are there snakes perched on your doorway ready to strike? Have they soured your disposition and challenged your faith? Get out a Bible and read Psalm 23 again. Read the words slowly and think about what it would be like for you to personally receive the Good Shepherd's anointing oil of protection. Wow! I feel safer already … don't you?

SEE THE LIGHT

When facing life's snakes we count on the Good Shepherd
to lovingly protect and care for us. When we face storms,
He is the Lighthouse that guides us safely home.

SHARE THE LIGHT

1. Life seems pretty humdrum at times but then something slithers
   up and threatens to bite. When was the last time this happened
   to you? How did you respond? Did you receive help? Did you look
   to God?
2. Good shepherds care for their sheep. How has God cared for you?
   What about your church? Your friends?
3. Read Psalm 23 and count the ways God cares for His sheep. How
   can these lessons be applied to your life?
4. Do you know anyone who is being threatened by a few snakes of
   their own? How can you share this lesson with him/her?

Notes:

_____

_____

_____

_____

_____

_____

_____

_____

_____

_____

_____

LIVE THE LIGHT: The Lighthouse in Action

Speaking of shepherds, how can we shepherd and protect the children in our care? Here are two practical suggestions that worked at our church:

Child Abuse Prevention Policy: This formal document outlines what our church does to prevent abuse. Policies include staff and volunteer screening, training guidelines, a two-adult rule, guidelines for classroom discipline, and an emphasis on open classrooms.

Nursery Pagers: This wonderful tool allows parents to leave their children in the nursery without worry. Each parent is handed a silent pager that will vibrate if there is a problem with his or her child.

Your Action Ideas:
How can you shepherd the children in your care/at your church?

1. _____

2. _____

3. _____

"I just wanted to take a moment to thank God and you for the wonderful devotions sent out this year. I know I'm not alone in saying how many times you have touched my heart. There are countless souls you have touched in the kingdom of God. Also, it has been a blessing to pray for those in need this year and I appreciate the prayers of others when I was in need."
—Sharon

"I requested prayer a few months ago for my wife, Cathy. She had cancer three times over the past twenty years and breast cancer for the past four years. She went for a CT scan this week and the doctor saw no sign of cancer. Praise the Lord!" —Danny

WEDNESDAY—Becoming God's Lighthouse

Everything begins with prayer.

*Listen to my voice in the morning, Lord. Each morning
I bring my requests to you and wait expectantly.*
Psalm 5:3

Does God answer prayers? When I posed this question to my class, the replies were quick and enthusiastic: "Of course!" "Yes, always."

"Then, why don't we pray more frequently?" I questioned. An uncomfortable silence filled the room.

Finally, the excuses poured out: "I'm too busy." "There is no time." "God's too busy to listen to me." "I don't know what to say!" "I'm not worthy." "I don't know how!"

Our individual reasons may sound different, but our predicament is basically the same. We do not fully appreciate the importance and power of prayer. Prayer should be as critical and functional as the steering wheel in a car. *"Without you, O Lord, I can go nowhere!"* Yet, for most of us, prayer is more like the spare tire — seldom used except when something goes flat. In other words: "Don't call us, we'll call You ... when we need You!"

Prayer is intended to be an ongoing relationship with our Creator — much more than presenting a wish list to a heavenly Santa Claus. But all good relationships require commitment and a willingness to invest time. Lots of time.

Suppose you tell a trusted spouse or friend you can't spend more time with them because you're too busy or you think they're too busy. Or because you don't know how to talk to them or you're not worthy of their attention? What kind of relationship would you have?

Here is God's promise on the subject of prayer: *"Don't worry about anything; instead, pray about everything. Tell God what you need and thank him for all he has done. If you do this you will experience God's peace, which is far more wonderful than the human mind can understand. His peace will guard your hearts and mind as you live in Christ Jesus."* (Philippians 4:6-7)

Our tendency is to worry isn't it? Yet we know worry solves nothing and even can cause emotional, physical and spiritual harm. Prayer means giving our worries to God, who in return promises a supernatural peace —

a peace far more wonderful than the human mind can understand. Could it really be as simple as that? Yes, it can. But we must commit to praying regularly. Let's look at a basic formula to help guide your prayer life:

1. **Praise God.** Praise sets the tone and reminds you who God really is. Try looking at some of the Psalms and reading them out loud to get you started. I suggest Psalms 8, 19 and 148.
2. **Confess.** A good relationship strengthens with honesty. No sane doctor would offer a cure without hearing what hurts. Admitting your faults promotes spiritual healing.
3. **Listen.** Sometimes, it's easier to talk than to really listen. Easy, but not smart. Quiet times are often when you will find direction. Listening allows God to speak to your soul.
4. **Ask for Help.** This part becomes more meaningful when you take the time to praise, confess and listen. This is when you literally learn to stop worrying and start praying.
5. **Give Thanks.** This step is not always easy, but giving thanks recognizes that God is looking out for you and has your best interest at heart. You are saying, "I trust you."
6. **Keep a Journal.** This may be the most important part of your prayer life. The journal is where disappointments, struggles, joys and miracles are recorded and remembered.

Does God answer our prayers? Yes; but are we doing our part? Consider this: Two people with similar difficulties begin to pray. The first expects instant results and finishes his prayer frustrated and confused. Months later, the problem and the prayer are forgotten. The second person prays looking to spend a few quiet moments with a trusted friend. She completes her prayer feeling more content and at peace. Over the next few months, while recording her thoughts in a journal, she notices progress with the problem itself and especially in her ability to cope. She thanks God.

Think about it. You have the opportunity to be in a relationship with God — one that can make an authentic difference in your life and the life of anyone who comes in contact with you. So, what are you waiting for?

As you seek to grow in your relationship with God, you will see that your prayers can have a rippling effect. When you throw a stone into a pond, there is a splash as the weight of the rock pushes the water away.

Then the splash is followed by a ripple, which is followed by another ripple, then another and so on. When you pray, there will be more ripples —
more circles — as God turns your prayer life into a prayer ministry.

The first circle begins with family. Prayer can start with grace at
mealtime. You can learn to pray with your spouse or a close friend. If you
are a parent, pray regularly with your children. *"Listen to my voice in the
morning, Lord. Each morning I bring my requests to you and wait expectantly."* (Psalm 5:3) Prayer can be the glue that holds a family together in a
world that's falling apart:

> At 6 a.m., Mom rang the bell to summon us to the prayer room.
> At 6:15 we better be there. We've been gathering every morning
> for over ten years. I used to hate it getting up so early, but now
> "Morning Prayer" time is a regular habit. Our family held together
> through good times and bad and what I cherish the most is our
> morning prayers. —*Ann*

The second circle involves a small group. Two key features of this
ministry are accountability and encouragement. Accountability represents
the desire to improve while warm, loving encouragement keeps you going
when accountability is impossible. *"Devote yourselves to prayer with an alert
mind and a thankful heart."* (Colossians 4:2) Prayer sustains and challenges us:

> Every Sunday morning at 7:30 a group of men meet at church to offer
> encouragement and prayers. It's the only time all of us can make it.
> We've helped each other through marriage problems, deaths and
> serious illness. Each week, we challenge ourselves to be a better
> Christian witness than the week before. It hasn't always been
> easy, but [I believe] this group made me a better person. —*Russell*

The third circle is your local church. Prayer should be a regular part
of worship, but there could also be regular prayer gatherings and occasional healing services. Many churches post lists and have at least one person praying every hour of every day. There also are prayer chains so more
urgent prayers can be passed on quickly. *"They devoted themselves to
prayer."* (Acts 2:42)

During worship I asked for prayer on behalf of a man in another state [who was] facing surgery. A candle was lit reminding us to pray, and a card of encouragement was mailed [to him] the next day. He called me later in tears. That prayer card was the first thing he saw when he woke up in the recovery room. —*Cathy*

Thirty-eight men recently attended a "Walk to Emmaus" weekend while others worked behind the scenes and hundreds more prayed. Some prayed at a certain hour for the success of the weekend, while others prayed for an individual. When the "walk" was over, thirty-eight men spoke of life-changing experiences. Why? There were many reasons, but underneath it all was prayer. —*Don*

The fourth circle is the wider community. Following the tragedy of September 11, 2001, communities gathered to pray for the victims and for solutions to the plague of violence and terror. *"I urge you first of all, to pray for all people."* (1 Timothy 2:1) A wider community of prayer can be expanded to include your neighborhood — and even the entire world — as the following letter illustrates:

A two-year old girl named Becky was struggling with cancer. A family friend ... began searching the Internet for prayer groups. To each group, she sent an urgent e-mail message asking them to pray for Becky. Within hours, thousands of people around the world were praying and sending e-mails offering love and encouragement. —*Jennifer*

Prayer ministry begins with you and spreads outward in ever-widening circles. The possibilities are endless and the potential is awe-inspiring. How is your prayer ministry doing?

SEE THE LIGHT

Prayer begins with you, but soon there will be more ripples, more circles, as God turns your prayer life into a prayer ministry.

- Prayer always starts with you.
- Are you praying with your family?
- Do you have a small group to support you?
- Does your local church have a prayer ministry?
- How are your prayers reaching the community and world?

SHARE THE LIGHT

1. We know that prayer is important and meaningful, so what keeps us from praying more frequently?
2. How can you use the prayer formula on page 21 to deepen your prayer life?
3. How can your prayer life turn into a ministry?
4. Share this lesson on prayer with at least one other person and ask them to pray for you and your ministry.

Notes:

LIVE THE LIGHT: The Lighthouse in Action

Every church should have a weekly prayer request sheet listing new and critical requests as well as on-going requests. In addition, at Timberlake we regularly include prayers for our government leaders and unique events and crises that arise. During worship, new prayer requests are spoken and a candle is lit to symbolize God's presence.

When our children and youth go on mission trips, each one leaves behind a paper hand with his or her name on it. Members of the congregation are invited to take home one of the paper hands and pray for that child throughout the week.

Sowing Seeds Ministry provides a web page for prayer requests and receives them from all over the world. Three times each week, these requests are e-mailed to thousands of prayer warriors worldwide. With permission, e-mail addresses are included so that each request receives e-mails promising continued prayer and support. (*For information, visit www.SowingSeedsofFaith.com*) Stories of miracles and changed lives continually remind us of God's presence and power.

Your Action Ideas:
How can you expand your prayer ministry?

1. _____

2. _____

3. _____

"I asked for prayer about attending church and becoming active after a long [time] away. I have been attending this wonderful church ... have signed up for ministries and [am] attending classes to strengthen my walk." — Joann

"Our Youth Group was excited about the opportunity to minister to those who e-mailed you. We spent our evening replying to the prayer list to encourage and share the love of Christ. I would like to receive as many e-mails as possible. Thank you for sharing them with us." —Terry

THURSDAY—An Attitude that Shines

Loving our Lord begins with prayer and continues with attitude.

I have learned the secret of living in every situation …
For I can do everything with the help of Christ
who gives me the strength I need.
Philippians 4:11-13

First: Thanks to special effects, no cats were actually harmed during the writing of this story. Second: This story is not original. I first heard about "Kicking Cats" from Zig Ziglar, a well-known motivational speaker. The story is so powerful — and the situation so common — I'd like to share it with you.

The steering wheel had never been gripped tighter as Jim drove to work on Monday morning. Jim was angry — really angry. Early that morning his wife told him, "I can't take your workaholic ways anymore. If you don't learn to spend more time with your family, we're leaving, forever! Maybe you should marry your company because you spend enough time there."

Still angry upon arriving at work, Jim stomped toward his office, smacked the intercom button on his telephone and shouted for his sales manager: "Bill, come to my office immediately!"

Bill was a first-rate manager employed for twenty three years, but sales admittedly were off. Jim raised his voice: "Bill, I'm tired of your poor production and pitiful excuses. I expect you to whip our sales staff into shape. If you can't, then I'll hire someone who can and I don't care how long we've been together. Do you hear me?"

"Yes sir." What else could Bill say? Plenty. He walked out mumbling: "That no good, sorry excuse for an owner! Where does he get off threatening me after I've worked so hard for him all these years? I made him the success he has become. We've seen rougher times than this before. The nerve of him giving me all this abuse because of a few bad months. What a jerk!"

Bill then barged into his top sales rep's office and shouted, "Robin, I'm tired of making you look good. You wouldn't be number one if I wasn't feeding you customers. Last month, when I really needed help, you let me down. If you don't do better, I'm replacing you with a real sales person. Do you understand?"

Robin understood all right. "He has a lot of nerve jumping on me after all the sales I've generated for this company. Everyone knows the only reason he became a manager is because of me!" As she sat and stewed, the phone rang. Robin picked it up and shouted: "Hold all my calls! If you were any kind of decent receptionist, you would know that I'm busy! Just remember — you, too, can be replaced!"

"Well, the nerve of that prima donna!" thought the receptionist. "Who does she think she is?" For the rest of the day, whenever anyone called, instead of a pleasant, "Thank you for calling. How may I help you?" the unfortunate caller was met with a gruff, "What do you want?"

When the grumpy receptionist finally made it home that evening, she walked in on her son, Tim, lying on the couch and watching TV. "Tim, how many times have I said that with me working all day, you need to carry more weight? This room is a filthy, disgusting mess. How dare you watch television while I spend all day working to support you. Go to your room. You're grounded — for life!"

Upset and angry, the boy hopped from the couch and stomped toward his room. "How dare she give me a hard time when I've had a tough day at school. I've already vacuumed and straightened up. I just took a short break." On the way to his room, Tim noticed Ellis, the family cat, lying asleep on the floor, minding his own business in the middle of the den.

Oh, oh! Can you guess what happened next? Before the poor critter could even utter a decent meow, the boy gave the cat a vicious kick which sent him flying across the room. Ouch!

Now this raises a question: Wouldn't everyone have been better off if Jim had just gone to the receptionist's house and kicked the cat himself? It also raises another question: Who's been kicking your cat? And even more to the point: Whose cat have you kicked lately?

We live in a negative, cat-kicking world, don't we? No one is immune. In order to deal with it, we need extraordinary strength and courage to keep our attitude focused in the right direction.

By the way, aren't we relieved no one ever "kicks the cat" in church? (*Let's share a long pause while we soak in that statement and chuckle together.*) Ouch! The truth hurts. Even in God's house we are not immune to a little cat-kicking. If you don't believe me, attend a few church committee meetings.

In his letter to the Philippians, Paul wrote: *"I have learned the secret of living in every situation. ... For I can do everything with the help of Christ who gives me the strength I need." (Philippians 4:11-13)* Wow! Paul seemed to have his act together. Wouldn't you love to have that kind of contentment? How? When someone kicks your cat, how can you respond like Paul, filled with gentleness and grace? First, let's look at some *wrong* ways to respond:

- Look for another cat to kick? *No, that's abuse.*
- Whine to everyone you know? *Again no. That's gossip.*
- Throw a temper tantrum? *No, it's immature.*
- Take your ball and go home. *No, that's quitting.*
- Use the silent treatment? *No, that would be weak.*
- Vow to get even. *No, that's revenge.*
- Do nothing? *No! That's unhealthy for them and for you.*

How can you and I apply Paul's words? Remember he said: *"I can do everything with the help of Christ."* Ah, there is the secret. I can do everything with the help of Christ. So how do we apply this valuable lesson?

First, let's look at the Bible. This time from Peter: *"Finally, all of you should be of one mind, full of sympathy toward each other, loving one another with tender hearts and humble minds. Don't repay evil for evil. Don't retaliate when people say unkind things about you. Instead, pay them back with a blessing. That is what God wants you to do, and he will bless you for it. For the Scriptures say, 'If you want a happy life and good days, keep your tongue from speaking evil, and keep your lips from telling lies. Turn away from evil and do good. Work hard at living in peace with others.'" (1 Peter 3:8-11)*

When someone kicks your cat, Peter reminds you to *"Work hard at living in peace with others."* What does that mean? Here is my checklist:

1. **Pray.** Talk to God and ask for help. You can even get angry! God can take it.
2. **Get some perspective.** In light of eternity in heaven, remember that God comes first.
3. **Share.** Spend time with a trusted friend or prayer partner. Talk and pray together.
4. **Seek.** Look for God's guidance on how to properly respond and then pray for courage.
5. **Confront if possible.** This should be done with love, confident that you are obeying God's will.

6. **Forgive.** This is a process but, ultimately, it's the only way to promote healing and growth.
7. **Pray again.** In faith, turn the solution over to God — regardless of the immediate outcome.

Is this easy? Absolutely not! Like Peter said: *"Work hard at living in peace with others."* Working hard is the key.

Now, let's apply lessons learned and revisit the "Kick the Cat" story for an appropriate ending:

Jim, after much thought and prayer apologizes to his wife and promises to be a better husband and father. He begins clearing his calendar to make time for his family. Jim also apologizes for taking his personal frustration out on Bill. Bill seeks out Robin and asks forgiveness for being so rude. Robin finds the receptionist and apologizes for her terrible behavior. On the way home, the receptionist orders pizza and, over dinner, promises to be a more understanding mother and not take her work frustrations out on Tim. And as for Ellis, the cat... He received quite a few extra treats.

What can we learn from God through Paul and Peter? The secret of living in every situation is to look to Christ for strength, love one another and work hard at living in peace. It sure beats kicking cats!

SEE THE LIGHT

We live in a negative, cat-kicking world. We may not be able to change that world, but we can change our attitudes. God revealed the secret through both Paul and Peter: Look to Christ for strength, love one another and work hard at living in peace.

SHARE THE LIGHT

1. We do live in a negative, cat-kicking world. Who has been kicking your cat lately? Whose cat have you kicked?
2. The list on page 28 gives several wrong ways to respond. What makes them wrong?
3. Re-read the checklist of right ways to respond. How can we put these methods into practice?
4. How can you share this story with your friends and find ways to have a Christ-like impact on a negative world?

Notes:

_____

_____

_____

_____

_____

_____

_____

_____

_____

_____

_____

_____

_____

_____

_____

_____

_____

LIVE THE LIGHT: The Lighthouse in Action

One way the church can help adjust your attitude is by providing numerous opportunities for lively fellowship. At Timberlake, our favorite form of fellowship is eating ... and boy, can this church eat!

Thursday night is "Nurture Night." This includes a meal cooked by one of our mission and ministry groups. You can eat a delicious meal and then join one of our many Bible studies or small groups.

On Sunday mornings, we offer our famous "Breakfast Cafe," which is open during the three worship services. Once again, one of our ministry teams prepares the breakfast. You just show up and enjoy the food and the opportunity to meet others.

Sunday evenings our many children and youth take over the church. Two kitchens full of volunteers serve a delicious meal, followed by small group opportunities and a youth-style worship service.

Your Action Ideas:
How can you/your church encourage positive attitudes and fellowship?

1. _____

2. _____

3. _____

"Often the church is referred to as light. Like a moth, I am drawn to the light. Sometimes I fly close to the light and enjoy the warmth. Other times I stray into the dimly lit area and fly my own way. God allows me to dart out into the dark but I am always drawn back to the light of the church." —Jim

"Thank you for responding so quickly to my prayer request! I felt a sense of hope, and quite literally knew that it was God's love and mercy working through you and your prayer team. What comfort it brings to me to know God still works in my life! ... I don't feel so isolated and alone and am happy to be alive. I know ... there is a network of spiritually-fit people who truly care and are praying for me at this very minute!" —Jennifer

FRIDAY—Simplify

Clutter usually involves a whole lot more than an office or home.

"I am jealous for you with the jealousy of God himself.
For I promised you as a pure bride to one husband, Christ.
But I fear that somehow you will be led away from your pure
and simple devotion to Christ, just as Eve was deceived by the serpent.
You seem to believe whatever anyone tells you..."
2 Corinthians 11:2-3

"I found a picture of your office on the internet," a relative mentioned when my wife and I were visiting.

"Oh really," I answered, wondering why she would be so interested.

"We've never had a chance to visit your church, so I decided to check it out online. I love the page that has a map of your church and I can click on any room and see a picture. Your sanctuary is beautiful and the Family Life Center is interesting. But have you seen your office?" she pressed on.

"Actually, I haven't. Why do you ask?" Now I was really curious. What was her point?

"I made a copy of the picture for you. Maybe you should take a peek," she said with a mischievous grin.

Preserved in glossy 8-by-11 technicolor was my office — in all its *(gulp)* glory. Maybe a better title for the picture would be "Extreme Clutter" or "Disaster Area" or "This site should be condemned!" Papers were strewn all over my desk. You could hardly see my computer for the mess. A lamp shade was tilted at a 45-degree angle. In the background were pictures, books and old mementos scattered all about.

I was embarrassed, ashamed and yes, humiliated. I knew something drastic needed to be done, but it wouldn't be right to eliminate my entire family, would it? *(Okay, Larry, get serious.)* There was no way around it. Something needed to be done about my office.

Clutter often involves more than just an office or a house. In his book, *So, You Want to Be Like Christ,* Chuck Swindoll wrote a chapter entitled "Simplicity: Uncluttering Our Minds." With tongue planted firmly in cheek, Swindoll shared five steps toward achieving a cluttered mind. As I read each statement, I was forced to declare myself ... guilty! Read his list and see where you stand:

1. Say yes every time someone asks you to do something.
2. Don't plan any time for leisure and rejuvenation.
3. Aren't satisfied with your accomplishments — keep moving.
4. Max out your credit cards beyond what you can repay.
5. Acquire all the latest technology so you can simplify your life.

Guilty! I say "yes" far too often. Guilty! I plan very little time for leisure and rejuvenation. Guilty! I am seldom satisfied with my accomplishments. I do keep moving. Guilty! I've taken on too much debt this year. Guilty! I've often acquired the latest technology hoping for a simpler life, only to find myself maintaining yet another gadget. Where does it all end? I confess! I am guilty of a cluttered office and a cluttered mind. In fact, every component of my life is cluttered. *(Sigh)*

Max Lucado wrote in *Cure for the Common Life*:

We are a nation that believes in having it all. In 1950 American families owned one car and saved for a second. In 2000 nearly 1 in 5 families owned three cars or more. Americans shell out more for garbage bags than 90 of the world's 210 countries spend for everything. In 1900 the average person living in the US wanted 72 different things and considered 18 of them essential. Today the average person wants 500 things and considers over 100 of them essential.

Our prosperity, however, carries a hefty price tag. Most of us feel the stress of a hectic, cluttered lifestyle.

Paul wrote in 2 Corinthians: *"I am jealous for you with the jealousy of God himself. For I promised you as a pure bride to one husband, Christ. But I fear that somehow you will be led away from your pure and simple devotion to Christ, just as Eve was deceived by the serpent. You seem to believe whatever anyone tells you ..."* (2 Corinthians 11:2-3) When our lives are cluttered we are more easily led astray.

In her beautiful poem, *Fate*, Ella Wheeler Wilcox wrote:

One ship drives east and another drives west
with the selfsame winds that blow:
'Tis the set of the sails and not the gales,
which tells us the way to go.

Two ships driven by the wind, yet one stays on course. Are you sailing where you desire or are you caught in the gales of a cluttered lifestyle? Ella continues her poem:

Like the winds of the sea are the ways of fate,
as we voyage along through life:
'Tis the set of the soul that decides its goal
and not the calm or the strife.

I was caught in the gales of a cluttered lifestyle. Perhaps you are, too. I believe the answer is found in one word: simplify. As Wilcox's poem reminds us, we must set our souls and decide on our goals; otherwise, we will find ourselves "blown around" by the whims of life. In short, we must learn to simplify our lives. The reward is a life less complicated, not more. We will have more time, not less. And the fruit is the opportunity to enjoy a long-lasting, satisfying, rewarding, intimate relationship with our Creator. After seeing that picture of my office, I recognized the need to simplify my own life.

So now you're probably saying, "This all sounds great but where do I start?" For me, simplifying started in my office. For a good part of three days I filled multiple trash cans with unused books, old gifts and files. Anything not needed — including furniture — was given away or thrown away. People walking by looked at me strangely and then, with worried expressions asked, "Are you moving?"

While cleaning my office was helpful, I need to do so much more. So, what's next?

In the parable of the farmer sowing seeds, Jesus says this about the seed growing in thorny ground: *"The thorny ground represents those who hear and accept the Good News but all too quickly the message is crowded out by the cares of this life, the lure of wealth and the desire for nice things so no crop is produced."* (Mark 4:18-19) Jesus is describing a cluttered lifestyle.

Swindoll's book also provides a good checklist for the *un*cluttered life:

1. Do you say "no" enough to keep from being overly committed?
2. Do you maintain a good balance between work and leisure time?
3. Do you enjoy appropriate satisfaction in your accomplishments?
4. Do you have spending and debt under control?
5. Does technology simplify your life rather than complicate it?

I'm learning to ask tougher questions of myself: How can I more effectively control my hectic schedule? Is there a creative way to adjust my time to allow more room for God, my family and myself? Can I learn to say no to more activities? How can I stop and truly appreciate my many blessings?

Max Lucado wrote about a farmer who was discontented with his farm. He griped about the lake on his property always needing to be stocked and managed. The hills ruined his roads and added wear and tear on his vehicles. And those fat cows lumbered through his pasture. There was all the fencing and the feeding. What a headache. He decided to sell the place and move, so he called a real estate agent and made plans to list the farm. A few days later the agent phoned, wanting approval for the ad she planned to list in the local paper. She read: "A lovely farm in an ideal location, quiet and peaceful, contoured with rolling hills, carpeted with soft meadows, nourished by a fresh lake and blessed with well-bred livestock."

The farmer paused and then said "would you read that ad to me again please?" After hearing it a second time, he said, "I'm sorry. I've changed my mind. I'm not going to sell. I've been looking for a place like this all my life." Maybe the farmer discovered the answer to a cluttered lifestyle.

Paul wrote: *"I have learned how to be content whether I have much or little."* (*Philippians 4:11*) Maybe the real secret to a simplified life is in learning how to be content with much or with little.

SEE THE LIGHT

Clutter often involves more than just an office. I confess that I am guilty of a cluttered office and a cluttered lifestyle. Fixing it the right way involves turning over my life and my lifestyle to God.

SHARE THE LIGHT

1. Are you guilty of a cluttered lifestyle?
   - Do you say yes every time someone asks you to do something?
   - Do you plan time for leisure and rejuvenation?
   - Are you satisfied with your accomplishments or do you feel you have to keep moving?
   - Do you max out your credit cards beyond what you can repay?
   - Do you acquire all the latest technology in hopes of "simplifying" your life?
2. The key word is simplify. But how do we begin cleaning up our lives? Where do we simplify first?
3. What does it mean to be content? How can you be more content?
4. How can you better turn your lifestyle over to God?
5. How could you share this message with someone else?

Notes:

_____

_____

_____

_____

_____

_____

_____

_____

_____

_____

_____

_____

_____

LIVE THE LIGHT: The Lighthouse in Action

Speaking of cluttered... Our church was cluttered with committee meetings nearly every night of the week. Church board meetings went on for hours, resolving every situation and leaving very little for the committees to do. I was worn out. We needed to clean up the clutter and get organized.

The solution: Every committee and ministry is grouped under one of four teams, with each team meeting on a different Monday each month. The teams are responsible for resolving situations and managing ministry opportunities. Our church board serves as overseer, simply encouraging the teams' hard work. The four teams are:

Ministry & Missions: Includes everything from mission teams to our local food bank. In addition, we have a worship and communications team to help us communicate our focus to the congregation.

Congregational Care: Based on the premise that the pastor cannot do it alone, this team provides prayer support, hospital and nursing home visitation, grief and divorce recovery, parish nurses, lay pastors and newcomer mentors.

Nurture: Our small group ministry is managed by this team which also includes children and youth ministry, Sunday school, and our young, single and older adult ministries.

Administration: Includes the more familiar committees: trustees, finance, pastor and staff relations and volunteer ministry. The Administration team provides vital and necessary support for our numerous ministries.

Your Action Ideas:
Are there areas in your church that are cluttered? How can you reduce the clutter and simplify?

1. _____

2. _____

3. _____

SATURDAY—Start Shining

A consistent walk with God requires endurance.

*I keep working toward that day when I will finally be all that Christ Jesus
saved me for and wants me to be. No, I am still not all I should be,
but I am focusing all my energies on this one thing:
Forgetting the past and looking forward to what lies ahead,
I strain to reach the end of the race and receive the prize for which God,
through Christ Jesus, is calling us up to heaven.*
Philippians 3:12-14

On just about any computer with the Windows operating system, you can find the card game, *FreeCell* — also known as "my stress reliever." When I come to a stopping place at work, I play a quick game. When faced with a tough situation, I'll pause for another round of *FreeCell*. When I'm feeling good or just when I have a few spare minutes, I'll whip out *FreeCell*. In fact, I'll use almost any excuse to play. I love this game.

So, what is *FreeCell?* According to Microsoft, "The object [of this game] is to move all the cards to the home area, using free cells as place-holders." The rules then add a mysterious extra note: "It is believed (although not proven) that every game is winnable." Really?

Maybe every game is winnable for a mathematical genius, but for most of us regular folks, well, winning's not such a sure thing.

Sometimes a game is so easy, anyone could play; the cards just seem to fall into place. Sometimes I only have to look ahead and make a calculated move or two before winning. Sometimes I make a mistake or a really dumb move and end up defeating myself. And sometimes, despite my best efforts, the game proves too challenging, forcing me to quit.

Oftentimes, however, I find myself in a tight spot in the middle of the game. I'm only one or two moves away from disaster. I want to quit and start over. So what now? I have reached a turning point. The temptation is simply to give up. It would be easier to start over, but if I quit, I lose. And if I quit often enough, the statistics kept by the computer will mark me as a *loser*. Ouch!

But if I refuse to give in — stop for a moment, regroup my thoughts and then approach the game with a fresh dose of creativity — I am often rewarded with renewed insight so that a small correction leads to a series of good moves, resulting in an immensely satisfying victory. If I refuse to quit, and I win enough of these turning points, the statistics kept by the computer mark me as *winner*. Hooray!

Consistent winners in the game of *FreeCell* refuse to quit in the midst of turning points. They continue to explore other options and frequently turn potential disaster into sweet victory.

So you're probably wondering by now, "What is your point? After all, *FreeCell* is just a game, isn't it? Who cares?"

Maybe all of us should care, because the stages of life's journey are a lot like a game of *FreeCell:*

1. At times life seems easy and all your decisions seem to turn out right.
2. At times you only have to make a few good choices to keep things going smoothly.
3. At times you make a mistake or do something really dumb that causes an obvious setback.
4. At times, despite your best efforts, your life can be a challenge and you're tempted to start over.

It's only natural. When you find yourself in a tight spot, the temptation is to quit and start over. You are only one or two moves away from disaster. So what now? You have reached a turning point. Do you give up? It seems easier to start over, but if you quit, you lose. And if you quit often enough, the statistics kept inside your brain mark you as a loser. Double ouch!

Now imagine the alternative: You refuse to give up. You stop for a moment, regroup your thoughts and then approach the situation with a fresh dose of creativity. When you do this, you often will be rewarded with renewed insight so that a small correction leads to a series of good moves resulting in an immensely satisfying victory. If you refuse to quit and you turn the situation around, the statistics kept inside your brain will mark you as a winner. Double hooray!

Consistent winners on the journey of life refuse to quit in the midst of turning points. They continue to explore other options and frequently turn potential disaster into sweet victory.

Remember Paul's words: *"I keep working toward that day when I will finally be all that Christ Jesus saved me for and wants me to be. No, I am still not all I should be, but I am focusing all my energies on this one thing: Forgetting the past and looking forward to what lies ahead, I strain to reach the end of the race and receive the prize for which God, through Christ Jesus, is calling us up to heaven.*" *(Philippians 3:12-14)*

In other words, whether it's *FreeCell* or the journey of life, don't quit. Keep exploring other options and taste the sweet victory.

SEE THE LIGHT

Consistent winners on the journey of life refuse to quit in the midst of turning points, continue to explore other options and frequently turn potential disaster into sweet victory.

SHARE THE LIGHT

1. What does playing *FreeCell* have to do with life?
2. How can understanding the stages of the journey help us?
3. Where does God fit in all this talk of *FreeCell* and life?
4. How can you share this message with a friend?

Notes:

_____

_____

_____

_____

_____

_____

_____

_____

_____

_____

_____

_____

_____

LIVE THE LIGHT: The Lighthouse in Action

"Say Christ" Chairs. At Timberlake, all of our youth have the opportunity to "let their light shine" by earning a director's chair with their name stenciled on the back. They earn the chair through a combination of attendance, mission projects and giving. The chairs are purchased by sponsors who have the opportunity to mentor and encourage the youth throughout their time at church. Every year our church awards approximately thirty to thirty-five chairs. Through these chairs, youth learn the value of mission and ministry and adults receive opportunities to be involved in the lives of our youth.

Your Action Ideas:
Like FreeCell, youth ministry can be difficult and challenging. What can you or your church do to bring new life to your youth ministry?

1. _____

2. _____

3. _____

"We had a youth group called 'The Way Station' which met every Friday night ... we would hear God's word, share testimonies and sing songs. My Christian life grew so much during that time. I often wonder if I would be a Christian today without that church experience." —Debbie

"I wrote to mention how your book is helping to transform the lives of many young people here in the church of Ethiopia. Thank you for your continued prayer for my ministry. May the Lord bless you with his blessings. You know that our young people have many problems across the world and your book deals with many of these social problems and it really helped me to teach 500 youth in the last month. Thank you for your support for me through your books and continue doing the same as the Lord puts in your heart." —Asrat

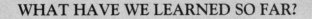

WHAT HAVE WE LEARNED SO FAR?

Monday—We need light
Before we can fully "Love our Lord," we must recognize
our spiritual blindness and seek the light of God's Lighthouse.

Tuesday—Opportunities to Shine
When facing snakes or storms we turn to the Lighthouse
to guide us safely home.

Wednesday—Becoming God's Lighthouse
Prayer begins with you, but soon there are more circles
as God turns a prayer life into a prayer ministry.

Thursday—An Attitude that Shines
Instead of "kicking cats," look to Christ for strength,
love one another and work hard at living in peace.

Friday—Simplify
Whether it's a cluttered office or a cluttered life,
fixing it involves turning your lifestyle over to God.

Saturday—Start Shining
Consistent winners refuse to quit in the midst of turning points.
They continue to explore other options and frequently
turn potential disaster into sweet victory.

Now, let's put it all together...

SUNDAY—Live the Light

God, breathe life into us!

Preach to these dead people and say to them, "Dead people,
hear the word of the Lord! This is what the Lord says to you
I will breathe into your dead bodies and you will come to life."
From Ezekiel 37

One dark, stormy night, I dreamed God placed me in a church to prepare for their Sunday worship service. God had me walk up and down the aisle among hundreds of people. They all looked *(gulp)* ... they all looked dead! There were all kinds of people: children with crayons in their hands, teenagers sitting among friends, mothers cradling babies and choir members holding music. They seemed normal enough — for dead folks. Then God asked me: "Preacher, can these dead people live?"

I replied, "Lord, you are the only one who knows."

Welcome to my modern translation of "The Valley of the Dry Bones" from the Old Testament prophet Ezekiel *(Chapter 37)*. The question asked by Ezekiel is: "Can these dead people live?" In other words, can today's church still make a difference in the world?

To answer this question, we need to understand several important trends shaping our church and society today:

1. Our nation is in severe crisis — ethically, morally and financially. The newspapers are filled with stories of corruption, corporate collapse and scandals of all kinds.
2. The events of September 11, 2001, and the continuing war against terrorism changed our nation forever. Church attendance was expected to increase — and it did at first — but not for long.
3. Interest in spiritual growth is increasing. Christian web sites, increased sales of Christian books and media attention on spirituality shows we are a nation interested in discovering God.
4. Church morale in general is low. Declining attendance, combined with higher costs, make it almost impossible for many churches to pay their bills. There is little left over for ministry to others.

The first two trends are somewhat obvious, but three and four seem contradictory. While interest in spiritual growth is increasing, the traditional source of our spiritual growth — namely our churches — is experiencing steady decline. Why is this? Surveys and opinion polls quote many typical Americans as saying: "I believe in God but I don't need to be in a church."

Those who seek deepened spirituality but do not use the resources offered by churches cite many reasons. Comments like these are heard frequently:

- "Worship services are boring and irrelevant."
- "Churches are always asking for money."
- "I need to do more than serve on a committee to be involved."
- "Churches don't seem to do much to serve our community."
- "Church people are too quick to judge and exclude." (They cite positions on divorce, homosexuality and abortion, to name a few.)
- "Church people are just a bunch of well-dressed hypocrites."
- "Churches are always trying to tell me what is right and wrong."

Are these statements true? No! Well, sometimes. But if those outside the church believe them to be true, then we as the church need to do a better job of communicating God's grace — not just judgment. We need to display the passion and the daily excitement of serving Christ. We must work to change the world's image of us and preach God's truth.

Continuing my translation of Ezekiel: Then God said to me, "Preach to these dead people and say to them, 'Dead people, hear the word of the Lord! This is what the Lord says to you. I will breathe into your dead bodies and you will come to life. You will begin to smile at one another and offer a hug. You will welcome the strangers, visit the sick and volunteer to help those who are helpless. Then you will know that I am the Lord.'"

Can God still breathe life into the church? Of course! But are we ready to receive it?

I imagine Ezekiel continuing: "So I preached to the dead people as God commanded. First one person began to smile and then another moved his head to look at me. One woman began to fold her hands together as if in prayer ... but there was still no twinkle of light in any of their eyes or color in their cheeks."

Good leaders never accept "the way it is." They dream of what could be and work to make it a reality. Ezekiel asked, *"Can these dead people live?"* In other words, can God still breathe life into our church? The answer is a resounding "Yes!"

So what can we do to enable our church to truly live? We start with the basics:

1. **Pray.** Everything begins with prayer. Pray for God to breathe new life into you. Start a small group dedicated to praying for your church. Emphasize prayer time during worship services.
2. **Listen.** Listen to the spoken and unspoken needs of your community. Do you live in a neighborhood full of single parents and children? How can your church offer help?
3. **Worship.** Worship should be relevant and exciting. Churches are forming worship teams to help their pastors explore creative ideas and better utilize the talents within their congregation.
4. **Teach.** Teaching in small groups offers new life. Many new ministries begin because someone within a Bible study or small group feels called by God to become more involved.
5. **Be Open.** Be open to new ideas and people. As your church grows, new people will feel inspired to offer suggestions. Will you listen with respect and be open to change?

Then God said to me, "Keep preaching to the dead and say this: 'Holy Spirit, come from the four corners of the globe and breathe life into their dead bodies.'" So I did as God commanded and there were strange noises throughout the congregation as people began first to breathe, then to sing — not like dead people —but with the excitement of folks possessed by God's living spirit. One man shouted, proclaiming that God healed him of the pain caused by a painful marital separation. Another left the church to seek a former friend and reconcile their differences. An elderly woman walked over to the youth and began to hug each of them. A businesswoman was led to donate a portion of her profits toward a homeless shelter. A teenager felt called to begin a Bible study at school, and on and on.

Wait! Is that all there is to it?

No! Now it's time for God to breathe life into the church. But how does this happen?

1. **Discover.** Churches, like individuals, need to discover their mission. No church can do everything, but every church can do something. What would God have your church do?
2. **Start.** Set an example by starting a ministry within your church that suits your particular gifts. This could be as simple as hosting a Bible study in your home or volunteering your time at a local literacy group.
3. **Evangelize.** Evangelism begins when you look for someone as a friend. Pray for them by name. Ask God to use you. Tell your story and even admit your struggles. Watch God work.
4. **Involve.** Ministry means matching needs with the talents of members. Our church consolidated thirty committees into four teams and challenged each team to design a new ministry.
5. **Celebrate.** Every church has events to celebrate and accomplishments to lift up. Ministries and people should be congratulated frequently. Celebrated success is contagious.

Here is how I believe Ezekiel's story ends: As the holy breath of God entered the dead bodies throughout the church, they each came to life and jumped to their feet — a vast army. Then God said: "These dead bodies represent my beloved church who feel cut off from Me and whose hope for living is gone. Therefore, preach to them and say: 'God promises to open your graves and give you life. Then you will know that I am God. I will put my Spirit in you and you will live!'"

May we all be challenged by the prophet Ezekiel to live again. For all of its shortcomings, the church is still the best place to find God's eternal healing and comfort. May God breathe life into our dead bodies and help us rise up again to become a mighty army — the church! *"Then you will know that I am God. I will put my Spirit in you and you will live!"* Wow! What a wonder to behold!

SEE THE LIGHT

What can we do to help our churches truly live? Start with the basics:
1. **Pray.** Everything begins with prayer.
2. **Listen.** Find the spoken and unspoken needs of your community.
3. **Worship.** Worship should be relevant and exciting.
4. **Teach.** Teaching in small groups offers new life.
5. **Be open.** Be open to new ideas and new people.

SHARE THE LIGHT

1. In this special translation of Ezekiel 37, we find dead people in the church needing new life. How is your church doing? Would you describe your church as dead or alive? Why?
2. Using the lessons learned this week, what is God calling you to do to bring new life to your family, your small group, your church or your community?
3. After completing the first week of learning how to "Live the LIGHT," what will you do to let your light shine brightly?
4. Draw up your action plan based on what you feel God is asking you to do.

Notes:

_____

_____

_____

_____

_____

_____

_____

_____

LIVE THE LIGHT: The Lighthouse in Action

Grief Ministry. We all face grief eventually. Most churches respond quickly and compassionately during the first few days following a death. But what happens after that? The grieving process itself can take a year or more. The finality of death is hard to accept and that's what grief ministry is all about. GriefShare, a special seminar and support group for people grieving the loss of someone close, is one excellent resource and there are many others. The GriefShare series includes a 13-session combination of video teaching and small group discussion that gives each group the opportunity to learn and share.

Your Action Ideas:
How can helping others grieve breathe new life into your church?

1. _____

2. _____

3. _____

"My church planted important seeds in my life, which came from my parents and those seeds, in turn, came from their parents and those seeds grew out of the great revivals." —Brian

"I wanted to let you know that the prayers of your team are really being felt! I don't have time to reply to [all of the e-mails] but would you let them all know that God is working on me even as I type and is rebuilding our relationship. I have [reason] to be scared and to feel helpless, but I don't. I know He is there. I appreciate all the prayers. Please don't stop! And thank you, because without this type of ministry, I might've fallen through the cracks and things could have been quite worse. God Bless all of You!" —Maria

WEEK TWO

INVITE

MONDAY—We Need Light

Who should we invite?

Therefore, go and make disciples of all the nations,
baptizing them in the name of the Father and the Son and the Holy Spirit.
Matthew 28:19

One day I received the following e-mail: "Dear Larry: All churches should make people feel there is a place for them. For example, there are millions of people who are single — not divorced, not widowed — just single. Churches lump those groups together. Other churches have singles groups but people who have gone to their stuff say you might as well go to a bar. It's like a meat market. They don't get anything out of it. The divorced whine while others cry. So the message for us: 'There is no place for you here.'"

The writer of this e-mail will remain anonymous but I know him through our prayer network. He is young, single and recently expressed interest in God, but claims no church affiliation. Over the next few days, through e-mail, he shared his frustrations and revealed valuable insight.

"In my whole life, I never heard a pastor with the guts to talk to single people about stuff they really face: like loneliness, sex and having to solve every problem on our own. What we actually hear is how our money is all ours and we have free time. We never hear about how there is only one income. Most of us aren't lawyers or doctors and barely make ends meet. And we would give up our free time in a second not to feel so lonely. But the church just wants us to volunteer for things like watching the kids in the nursery so parents can get spiritual lessons."

He also sent me an article by Julia Duin, "Why Singles Boycott Churches." Duin wrote: "*Single Adult Ministries Journal* reports that the largest group of nonchurched people are singles. Church attendance is undeniably shrinking while the number of singles in America is skyrocketing. More and more Christian singles are quietly boycotting their churches."

My e-mail friend was blunt: "Every church talks about family but never about singles. So if you go to hell for not going to church, millions of singles will be there. But don't listen to me. I don't even go to church and probably never will. Church is for families like everything in this stupid world."

Julia Duin adds her own list of discontented singles: "A female government worker friend of mine in Northern Virginia; an evangelical male journalist in Seattle; another Christian male journalist in Wyoming; a male acquaintance in Richmond; a female journalist in Oregon — all of these are real singles who have put up and put out and have now opted out of an irrelevant church."

The e-mail writer continued: "I haven't served a church for years. So why do I read the Bible you sent or try to learn about God and watch religious shows? I even saw Billy Graham and regularly listen to a Christian radio station. Why do I do all that but avoid going to church?"

Why indeed. Churches like ours can brag about vision and Bible studies, programs and missions; but if a large portion of our population opts out, something is terribly wrong. So maybe we need to stop preaching and listen to those who opt out. In Matthew, Jesus told his disciples: "*I have been given complete authority in heaven and on earth. Therefore, go and make disciples of all the nations, baptizing them in the name of the Father and the Son and the Holy Spirit. Teach these new disciples to obey all the commands I have given you. And be sure of this: I am with you always, even to the end of the age.*" (Matthew 28:18-20)

If we're serious about following Jesus' command to go and make disciples, maybe we should listen more carefully to those who claim to love Jesus but not the church.

The e-mail writer continues: "For one thing, it's hard to go into an environment you are not familiar with by yourself. I feel that I would stick out like a sore thumb. Maybe people would say 'hi' but then would go off and sit by whomever. I'd probably have an anxiety attack. I would never go to 'Nurture Night' at your church; not that it's bad, but I would wonder who would sit by me and who I would talk to. Would I feel all alone, head out the door and no one even notice I'm gone?

"All those fears keep me away. Right now, I don't care about singles groups. I know enough singles. I want to learn about God. I want support. You said people in church can be your family. That's what I want. Social events are fine but not what I need. I have events. I need the church."

Wow! Maybe he has a point. Shortly after these words were first published in one of my columns, I was literally bombarded with e-mails. Here is an abbreviated sampling of the responses:

I am a strong Christian. I love the Lord. I love His word. However, I don't go to church. I think churches have missed the boat. Church is about fellowship and giving encouragement and strength to fellow believers. Instead, we sit next to a perfect stranger for an hour and "worship." We stay isolated and alone — only now we are alone within a crowd. —*Alicia*

I relate to the writer of the e-mail so much I could have written it myself. Reading through it, I'd think, "Exactly! That's just how it is! I agree! I feel that way too!" As you can tell, I'm single (not divorced, not widowed, not a parent — just single). I can't tell you how refreshing it was to read something from a pastor that finally addresses this issue. Believe me, it's a *big* issue. I don't go to church for many of the same reasons your writer addressed. —*Anon.*

This message really touched me. I am not sure I would be involved or attending church if I did not have kids. It is hard to be thrown into a family environment when you are single. It helped that I had friends who helped me. — *Jodi*

Jodi is unknowingly testifying to the secret of witnessing to someone outside of the church. "I had friends who helped me." We need to be a friend willing to help another adjust. Jesus says: *"You are the salt of the earth. But what good is salt if it has lost its flavor? Can you make it useful again? It will be thrown out and trampled underfoot as worthless. You are the light of the world — like a city on a mountain, glowing in the night for all to see. Don't hide your light under a basket! Instead, put it on a stand and let it shine for all*

In the same way, let your good deeds shine out for all to see, so that everyone will praise your heavenly Father." (Matthew 5:13-16)

Salt adds flavor and zest to any food. But if salt stays in the container, what good is it? A flashlight is a necessity when you lose your electricity; but if you keep it in a drawer or forget to replace the old batteries, what have you got? You have another piece of junk wasting space. At the same time, if you or your church expends no effort to be salt and light to those outside your doors, what good are you? Your salt is still in the container. Your flashlight lies unused in a drawer. Where is your usefulness? Are you really serving Jesus Christ?

Is the answer to becoming a more effective witness really so simple? Just be a friend? Well, it's a great start; but the person being helped also has to make an effort as the following e-mails suggest:

> I find it difficult to go into a place not knowing many folks, but sometimes you have to take that step and check out the possibilities. A wise woman told me, if you have an opportunity to go out then go. If you don't enjoy yourself, then at least you've gotten out even if for a short while. When the next opportunity presents itself, go out and do it all over again. Each time, it gets easier. —Anon.

> I feel it is very important to establish your own identity and work toward a common goal with your church, which is to have a closer relationship with God. I think the least we can do as "singles" is force ourselves into a situation that may seem uncomfortable at first. You'll be surprised to see that it may not be uncomfortable whatsoever! —Lora

> I joined a church four years ago because of our children. I was an alcoholic for 18 years and got sober in AA. My excuse for not attending church was because of those "hypocrites." But I was the biggest hypocrite. God wants a relationship with all of us. —Warren

In other words, the people we want to reach must also be willing to make an effort.

Churches as institutions also need to be more aware and assertive about responding to the needs of the communities they serve as the following e-mails point out:

I am a registered nurse and work weekends and nights. Church should not be about me fitting into a Church's schedule. The "church" needs to serve the community. I think we could take lessons from organizations such as Alcoholics Anonymous, which has meetings all the time. I need a supportive community of believers as much as others need support for addiction. —*Joanne*

For two years, we were more like visitors at church because we were often away taking care of my parents. Now when we go, I feel very isolated. What is it about church that makes us feel that way? It should be a warm inviting place for all members of the family of God. —*Susan*

My husband recently started coming to worship service with me but, before that, I felt so alone. I once thought about reserving a couple of rows for pew pals: A place for those who come alone. Then they can have people to sit with each week. —*Anon.*

I was single so long and remember well the loneliness and feeling uncomfortable. A singles group with good leaders helped a lot. Teachers who would talk about anything and everything, events that were not "date-oriented," preaching that dealt with how to live as singles — all helped me. Getting active in helping others helped me get my mind off my singleness. —*Lisa*

So here is what I've learned so far:

1. All churches should aggressively look for ways to make everyone feel there is a place for them.
2. Single adults, a rapidly growing population group, especially feel excluded by the church.
3. Single adults do not need groups or events as much as they simply need the church.
4. The best way to be a witness for Jesus Christ is to be a good friend.
5. The people we want to reach must also be willing to make an effort.
6. The church should be aware and responsive to the needs of its community.

The original e-mail writer who started this article wrote back and offered his own answers:

"I want to be mentored by someone who will help me because I don't have a church background. I don't want to walk in and right away be told what I should do in the church. It's not that I would never be willing. It's just not where I am right now. When you start a job, you have a supervisor who introduces you to the people you work with. The work environment is better at saying 'you belong' than a typical church. So, people already in a church could sponsor people who aren't."

Most churches, including ours, have ushers and greeters at the door to help visitors feel welcome. But what happens after someone enters the worship area? Who will introduce them to others sitting nearby or help them understand what's in the bulletin? Some like to sit alone but most don't. Most churches have a visitor center packed with brochures but is someone also ready to talk to visitors?

"Maybe the church could say, 'If you want someone to sit with and show you the ropes, call us.' Then he/she could meet with you and help out. I would volunteer to be a mentor if I was already in a church. It wouldn't even take any special skills really — just a willingness to sit and talk to someone who doesn't want to be alone. It would help so much to have committed church members take you under their wing. It wouldn't be forever — just someone to sit by in the service.

"I know people who don't go because churches have you greet each other. You may say what's wrong with that? It's hard and awkward for a shy person who is alone. We see people talking and laughing then giving a cursory handshake. It wouldn't be as hard if you had someone to sit by."

As a church, we are working hard to expand our small group opportunities because we know if you are in a small group you can better strengthen your relationship with God. We want to better communicate our vision so you will be more excited about our ministry. But none of our groups or visions will be especially helpful if we are not helping you feel welcome and valued.

My e-mail friend also made a suggestion for preachers: "I saw a minister walk out with a black smudge on his face. He pretended not to know it was there. Then a woman in front passed him a mirror. He used the mirror to notice the smudge. Then he took a red washcloth and wiped it off. The black mark represented sin. The mirror represented the law and why we need it. The red washcloth represented the blood of Jesus. How it wipes away our sins. If he only said all that, I probably wouldn't remember any-thing but the visual made me understand and remember."

He concluded: "I am only brainstorming. I probably sound ridiculous, but look how motivated I am and I don't go to any church. But you didn't turn a deaf ear. You are hearing me. Do you know how motivating that is? It feels good. It makes me want to help because you help me just by hear-ing what I am saying. You didn't shut the door on me. If you did, for sure I would never go to church."

So what can we do?

1. Churches can provide mentors or sponsors to provide loving guidance for newcomers.
2. Mentors and sponsors should share similar interests and backgrounds in order to relate.
3. Preachers and worship leaders need to be more creative in expressing their messages.
4. Don't turn a deaf ear to those who are not active. Their ideas and their opinions matter.

Dan Hassett, author of *God Uses Who He Chooses* writes: "A few years ago, I found myself single in a new town working a new job with a new company. I told God, 'It's you and me, Lord. I simply want to seek and serve you.' After a few fits and starts I felt led toward a church. Surprise! I found myself warmly welcomed, invited to dinner, to a Bible study, to take part in a play, to join the choir and to get involved in an addiction recov-ery ministry. I said yes to all the invitations and soon found myself feeling 'part of' the family of God. I even volunteered to drive a church van to pick up people from the halfway houses for recovery services. Paul lauded the single life and urged singles to immerse themselves in Christ and His service. My advice is the same: Seek God and service in His kingdom and He will fill your life with joy and satisfaction too."

SEE THE LIGHT

As a church we are working hard to expand our small group opportunities because we know if you are in a small group you can better strengthen your relationship with God. We want to better communicate our vision so you will be more excited about our ministry. But none of our groups or visions will be especially helpful if we are not helping you feel welcome and valued.

SHARE THE LIGHT

1. All churches should make people feel there is a place for them. How are you helping your church make a place?
2. The largest group of nonchurched people is single. Why?
3. If you are single, how does this story touch you? How should you respond?
4. If you are a church leader, how could you respond more effectively to single adults?
5. How could you reach out to someone new in your church?

Notes:

_____

_____

_____

_____

_____

_____

_____

_____

_____

_____

LIVE THE LIGHT: The Lighthouse in Action

After reading this story, one young single adult decided to take matters into her own hands. She began inviting her friends, suggesting they sit together. Later she asked them to meet her for breakfast first. I heard that she simply would not take no for an answer. Within a few short weeks she had approximately twelve friends joining her for breakfast and church. So far they are still attending and, best of all, they are still friends.

Divorce Recovery. Most of these single adults are not young but they are very much in need of church support. We sponsor this vital ministry at least twice per year to let those going through the trauma of separation and divorce know that they are loved and supported.

Your Action Ideas:
How can you welcome and support singles and others who may feel alone in the church?

1. _____

2. _____

3. _____

"I just wanted to thank you for the great blessing that your prayer ministry had in my life. Besides being honored by God to have the privilege of prayer to Him on behalf of others, I have also requested prayer and God has been so very faithful. My mother, who is battling Alzheimer's, is now doing so much better since I requested prayer. My husband who hurt his back has now returned to work and the Lord supplied our needs in every area while he couldn't work. A girl named Chris who broke her back while snowmobiling is still alive and amazing the doctors with her recovery. These are just a few of the praise reports I wanted to share with you." —Maureen

TUESDAY—Opportunities to Shine

The best opportunities to invite often come by surprise.

And now dear children, continue to live in fellowship with Christ
so that when he returns, you will be full of courage
and not shrink back from him in shame.
1 John 2:28

I was not looking for an opportunity to be a preacher. All I wanted was to purchase some mulch at the discount store and go home. But there was a hole in the bag, so the cashier sent someone to replace it. Hence, we waited. Then a shirt I was purchasing was missing a price tag, so the cashier once again sent someone to find the correct price. We waited some more. While we waited the cashier talked. Boy, did he talk!

To pass the time, I started filling out the check and innocently asked, "What is today's date?"

"I don't know. I don't care. All I know is that today is Friday!" he said with emphasis and a grin.

In a feeble attempt to be polite I replied, "So, you like Fridays?"

"Oh yeah," he said with obvious enthusiasm. "I love Fridays because it's party time and I love to party! I live to party!"

Before I could respond he continued, "I drink and party all night long! Yep! My friends and me love to have a good time. We try to do it every night. That's what I live for: friends, drinking and partying."

I thought to myself: "Why is he saying this to me? Should I respond? Should I tell this young man he's making a big mistake? Should I tell him there is another way to enjoy life? Should I talk about God to a stranger in a crowded department store? I really don't want to be a witness right now, Lord. I just want to make my purchase and go home. Is there anything wrong with that?"

Yet, if I say nothing it looks as if I approve or at least condone his outrageous behavior. But if I say something, how do I say it without sounding judgmental and arrogant? In essence, I was in a fix.

There is a great verse in the Bible that seems appropriate: "*And now dear children, continue to live in fellowship with Christ so that when he returns, you will be full of courage and not shrink back from him in shame.*" (*1 John 2:28*) I needed a dose of Godly courage and wisdom to say something appropriate to this young man and let him know I did not approve his actions, but that I loved him as a child of God.

After a pause, I looked at the young cashier and flashed my biggest smile. "Thank you for telling me about your parties. You just made my day!"

This time, it was his turn to pause. "What do you mean?" he asked with a look of confusion.

"Well, I'm a preacher and I have been looking for someone who needs prayer today — and you're it!"

His mouth opened in astonishment and he stared at me for a long moment before a smile began to appear. Then he laughed and said: "You won't believe this, but that is what my preacher said to me!"

For the next few moments my new young friend talked about his preacher and church. Recently, he had left home to make it on his own. You could see a trace of loneliness in his eyes as he said, "My pastor is a great guy. He writes me occasionally and the church still sends newsletters."

I left the discount store with a bag of mulch and a new perspective on the importance of creatively communicating God's message to each other. What we say and how we say it can mean the difference between healing and hurting. *"Evil words destroy one's friends; wise discernment rescues the godly." (Proverbs 11:9)*

Whether you are standing in line at a department store or participating in a church committee meeting, God is continually offering opportunities to witness your faith. What will you say? How will you say it? Take a deep breath, pause, say a short prayer and remember God's promise: *"Continue to live in fellowship with Christ and you will be full of courage."* As for me, I have a new friend to pray for. Isn't that what being a follower of God is all about? Now, if I could only get someone to spread this mulch!

SEE THE LIGHT

"And now dear children, continue to live in fellowship with Christ so that when he returns, you will be full of courage and not shrink back from him in shame." (1 John 2:28) I needed a dose of Godly courage and wisdom to say something appropriate to this young man and let him know I did not approve his actions, but that I loved him as a child of God.

SHARE THE LIGHT

1. We seldom look for opportunities to be a witness but God gives them to us just the same. The question is: Have you noticed? What opportunities has God given you lately?
2. How can you talk to someone about Christ without sounding judgmental or condescending?
3. How can you help your church be more aware of the everyday opportunities God gives to be a witness?

Notes:

_____

_____

_____

_____

_____

_____

_____

_____

_____

_____

_____

_____

_____

_____

_____

LIVE THE LIGHT: The Lighthouse in Action

Give stuff away. One Father's Day we gave every man in church a golf shirt with our lighthouse logo and mission statement: "A light to guide you safely home." It's been several years and I still see men throughout town proudly wearing that shirt. I've also heard numerous stories of people walking up to them, pausing to read the shirt and then commenting. It has presented numerous opportunities to witness.

What else do we give away? Let's see... Each child who is baptized in our church receives a cross-stitched baptismal banner. There is a book table near the sanctuary that is stocked with free books on various topics. Newcomers receive a coffee mug with our church name and logo, and first-time visitors are greeted at home on the afternoon of their visit by a volunteer who gives them a plant and invites them back.

Your Action Ideas:
What can you or your church give away as a witness opportunity?

1. _____

2. _____

3. _____

"My church is an anchor when winds howl, storms come and turbulent seas become too rough. As I head toward the Lord's Day, I can see a lighthouse guiding me and the anchor that holds me fast. When I step through those church doors I feel peaceful and realize I was never alone in the storm: One greater than I was there all along." —Nancy

"I wanted to let you know that your devotion ... hit me like a ton of bricks at precisely the right moment. Currently I am struggling with getting back on my feet after my move back home. I have had a very difficult time finding suitable work. So that devotion and scripture were both fitting and comforting at this time. ... No, it is not what job I have. And no, its not how much money I make. What is important is that this present situation in my life is a God-given opportunity for me to learn from my mistakes and grow in character and in Him. Thank you for reminding me of that!" —Suzanne

WEDNESDAY—Becoming God's Lighthouse

A true willingness to invite must include respect for others.

Shout with joy to the Lord, O earth! Worship the Lord with gladness.
Come before him, singing with joy.
Psalm 100:1-2

Did you know "Amazing Grace" can be sung to the tune of "Gilligan's Island" or "House of the Rising Sun"? Hymn writers sometimes used other melodies — even those sung in local taverns — to make it easier for people to recognize and sing their hymns. Imagine that! Some of our most popular hymns used melodies sung in a bar.

Speaking of bar tunes ... Many years ago, when my aspiring writer and musician son Stephen was 13, he asked me to listen to his favorite style of music: rap. I listened carefully and honestly told him I didn't like it. But then I challenged him: "Why don't you write a Christian rap song and sing it for our church?"

Why did I say that? Our church was a typical country church which sang mostly hymns written over one hundred years ago. How would these precious people respond to a rap? Oh well. Why worry? My son would never write a Christian rap song and he certainly never would sing it in church ... would he? Oh, yes! He would. Stephen wrote that song within a week, so I fulfilled my part of the promise. One Sunday he stood before our entire congregation and sang, or rather, *rapped*, "Stand Up for the Lord."

When the service was over, young people surrounded Stephen, eagerly telling him it was the best song they ever heard in church. Others asked for the words. At this point, I figured it would be smart to take another look at Stephen's rap for Jesus: "Stand Up for the Lord."

Take it to the top, not just another Christian rappin'
Here to tell you what's really happenin'
All this violence in the streets, I don't want to hear it
It's time that the people got the fever for the spirit.
He gave us our life and He gave us our choice
But we are the youth and we've got the voice
For serving Christ is a price we can all afford
C'mon y'all, oh yeah, stand up for the Lord.

As I read the words, the message coming from a youthful perspective really hits home. Stephen was clearly pointing out world-wide problems and urging Christians to action. "All this violence in the streets ... It's time that the people got the fever for the spirit." But more importantly, my son saw the relationship and the choice Christ offers us all, even today: "He gave us our life and He gave us our choice." Stephen declared that our youth do have a voice and we all should, "Stand up for the Lord."

> Think twice about the way you live your life
> You don't go to heaven or hell with a roll of the dice
> Jesus Christ loves everyone and all
> Just think of his grief when he feels us fall
> Out of his hands, into the devil's deed
> And by him dying on the cross we were all freed
> We're just sparks and God is the fire
> The one and only God-preacher, teacher, Messiah
> I know you wanna, you know you wanna, so why ain't you gonna?

Okay, okay so it's not a classic hymn. But when Stephen stood before the church and sang — and all of us old people mostly stared — I noticed that the youngsters began nodding their heads in rhythm with the beat. And by the smiles on their faces, I knew they were enjoying and understanding the message.

Stephen said something simple but profound in the second verse: "Think twice about the way you live your life. You don't go to heaven or hell with a roll of the dice." In other words, there is a real God who celebrates our joys and grieves over our failures. "Just think of his grief when he feels us fall." My favorite line in the song however, is this one: "We're just sparks and God is the fire." What a wonderful way to describe our mission as Christians. "I know you wanna. So why ain't you gonna?"

> C'mon, let's stand up for the Lord.
> Makin' controversial music and pullin' the money
> But after a little while, you just ain't funny
> Just give your life to the Lord
> The person who all your life you've ignored
> The world is full of crime and sin
> Don't ya think it's about time we let the Lord in?

You'll see the light if you open the door
C'mon ya'll, oh yeah, stand up for the Lord.

Stephen takes a satirical poke at musicians in this verse: "Makin controversial music and pullin' the money," accurately describes the state of our popular music industry today. Eventually however, you soon find the money and attention are never enough. "You just ain't funny." My son once again emphasizes another solution, another way. "Just give your life to the Lord. Don't ya think it's about time we let the Lord in?"

Stand up, Stand up, Sit down, Psyche
Too busy preachin' the word on the mic
He's got the whole world in His hands
But some people just don't understand
Believe in the Lord and you'll find out
That he'll put joy in your life and there's no doubt
That followin' Jesus never leaves you bored
C'mon y'all, oh yeah, stand up for the Lord.

Music is a tool — a wonderful tool used for expressing our deep love for God. No generation should ever claim to know which music is proper. After all, one generation's barroom melody could soon be another's sacred hymn. We need to learn to value all styles of music, realizing that many people feel, "If you respect and appreciate my music, you also respect and appreciate me." *C'mon y'all, oh yeah, stand up for the Lord.*

SEE THE LIGHT

Music is a wonderful tool used for expressing our deep love for God. No generation should ever claim to know which music is proper. After all, one generation's barroom melody could soon be another's sacred hymn.

SHARE THE LIGHT

1. How does music help you draw closer to God?
2. How can music help you talk to someone else about God?
3. How can your church use a wider variety of music styles to express their worship of God?
4. How can you and your church say to the world: "C'mon y'all, oh yeah, stand up for the Lord."

Notes:

_____

_____

_____

_____

_____

_____

_____

_____

_____

_____

_____

_____

_____

_____

_____

_____

_____

_____

_____

LIVE THE LIGHT: The Lighthouse in Action

Because music plays such a pivotal role in worship, we offer variety within our four Sunday services. There is traditional, contemporary and, at our youth-oriented service, rock. On occasion, we even switch the musical groups around so our congregation can appreciate the gifts and talents of our many musicians. What we've learned, however, is that the style of music itself is never as important as the love and sincerity of the people involved.

When our church was smaller we invited a wide variety of musicians to share their talents and a short testimony during worship. We also encouraged people in the congregation to do the same. As we became larger this became more difficult, but we still invite them to share their gifts in our many small groups. We find this openness attracts creative people who would otherwise feel their talents and gifts were ignored.

Your Action Ideas:
How can your church use music to welcome un-reached groups?

1. _____

2. _____

3. _____

"Outside the church doors, there are so many distractions and so many people who are different in their interests, beliefs, values, priorities. Inside is a safe-haven, a place to commune, worship and learn. I thank God we have the privilege and freedom of going to church." — Anonymous

"I found your website when I was going through a particularly troubling time in my job and your weekly devotions helped me rededicate my life to Jesus and deal with a very troublesome co-worker. I was able to stop using antidepressants — what a wonderful feeling to be free of that burden. My family is searching for a church to attend that meets all our needs and only wish you were closer so we could attend. Thank you for being there; I truly feel it was divine intervention finding you." —Jody

THURSDAY—An Attitude that Shines

When you seriously invite, there is often controversy.

Do for others what you would like them to do for you. This is a summary of all that is taught in the law and the prophets.
Matthew 7:12

Just as the worship service began, a middle-aged, African-American man, neatly dressed in a blue suit, entered the sanctuary and quietly took a seat near the door. He smiled but did not speak to anyone during the service. When the final hymn concluded, he quietly slipped out. Later, an usher whispered to the minister that the man's name was Walter, that he was a local problem in the area and, as an aside, added that his breath reeked of alcohol.

Week after week, the story was the same. Walter would enter just as the service began, usually wearing the same suit, the same smile and the same odor of alcohol. Several church members began to complain. One woman stopped attending. "Deep down, I know it's wrong," she said, "but I just can't bear to see what is happening to our little church!" More people complained. "He's a drunk!" they said. "We can't have alcoholics fouling up our church service!"

"What about John?" the minister said. The son of a prominent member, John also attended regularly and also was an alcoholic. But he was also very white. "That's different!" the church leaders quietly but firmly stated. Meanwhile, unaware of the controversy swirling around him, Walter continued attending, saying little and at the final hymn, silently slipping out the side door.

What would you do? What should the church do? What would Jesus do? Should you:

1. Politely ask him to leave? His presence is disruptive and a bad influence on the church, especially the children.
2. Do nothing? Leave him alone. He's doing no harm and maybe he'll leave soon.
3. Get involved and look for ways to offer help? But how?

Jesus teaches: *"You are the salt of the earth."* (Matthew 5:13) The salt represents our willingness as God's witness to add flavor and zest to the world around us. God was giving that little church a unique opportunity to be salt and light to someone in need. The question is: What kind of witness will we be?

Jesus is also very blunt on judging others: *"Stop judging others and you will not be judged. And why worry about a speck in your friend's eye when you have a log in your own?"* (Matthew 7:1,3) So, if we are to be salt of the earth and not judge others, how should we witness God's love to Walter?

Good question but first let's look at another example.

Bill and Linda Smith had been members of the same church most of their lives. Bill was head of the governing board while Linda sang in the choir. As a couple, they were an indispensable part of the church body. Anyone who needed help often received it from the Smiths. Friends and family assumed their marriage was as strong as their faith — rock solid.

One Sunday morning, Bill and Linda were not in church and no one knew why. During the week, rumors circulated among church busybodies. "Bill left home and is living with another woman. Money was stolen from the business Bill managed." Other rumors circulated: "Linda is so depressed that she sits at home with the lights out and the shades drawn, crying, drinking and popping pills." (Most of these stories were later found to be untrue.)

The next Sunday, Bill and Linda Smith were still gone. More rumors circulated around town. Then, another Sunday passed with more gossip but no real answers and no Bill and Linda Smith.

What would you do? What should the church do? What would Jesus do?

1. Be proactive and send Bill and Linda a letter asking them to resign from all of their church positions?
2. Do nothing? Leave them alone. After all, it's their problem. Let them work it out.
3. Get involved and look for ways to offer help? But how?

Jesus teaches us to be the "light of the world." (Matthew 5:14) The light represents our willingness to witness with our good deeds not just our talk. With Bill and Linda there was too much "talk" and too few "good deeds." So, if we are to be light to the world instead of spreaders of idle talk, how could we become God's witness for Bill & Linda Smith?

So, back to Walter, a middle-aged African American man who also happens to struggle with alcoholism. Walter starts attending a small all-white church. He doesn't make a scene or disturb anyone, but as his visits continue, others begin to complain. Bill and Linda Smith, a very active couple in the church suddenly stop coming. The gossip is as thick as molasses with talk of adultery, theft and even drug abuse. But so far no one knows what actually happened.

What would you do? What should the church do? How would Jesus respond?

Jesus' Sermon on the Mount (Matthew, chapters 5-7) offers sound spiritual guidance. Most of us readily recognize parts of the sermon but, until recently, I never noticed how all three chapters fit together to form one provocative message. Chapter five points out how we should behave in order to receive God's blessing: We are to be as salt and light. Knowing we cannot be perfect, Jesus then provides spiritual tools in chapter six designed to help us strengthen our relationships with God. Then we come to chapter seven.

At first, chapter seven seems to be a collection of sayings with no real relationship to each other. But upon further study, I was amazed to discover that Jesus is actually teaching us how to apply what's already been learned in chapters five and six to real world situations. I found six helpful steps:

1. **Don't judge.** "Stop judging others and you will not be judged."
2. **Be realistic.** "Don't give what is holy to unholy people."
3. **Seek God's will.** "Keep on asking and you will be given what you ask for."
4. **Give respect.** "Do for others what you would like them to do for you."
5. **Sacrifice required.** "You can enter God's Kingdom only through the narrow gate."
6. **Produce good fruit.** "A healthy tree produces good fruit."

So how do these six steps guide our decisions? Let's take a look at the situation with Walter:

Don't judge. After several weeks, the pastor called a church meeting and asked point blank: "What are we going to do for Walter? He has a right to be here and we need to help him."

Be realistic. Everyone tried to be diplomatic, so the word "black" was never mentioned until one gruff old man stood up and said, "Admit it. If this young man was white we wouldn't even be here talking. He's black and you don't like him. The alcoholism is just a sorry excuse to run him down!"

Seek God's will. One woman tentatively raised her hand: "Preacher, would you lead us in prayer so God can show us what to do?" After the prayer, a quiet hush fell over the room.

Give respect. Another leader responded, "We have not treated this young man properly. We should make more of an effort to welcome him to our church. I think this is where we start."

Sacrifice required. Several spoke up after that: "I'll sit beside him next Sunday and introduce him to a few folks." Another spoke of his struggle with alcoholism and vowed to call Walter.

Produce good fruit. The following Sunday, Walter visited the same building for worship but was welcomed by a noticeably new church empowered by the love and grace of Jesus Christ.

During Sunday school, a member of the class Bill and Linda Smith attended said: "I am concerned for Bill and Linda. I've heard the rumors about their marital problems, but has anyone from our church actually talked to either of them?" There was a prolonged silence as first one, then another, shook their heads. "I for one am not prepared to abandon them when they need us most. Why don't we pray for them right now as a class and maybe God will show us what to do next?"

Later that afternoon, two women from the class visited Linda while two men searched for Bill.

Jesus ends the sermon with the promise, *"If we listen and obey, we will be like the wise man who built his house on solid rock. The storms come but the house will not collapse. It is the foolish person who takes the easy way and builds on the sand. When the inevitable storms come the house will fall with a mighty crash."*

At times you will face difficult situations that challenge your faith. The question is: Will you remember to listen to the counsel of Christ? Is your foundation built on solid rock or on shifting sand? What will you do? What will your church do?

SEE THE LIGHT

If we're going to be serious about following Christ, there will be many opportunities to respond to a wide variety of situations. What will you do? What should the church do? How would Jesus respond?

SHARE THE LIGHT

1. How can we apply the formula Jesus teaches in Matthew 7?
   - **Don't judge.** "Stop judging others and you will not be judged."
   - **Be realistic.** "Don't give what is holy to unholy people."
   - **Seek God's will.** "Keep on asking and you will be given what you ask for."
   - **Give respect.** "Do for others what you would like them to do for you."
   - **Sacrifice required.** "You can enter God's Kingdom only through the narrow gate."
   - **Produce good fruit.** "A healthy tree produces good fruit"
2. How can you share this message with others?

Notes:

_____

_____

_____

_____

_____

_____

_____

_____

_____

_____

_____

LIVE THE LIGHT: The Lighthouse in Action

"Disciple" is a highly interactive Bible study published by Abingdon Press. Students often finish the course with a greater understanding of the Bible and God's purpose for their lives. I teach this course every year as a part of my ministry and the ten or twelve who take the journey with me inevitably end up becoming leaders within our church.

Bible studies help us wrestle with issues such as the one in this story, providing Godly principles for guidance.

Your Action Ideas:
List three biblical principles that have guided how you interact with others.

1. _____

2. _____

3. _____

"I am a retired Marine. The church is important to us because in the twenty years I served our country, traveling around the world, it became the family we left behind. No matter where we went, our family was there waiting for us." —Mike

"I pray that the Holy Spirit sends Godly people into your life who will refresh your spirit with their friendship and encouragement. What you are doing in this ministry cannot be measured by earthly standards. Only when that blessed day comes when you stand before our Lord and Savior, Jesus Christ will you really have any idea of how many lives you've touched by this outreach. This makes me feel great because nothing I can really say can truly express my gratitude for the prayers that I am receiving from all over the world." —Nancy

FRIDAY—Simplify

A church that invites often needs to change priorities.

And let us not neglect our meeting together, as some people do,
but encourage and warn each other, especially now that
the day of his coming back again is drawing near.
Hebrews 10:25

I hate meetings! I'm not kidding! One thing I didn't anticipate when becoming a minister is the absurd number of meetings that come with church life. Have you ever been to a board meeting with the main topic being whether to pay someone to cut the grass or use volunteers? Churches often have hundreds of committee meetings, each jam-packed with issues. For example: Who left the lights on in the men's bathroom last week? (Wasting money); Did you hear what happened to Martha last night? (Gossip); There's a bunch of spoiled food in the refrigerator. (Clean-up); Who's cooking the hot dogs after church this Sunday? (I do like that one!)

Do you see the picture? It's not pretty. But after many years of ministry, I've learned an amazing truth. Are you ready? This will surprise you! The issue isn't meetings at all. Nope. The real problem is my leadership and my bad attitude. As pastor, I needed to mend my ways — and fast.

"Without wavering, let us hold tightly to the hope we say we have, for God can be trusted to keep his promise. Think of ways to encourage one another to outbursts of love and good deeds. And let us not neglect our meeting together, as some people do, but encourage and warn each other, especially now that the day of his coming back again is drawing near." (Hebrews 10:23-25)

In other words, we gather at a meeting in order to hold tightly to the hope God has promised us. Meetings should be used to encourage one another to outbursts of love and good deeds. The idea is not to stop meeting, but rather to use meetings as a source of encouragement, an opportunity for teaching and especially a call to Godly action. Wow! I had been missing the point. So, I changed.

Before any meeting I have learned to ask four simple questions:

• **Is God invited?** This is about priorities. More than a perfunctory prayer or devotion, this question is a spiritual challenge: Are we vigorously seeking to follow God's will?

- **Do you know where you're going?** This is about organization. What will you accomplish? Is there a clear agenda to follow? Are you prepared to answer reasonable questions?
- **Are the committee members with you?** This is about communication. Does the committee have enough information? Is everyone participating in a healthy and creative discussion?
- **Will the meeting end with smiles or frowns?** This is about encouragement. Does the meeting end with the anticipation we are following God's will for our church?

Want something more specific? Maybe these questions will help:

- Do you begin every meeting by seeking God's direction?
- Do you start and finish on time?
- Is there a written agenda?
- Do you provide adequate information?
- Are you making reasonable decision-making progress?
- Does the atmosphere encourage creative thinking?
- Do you offer opportunities for friendly disagreement?
- Is there reasonable consensus with the direction of the group?
- Has the overall atmosphere been encouraging?
- Do you end by seeking God's blessing for your action?

Oh, one more thing. We changed our church structure, too. Recently, we reorganized all of our committees into four teams:

- Ministry & Missions
- Congregational Care
- Nurture
- Administration

Each team focuses on how we can best fulfill our mission statement: "A Light to Guide You Safely Home." As a church we strive to be a lighthouse to our community and our world, providing a steady and comforting light to guide the lost into the safety of God's harbor.

Now, after carefully following all the lessons learned, I love meetings! (*No I don't.*) We never argue! (*Yes, we do.*) Our discussions are always relevant!

(No, they aren't.) But we are making solid progress and God's hand is gently guiding our ministry. I just need to know one more thing: Who's cooking the hot dogs?

SEE THE LIGHT

We gather at meetings in order to hold tightly to the hope God promised. Meetings should be used to encourage one another to outbursts of love and good deeds. The idea is not to stop meeting, but rather to use meetings as a source of encouragement, an opportunity for teaching and especially a call to Godly action.

SHARE THE LIGHT

1. Do you hate meetings too? How can you adjust your attitude?
2. How can you help the meetings you attend "hold tightly to the hope God promised?"
3. Apply the four questions on pages 73-74 to your next meeting and then look for ways to use them more effectively.
4. How can you share this message with fellow committee members and others in your church?

Notes:

_____

_____

_____

_____

_____

_____

_____

_____

_____

LIVE THE LIGHT: The Lighthouse in Action

Our church reorganized its meetings to take place on Monday night. At times there are three to five meetings going on at the same time. This forced the church to make several necessary adjustments.

First it is almost impossible to serve on several committees, so we have learned to seek out more people. They often contribute new and fresh ideas. Second, our other nights are now free for Bible Studies, small group opportunities and even recreation. The message to our congregation and to the community is that we are mostly a church full of ministries and small groups instead of committees.

Because of our encouragement to offer more than just a meeting, committee leaders have become better organized and ministry focused. Special attention is given to recognizing and appreciating the efforts of participants.

Your Action Ideas:
How can we better use our church meetings to be a source of encouragement for others and a more effective witness for God?

1. _____

2. _____

3. _____

"I was a Youth Pastor when my marriage fell apart. I stepped down because I couldn't serve God effectively and go through the pain. The following months, I pulled away from God and everyone around me. I fell into a depression and couldn't see any reason to continue living. It was my relationship with God, and the church family that continued praying for me, that pulled me out. I now lead a divorce care group." —Darrell

"I signed up on your prayer website years ago. I was in a crisis You were so kind to me and even personally e-mailed me. I receive prayer requests every week! I can't imagine not getting the weekly prayer requests. I pray for the ones God puts on my heart and I write encouragement to those God tells me to write. Your site is so special and unique." —Deb

SATURDAY—Start Shining

A church that truly invites is exciting and growing.

Look! I am going to breathe into you and make you live again!
Ezekiel 37:5

This is the type of e-mail that warms a pastor's heart: "Thanks so much for the e-mail welcoming me to the church. As you know I have been a returning visitor when I am home, and am now back for the summer and have been in the college Bible study class. I would very much like to become a member. I really enjoy your services and have a strong respect for your ministry. I have not been a member of a church in a long time simply because I haven't found one that signifies what I think it should be. I think you all have a great thing, by the way you try to help others — and genuinely try to do so — through prayer and any other means you can. That is one of the big reasons I have respect for you. I would again just let you know that I would like to be a member as I already consider myself one, and would like to help out in church activities any way I can. Let me know if you need anything; if not I will see you Sunday!"

It's been several years since I first arrived to serve as pastor of Timberlake United Methodist Church in Lynchburg, Virginia. Much has changed. People may not always agree or be happy about our church but one thing is sure: these past years were seldom dull.

Recently we celebrated Pentecost, which marks the birth of the church. Christ's disciples were filled with the Holy Spirit as tongues of fire settled over them. They rushed out proclaiming in many languages "Jesus is Lord."

Quoting from the prophet Joel they said: "*I will pour out my Spirit upon all people. Your sons and daughters will prophesy. Your old men will dream dreams. Your young men will see visions. In those days, I will pour out my Spirit even on servants, men and women alike.*" (Joel 2:28-29)

Pentecost was an exciting time to be the church. But our own church growth has registered Pentecost-like numbers with new buildings, hundreds of new people, many newly-formed small groups, lots of children and youth and many different missions, programs and ministries. This church has always been exciting, but the last few years have been astonishing.

One off-beat but interesting method of charting our growth is in our back yard: our trash pick up area. *(No, I'm not kidding!)* Five years ago, we had three or four regular-size trash cans in the back lot which were picked up once a week as a courtesy. Soon we added a small dumpster; then it became a big dumpster. And now the big dumpster is picked up twice a week although, unfortunately, the trash service is no longer free.

So, we've either gotten much bigger or we are one very trashy church. *(You can laugh now.)*

But, the best way to understand church growth is through what God teaches. Since I've been studying the Old Testament lately, I will use those books as I submit ten action words to describe a healthy church. Together we can apply them to our churches and see how we measure up.

1. **Praise.** Do we understand and appreciate the almighty God we serve? *"To all who mourn, he will give beauty for ashes, joy instead of mourning and praise instead of despair." (Isaiah 61:3)* Praise is our way of admitting and submitting to God's authority over our church and our lives.

2. **Prayer.** Do we pray regularly as individuals and as a church? *"He went home and knelt down as usual in his upstairs room and prayed just as he had always done." (Daniel 6:10)* Prayer is recognition of God's authority and a willingness to listen for God's guidance.

3. **Open.** Are we open to growth opportunities, new people and new ideas? *"Then the Lord told Abram, 'Leave your country. I will make you a blessing to others.' So Abram departed as the Lord instructed." (Genesis 12:1-4)* Listening to God's voice often requires change.

4. **Hospitality.** Do we genuinely welcome God's people? *"You welcome me as a guest, anointing my head with oil." (Psalm 23:5)* Anointing means to provide honor and protection, so genuine hospitality has to be more than a smile and polite, "How are you?"

5. **Obedient.** Will we be obedient to God's purpose for us? *"The people said to Joshua, 'We will serve the Lord our God. We will obey.'" (Joshua 24:24)* We all fit into God's master plan. As individuals and as the church, we are called to be obedient to God's purpose for our lives.

6. **Alert.** Will we notice the unique growth opportunities God offers? *"Intelligent people are always open to new ideas. In fact they look for them." (Proverbs 18:15)* Organizations and people all around us are facing challenges and difficulties. We try to offer what they need.

7. **Assertive.** Will we, while trusting in God, aggressively pursue opportunities? *"'Don't worry about a thing,' David told Saul. 'I'll go fight Goliath.'" (1 Samuel 17:32)* Sometimes we must face Goliath-size challenges in order to fully appreciate God's awesome power.

8. **Risk-Taker.** Every opportunity also has a cost. Are we willing to pay? *"God will rescue us but even if he doesn't we will never serve your gods." (Daniel 3:17-18)* From changing careers to giving up our lunch hour for a Bible study, there is always a cost involved with growth.

9. **Persistent.** Will we hang in there when the going gets tough? *"Look! I am going to breathe into you and make you live again!" (Ezekiel 37:5)* Facing and overcoming obstacles is a normal part of the growth process. God promises to breathe new life into us.

10. **Thankful.** Do we remember and give thanks to the One who is so critical to our success? *"Enter His gates with thanksgiving; go into his courts with praise." (Psalm 100:4)* What a shame, after coming so far, not to stop for a moment and say thank you!

I believe these ten action words faithfully describe our church and me as their pastor. The last several years have been a roller coaster ride filled with many ups and a few downs; but we struggled together to serve God. Our reward has been the opportunity to witness many miracles, including hundreds of lives changed within our church, community and even other parts of the world. Wow! Now onto the next five years ... Hang on, because the best is yet to come!

"Larry, I just wanted to take the time to thank you and Timberlake UMC for showing me and my family the love and welcome you have shown in our first few visits. As members of another church that went through drastic changes and forgot what God's family is, your church is a breath of fresh air."

SEE THE LIGHT

The best way to understand church growth is through what God teaches. A church that truly invites will find itself in the midst of an exciting, growing ministry.

SHARE THE LIGHT

How can you apply the ten actions words to your church?
1. **Praise.** Do we appreciate the almighty God we serve?
2. **Prayer.** Do we pray regularly as individuals and as a church?
3. **Open.** Are we open to growth opportunities, new people and ideas?
4. **Hospitality.** Do we genuinely welcome God's people?
5. **Obedient.** Will we be obedient to God's purpose for us?
6. **Alert.** Will we notice the unique growth opportunities God offers?
7. **Assertive.** Will we aggressively pursue those opportunities?
8. **Risk-Taker.** Opportunities have costs. Are you willing to pay?
9. **Persistent.** Will we hang in there when the going gets tough?
10. **Thankful.** Do we remember and give thanks to the One who is so critical to our success?

Notes:

LIVE THE LIGHT: The Lighthouse in Action

One of our church families with two elementary school children felt we needed an after-school program. Several years ago we tried but failed. This family, however, would not take no for an answer. Reluctantly we gathered people and started looking into the possibilities. Over the past few years, circumstances had changed and the prospects were more promising.

The more we looked, the more excited we became. Within a few months we started a new after-school ministry and this time we expect to be successful. But if we had not listened to this one family, we would have missed the opportunity to serve God and the children of our community.

Your Action Ideas:
Ask members of your congregation or people in the community: "What do you need that our church does not offer now?"

1. _____

2. _____

3. _____

"I'd been a Buddhist when we went to a September 11 memorial service. I cried through the whole thing and never felt so at home. I knew this was where I belonged. Next week, we returned and I accepted Jesus as Lord. I am disabled and have massive financial problems. Yet, I am at peace and happier than ever. I feel the power of Jesus and trust him with all my heart and soul." —Darlene

"I logged onto the search engine and typed 'Why is God denying me?' That eventually led me to your prayer website where I typed in my heartfelt desires. I went to bed with an anguished heart and tormented soul, but woke with a deep sense of peace. ... I was overwhelmed by the prayers and words of encouragement [e-mailed] to me by people in the U.S., India and West Africa. I live in South Africa and was surprised and humbled that the world prayed for me. I'm so grateful for Sowing Seeds Ministry." —Lerato

WHAT HAVE WE LEARNED SO FAR?

Monday—We need light
None of our small groups or visions will be especially helpful
if we are not inviting and helping our guests feel
welcome and valued.

Tuesday—Opportunities to Shine
Opportunities often come by surprise and we need a dose
of Godly courage and wisdom to make the most of them.

Wednesday—Becoming God's Lighthouse
Music is a wonderful tool for expressing our deep love for God.
No generation should ever claim to know which music is "proper."

Thursday—An Attitude that Shines
If we're serious about offering invitations in the name of Christ,
we must be prepared for controversy. What will you do?
What should the church do?

Friday—Simplify
We gather at meetings in order to hold tightly to the hope
God promised. Meetings should be used to encourage
one another to outbursts of love and good deeds.

Saturday—Start Shining
The best way to understand church growth is through what God
teaches. Together we can apply God's teaching
and see how we measure up.

Now, let's put it all together...

SUNDAY—Live the LIGHT

A church that truly invites will savor the fruits of its labor.

The master said, "Well done, my good and faithful servant.
You have been faithful in handling this small amount, so now
I will give you many more responsibilities. Let's celebrate together!"
Matthew 25:23

On June 27, 2004, a miracle took place. We celebrated the dedication of a new church! But this story is about much more than a building. It's about a tornado, a "black church" and a "white church" joined as partners, and the outpouring of love from an involved community. Oops! I almost revealed the end of the story. Read on.

Early one Saturday morning Cordelia Alexander awoke to the sounds of a concrete truck and men talking. The sounds coming from just outside her bedroom window were music to her ears. "It's going to happen," Alexander said. "The sun came out and it was like God saying, 'This is the day.'"

It was just two years ago when Alexander watched in disbelief as a tornado ripped through her community and destroyed the church in which she has been a member since the age of 12.

Throughout the day, the buzz of saws and the banging of hammers could be heard from the hilltop, where the small church once stood. By day's end, the building was beginning to take shape. The concrete foundation had been poured and two of the walls were finished.

Alexander and more than 50 other members of Lawyers Missionary Baptist Church have dreamed of the day when construction on a new church building would begin.

That dream is now a reality thanks to a unique bond of stewardship formed between Timberlake United Methodist Church and Lawyers Missionary Baptist Church.*

Our church received a unique opportunity — in the unlikely form of a tornado — to help another church and practice good stewardship of our resources.

The day after the tornado hit, the picture in the newspaper showed the damaged church with both side walls and the roof completely blown away. Yet, you could plainly see exposed pews with bibles and hymnals still in the racks. The pastor, Rev. Carlton Johnson, spoke of rebuilding but didn't say how it would be accomplished.

Larry Davies, pastor of Timberlake UMC said, "I couldn't take my eyes off that picture. An inner voice kept asking: 'What will they do next Sunday? Where will they go? Our church is only a few miles away. Surely we can do something ... but what?'" Shortly after that, Rev. Davies made a phone call.

Davies said: "Our church is in the process of building a new worship area. The current sanctuary is too small for the 11 a.m. worship service so we meet in the Family Life Center at the other end of the building. Lawyers Missionary Baptist Church desperately needed a sanctuary. We had one. We aren't using it. How can we possibly say no?"

Later that same morning, Rev. Johnson of Lawyers Missionary Baptist Church, Rev. Drinkard, a United Methodist District Superintendent, and Rev. Davies of Timberlake UMC stood in the sanctuary among the exposed pews and tried to imagine what force of nature could possibly cause this much damage. One member was sorting through the debris looking for anything salvageable. You could see the hurt in his eyes as he spoke of the church he loved.

"Rev. Johnson," Davies said, "We have a church sanctuary and we would be delighted to have you join us."

The following Sunday, the two congregations met as one church. In the hallway connecting the two sanctuaries were tables filled with food and coffee. As members of Lawyers Missionary Baptist Church arrived, members of Timberlake United Methodist were there to greet them and show them around. At 11 a.m., several Timberlake members volunteered to attend the Lawyer's Missionary worship service to show support.

Darrell Laurant, a local newspaper columnist wrote: "As movie reviewers love to say, this is the 'feel-good story of the year.' The crisis-enforced partnership between Timberlake United Methodist Church and Lawyers Missionary Baptist Church says so much about the true New

Testament message and the evolving relationship between races in this part of the world that it almost makes my hair stand on end."

For over two years Timberlake United Methodist and Lawyers Road Missionary Baptist Church shared the same building and more. There were concerts and dinners to raise money for the new building. There were joint worship services. The two youth groups were involved in mission projects together. But there seemed to be little progress toward actually rebuilding Lawyers Missionary Baptist Church.

Then along came "The $10 Challenge" and Jim Adams, a contractor and member of Timberlake UMC, responded. "Timberlake issued this challenge to see what you could do to make ten bucks grow," Adams said. "I'm not a wealthy person, but they asked us to use our talents." After pondering the issue, Adams decided he would use his $10 and talent to rebuild Lawyers Missionary Baptist.

"I'm not a real regular Sunday morning church person," Adams said. "I feel like if you believe in Christ, then you need to be doing something. It was my personal conviction that I needed to do more."

Rev. Davies remembers receiving a phone call from Adams one Saturday evening telling him what he was going to do. "The next morning, during one of our worship services, Jim stood up and said 'For my $10 Challenge, I'm going to rebuild Lawyers Missionary Baptist Church.' You could have heard a pin drop, it was so quiet. We witnessed a miracle that morning. Building a church for Lawyers Road Baptist is something we will all take pride in for the rest of our lives."

Since that time, Adams has been meeting with members of Lawyers Missionary to discuss plans for the church as well as searching the community for volunteers and donations. He said: "These people were evicted by a tornado and we should help them get back in their home."

A local company donated a beautiful stained glass window. Another company is installing heating and air-conditioning free. One church donated a baptismal pool. Timberlake UMC donated the pews from their old sanctuary and raised the money to buy their new steeple. Hundreds of volunteers are donating time and talents working on the building or supplying food for the workers.

Several members of Lawyers Missionary Baptist Church were on hand for the first day of construction. "We have a tremendous love for Timberlake UMC," Cordelia Alexander said. "We thank God for Jim Adams. God put it on his heart to do this. We are truly blessed."

Lawyers Missionary Pastor Carlton Johnson said, "I'm very excited and overjoyed. We've been looking forward to this day and praying it would not rain. This is the day the Lord has made. This is bringing people together, black and white, Baptist and Methodist. It's wonderful."

As the sun slowly set in the distance, the two pastors, Jim Adams and several members of both churches stood together on the foundation of the new church building sharing the experiences that brought them to this memorable day. Rev. Davies said: "Thanks to a tornado, our lives and our churches will never be the same. God taught us a valuable lesson on stewardship and love."

Phillip Mason, a lifelong member of Lawyers Missionary Baptist Church, said, "My hope for the future is to get the church built and more people will join us to do work for the Lord. I hope we keep in touch with Timberlake. We will never forget what they have done for us."

Could this be why God brought both of our congregations together? The Apostle Paul wrote: *"For the whole law can be summed up in this one command: 'Love your neighbor as yourself.' But if instead of showing love among yourselves you are always biting and devouring one another, watch out! Beware of destroying one another."* (Galatians 5:14-15) Two churches once separated by denomination and race learned to work together and discovered the real meaning of loving our neighbor as ourselves.

Yet amidst all the celebration of the new building, another miracle of God occurred during our final church service when the two churches came together. And the best part of all is that virtually no one even noticed.

During worship, we shared the sacrament of Holy Communion which is a sacred moment in the life of any Christian congregation. Rev. Carlton Johnson, the black pastor of Lawyers Missionary Baptist Church, and I, a white United Methodist pastor, stood together and served the juice and bread while, on the other side of the sanctuary, the lay leaders from each of our churches stood together and also served communion to our two churches as they came forward together as one united congregation.

What I just described would simply be unheard of as recently as 30 or 40 years ago, yet no one even considered challenging this hallowed moment. In fact, quite the opposite judging from an e-mail I received: "Larry, we thought the worship service was one of the best. Communion was very moving for us. All the different denominations and races pointing to one goal: worshiping our Father together. That is the way it should be. We all felt the same way. It made us feel good to be members of Timberlake United Methodist Church."

"A member of our congregation pulled me aside recently," said Davies, "and asked point blank if I was responsible for inviting Lawyers Road to our church. I remember being a little nervous, not knowing what he would say next, but I nodded my head, acknowledging responsibility. He smiled and said with obvious emotion: 'Thank you! I've never been more proud to be a member of this church!'"

*Special thanks to Suzanne C. Hickerson for permission to reprint this article which originally appeared in *The Bedford Bulletin*, Bedford, Va.

There are several people who deserve special mention for their role in bringing our two churches together.

Rev. Carlton Johnson has been the leader of Lawyers Missionary Baptist Church for many years, and it was his guidance that led our two churches to come together.

Jim Adams stood up in the middle of our $10 Challenge worship service and announced that he would build a church. And with help, he did.

Charlie Droog was sent by God to "go get." Whatever the church needed, Charlie was the one to go get it. And most of it was donated.

Also, to Rick Tomlin, Lester "Curly" Harris, and many other selfless volunteers who gave up so much to help a church in need. Thank you for giving of yourself for the Lawyers Missionary Baptist Church and the glory of God.

SEE THE LIGHT

The Apostle Paul wrote: "For the whole law can be summed up in this one command: 'Love your neighbor as yourself.'" Inviting means stepping out of your comfort zone to share the love of Christ whenever and wherever the opportunities present themselves.

SHARE THE LIGHT

1. The church is most effective when helping those in need — whether it's in your community or a distant corner of the world. Who is in need? What can you do to help?
2. Learning to invite can be as simple as having someone to your house for dinner, asking someone to join you for a cup of coffee or offering to meet someone at your local church. Name one person you can invite this week.
3. A tornado brought two different churches together in a beautiful way, but churches do not need a crisis in order to share experiences together. What can you and your church do to develop a closer relationship with other churches in your area?

Notes:

LIVE THE LIGHT: The Lighthouse in Action

MOPS. On a visit home, shortly after my father died, I noticed several young women looking after my mother. When I asked who they were, I was told they were "MOPS" — Mothers of Pre-Schoolers. My mother was the mentor for this group of young moms and now they were looking after her. Intrigued, I looked them up.

MOPS is designed to provide a caring, accepting atmosphere of support for mothers of pre-schoolers. Moms have an opportunity to share concerns, explore areas of creativity and receive instruction on areas of common interest. The groups are organized and run by the moms themselves. I was so impressed that I helped our church start a MOPS chapter of its own. You can, too. Visit www.tumc-mops.com.

Your Action Ideas:
Who needs help in your neighborhood or community? How can you or your church respond?

1. _____

2. _____

3. _____

"The church has been an important part of my life in many different ways, but most recently they taught me to really look in the faces of others for signs of pain or grief, to really listen when someone's talking to me, to not judge or condemn regardless of circumstances, to believe in miracles again and to see God in the faces of strangers." — Anonymous

"I live in India. I was depressed and concerned over problems of people I love. Your site caught my eye. I signed up and have been receiving prayer requests. … I remember one lady who said she was just about to commit suicide. She had three children whom she didn't want to hurt but was determined to take her life. God touched my heart to write to her. Her reply came back to me the next day. 'The birds are singing, the sun is shining, my heart is filled with joy and I am happy. Thank you so much for your prayer.' Since then, I always send out prayers in response to the requests I receive." —Shashi

WEEK THREE

GROW

MONDAY—We Need Light

Without storms we seldom look for the light.
Without storms we cannot grow.

I know that you can do anything, and no one can stop you.
You ask, "Who is this that questions my wisdom with such ignorance?"
It is I. And I was talking about things I did not understand,
things far too wonderful for me.

Job 42:2-3

John was born and raised within a large family in England. His father worked as a small town preacher so John experienced poverty first hand. His mother home-schooled all the children with discipline as rigorous as the best schools in the area, so John was raised in a strict environment. As a young boy, he was rescued from a burning second-story window moments before the roof caved in. John would refer to this incident repeatedly as testimony that he was delivered by the hand of God for a unique mission.

Soon after graduating from seminary, John felt the call to become a chaplain and missionary across the sea, in a newly-developed colony which included prisoners and a local tribe of Indians. Fresh out of the disciplined life of school, he was not prepared for the harsh living conditions deep in the country. Often, John wore his formal attire even when working in the woods. His insistence on holding worship services as if he were in London seemed odd. The Indians and everyone else mostly laughed at him.

On top of all this, John fell in love but couldn't seem to make up his mind whether to marry. He should have, but he didn't. He could have, but he wouldn't. Tired of waiting, his sweetheart gave up on him and married someone else. Furious, John later refused to serve communion to the newly-married couple. This unfortunate incident turned out to be the last straw for everyone; soon John was run out of town and found himself back on a ship headed toward England.

On the journey home there was a ferocious storm. The ship tossed erratically amidst the monstrous waves. John, feeling depressed because of his failed mission, was heartbroken, seasick and scared out of his wits. Yet, it was at this point that John's life was about to turn around.

In another time and place, a man named Job also was caught up in a severe storm. Job was a prosperous farmer living in the land of Uz. He was described by God as *"the finest man in all the earth — a man of complete integrity."* (Job 1:8) But Job, through no fault of his own, lost his possessions, his family and even his health. He was left desolate and alone, sitting on an ash heap scraping his itching, boil-covered skin with a broken piece of pottery. (Oh yeah — sitting with him were three friends: Eliphaz, Bildad and Zophar. Friends? Some friends!)

Job cried out to God, proclaiming his innocence, while the three stooges — er, friends — began spouting their litany of possible explanations for Job's plight:

Maybe you did something wrong, Job.
Could it be your children's fault?
Somebody must have done something wrong!
You are simply being disciplined.
Don't be angry with God, it's your fault!
Shut up Job; you have no right to complain.

Whoa! With friends like these three, who needs enemies? Although, come to think of it, we can't become too smug because Job's friends represent our own well-meaning responses when people around us find themselves caught up in vicious storms. Instead of compassion, we offer cheap explanations. Instead of help, we offer unwanted criticism. Instead of empathy, we offer slanderous gossip.

Meanwhile Job, confused and even angry at times, continued crying out to almighty God: *"'If only I had someone who would listen to me and try to see my side!' says Job. 'Look, I will sign my name to my defense. Let the almighty show me that I am wrong. ... I would face the accusation proudly.'"* (Job 31:35-36)

In other words, where is God when I'm caught in a storm? Good question! *"Then the Lord answered Job from the whirlwind. 'Brace yourself because I have questions for you. ... Where were you when I laid the foundation of the earth? Who defined the boundaries of the sea? Have you ever commanded the morning to appear? Where does the light come from? Can you hold back the movements of the stars?'"* (Job 38, excerpts)

Instead of answering Job's questions, God asked a few penetrating questions of his own. But how can this possibly help Job — or John — deal with tragedy? Two men with no common bond except a name beginning with the letter "J"shared similar calamities. Both were enveloped in vicious storms, looking for answers and a sign of hope from God.

John was heading home on a ship, disgraced and depressed because of his failed mission. He was heartbroken, seasick and scared out of his wits.

Job, after losing everything, was sitting on an ash heap, scraping his itching, boil-covered skin with a broken piece of pottery. Both men would have life-changing encounters with God.

It was the savage grip of the storm which provided the first clue that John's life would take a noticeable turn for the better. While on deck, holding desperately to anything solid, John noticed several families near the stern serenely singing hymns. He couldn't believe it! How could they conduct worship and sing in the midst of such a terrible storm? Why weren't they more frightened? John marveled at their faith and vowed to learn more.

Job cried out to God in the midst of his predicament and was visited by the Lord from a whirlwind. Instead of answering Job's questions, God asked a few penetrating questions of his own. This seems impressive, but why didn't God answer Job's question? Why was Job suffering so much having done nothing wrong? Yet, somehow, Job seemed to comprehend who God really is. Job said, *"I know that you can do anything ... and I was talking about things I did not understand, things too wonderful for me. ... I take back everything I said."* (Job 42:2-3)

What was Job's newfound revelation of God?

Weeks after arriving home, John continued contemplating his own mess of a life in contrast to the people contentedly singing in the midst of the storm. One night he heard someone reading a commentary on the book of Romans and began to understand what he was missing: "Since we have been made right in God's sight by faith, we have peace with God."

As John heard these words describing God's amazing grace, John would later write: "I felt my heart strangely warmed."

What warmed John's heart was the realization that faith was not earned by hard work or intellectual research. Both are helpful, but real faith comes from the heart and from committing to an ongoing relationship with God through Jesus Christ. We think religious satisfaction only comes from doing. John learned that real faith comes not from *doing* something but from *being* something. Wow!

If God never directly answered Job's questions on why we suffer, why was Job satisfied? Is it because there really are no sufficient answers to explain suffering? Maybe Job was searching for something more important than mere answers. Job was looking for a relationship with a God who would bring faith in the midst of life's worst storms. *"I heard about you before, but now I have seen you with my own eyes. I take back everything I said and I sit in dust and ashes to show my repentance."* (Job 42:5-6) Job learned real faith comes not from mere answers but from God's presence.

John soon began preaching again, but this time his passion was evident as he spoke of faith through God's amazing grace. Local preachers, feeling uncomfortable with John's newfound enthusiasm, refused to invite him back. But it no longer mattered, for John was soon preaching throughout the countryside. In fact, John began preaching so often that groups or societies began to form around the country. Other churches and leaders tried to stop the movement but, the more they tried to stop him, the stronger and more popular he became.

Near the end of his life, no one in all of England — including the king — was more recognizable than John: John Wesley. He rode between sixty and seventy miles a day by horseback. He would get up at four in the morning, preach at five and by six he was in the saddle and on the road. He did this until well into his eighties.

John Wesley delivered more than 42,000 sermons in fifty years, which is an average of over fifteen sermons a week. More than a preacher, however, John Wesley was also an organizer. His societies eventually became the United Methodist Church, which is one of the largest Christian movements in the world today and the church I proudly serve as a pastor.

Two men with nothing in common but names beginning with "J." Both found their true relationship with God in the midst of a storm.

SEE THE LIGHT

Job learned real faith comes not from mere answers but from God's presence. What warmed John's heart was the realization that faith was not earned by hard work or intellectual research. Both are helpful, but real faith comes from the heart and from committing to an ongoing relationship with God through Jesus Christ. We think religious satisfaction only comes from doing. John learned that real faith comes not from *doing* something but from *being* something.

SHARE THE LIGHT

1. We all face storms in our lives. Describe yours.
2. Why was Job satisfied with God's answer?
3. How did a storm help change John Wesley's life and ministry?
4. Have you ever turned away from God in the midst of a storm?
5. Describe a storm in which you found comfort in God's presence?
6. What could you do to help someone else who may be facing a storm?

Notes:

_____

_____

_____

_____

_____

_____

_____

_____

_____

_____

_____

_____

LIVE THE LIGHT: The Lighthouse in Action

Parish Nurses. Few storms in life are as deadly as those caused by disease and poor health. Healing and caring for the sick traditionally has been the role of faith communities. At Timberlake, parish nurses actively participate in the healing ministry of the church. They are called to serve as personal health counselors, educators and even referral agents. A nurse can listen, comfort and even accompany those who are sick. Talk to a nurse in your church and ask him or her to look into the possibility of becoming a parish nurse for your congregation.

Your Action Ideas:
How can your church provide light and point others toward the Light in the midst of a storm?

1. _____

2. _____

3. _____

"I just want to say a big thank you to you and your prayer partners around the world for their prayers and kind words of encouragement. According to Romans 8:28: 'All things are working for our good and His Glory,' and that is what is happening in our lives. It is not easy to understand this initially, when everything seems to be working against us and Satan seems to be winning, but praise and thank God for turning things around for our good and favor and building us up through tough and hard times and giving us His victory according to His promise in His word. He is helping us to be more than conquerors through Christ who strengthens us and takes care of all our needs. I feel more close to God than ever before and it is so peaceful and wonderful." —Murali

"My church shows the love of God. There is no basket hiding the light of God here." —Randy

TUESDAY—Opportunities to Shine

Our lights shine brighter when encouraged.

Without wavering, let us hold tightly to the hope we say we have,
for God can be trusted to keep his promise. Think of ways to encourage
one another to outbursts of love and good deeds.
Hebrews 10:23-24

In 1971, a roadside food-stand called Pierce's Pitt Bar-B-Cue opened near Williamsburg, Virginia. This so-called restaurant was nothing more than a shack with an order window. Only one meal was served: barbecue on a bun, with coleslaw or without, plus fries and a drink. No one complained because Pierce's Pitt simply served the best barbecue in the world. Their meat was slow-cooked in a special pit behind the store and mixed in a tomato sauce that can only be described as heavenly. Truckers from Florida to New York spread the word on their CB radios and the rest, as they say, is history.

Several years later, the two-lane highway became four lanes and a wire fence was erected, cutting off Pierce's Pit Bar-B-Cue from the road. But by then, it made no difference. Cars and trucks by the dozen simply stopped along the side of the road while people scaled the fence to walk over and place their orders. Later, an exit ramp was built nearby, in part because of the traffic jams caused by this little food-stand.

Over the last thirty years, the roadside stand has become a full-service restaurant and the surrounding area is now full of outlet stores, hotels, restaurants, Christmas shops and many other attractions in addition to nearby Colonial Williamsburg.

Was the success of Pierce's Pitt Bar-B-Cue the only reason why all the change occurred? Of course not. But it is an interesting part of the story.

Why am I telling you this? Because I discovered Pierce's Pitt in 1971 while traveling from home to college. I was one of those nuts who parked his car on the side of the road to climb the fence and place an order. At least once a year, I still visit the Williamsburg area and you can bet that I will find an excuse to eat one of those delicious barbecue sandwiches. (*Are you getting hungry yet?*)

Also in 1971, I preached my very first sermon in church. Now don't get any ideas. I was not yet a minister. You may wonder if I was even born in 1971 because I look so young. (*Please don't laugh. Just let me enjoy the fantasy.*) Actually, I was in my first year of college and not doing well at all. I was lonely, homesick and scared. My grades were terrible and I was worried about telling mom and dad.

One night, the pastor of my home church called and asked me to preach for youth Sunday in December. His invitation changed my whole outlook. Never once had I seriously imagined myself standing in a pulpit. Preachers were people to admire, but me ... actually preaching? Never! Suddenly my life had meaning again. The library, rather than the local tavern, became my next stop that night in order to research a message topic. Within days there were seven pages of notes in my folder. I was ready.

On the big day, I wore my finest (and only) suit. The service seemed to last forever before finally coming to my part. When the big moment came, I confidently strode to the pulpit, laid out my notes and began to speak. There was so much to say about my hopes and dreams; what a real church should and could be.

Was it me or did time fly? I finished, sat down, looked at my watch and gasped. It was only 11:30. My entire sermon lasted six minutes. Six minutes! It was probably the shortest worship service ever. People still remember how early they got out of church that day, because of me.

Many years would go by before I would stand in the pulpit again. I never had any intention of becoming a preacher. Looking back, however, I've discovered that every experience along the way was crafted by God to shape and mold me toward ministry. The encouragement of a church and a pastor who believed in me was an invaluable aid toward shaping my future. I will always be grateful.

In 1971, I had a lot in common with that little roadside stand, Pierce's Pitt Bar-B-Cue. We were both just beginning and our future success depended upon so many factors. Looking back, I realize the reason we both are still around is because of the support we received along the way.

SEE THE LIGHT

I discovered that every experience in my life journey was crafted by God to shape and mold me toward ministry. The encouragement of a church and a pastor who believed in me was an invaluable aid toward shaping my future. Our lights shine brighter when we're encouraged. They also shine brighter when we allow ourselves to be used by God to bring hope and encouragement to others.

SHARE THE LIGHT

1. Often, seemingly insignificant events can be turning points in your life. Can you name one or two that were turning points for you?
2. Who encouraged you to be the person you are today?
3. What can you do to thank him/her?
4. How will you encourage someone else?
5. How can you help your church be more encouraging?

Notes:

_____

_____

_____

_____

_____

_____

_____

_____

_____

_____

LIVE THE LIGHT: The Lighthouse in Action

Support Groups. A man in our church was diagnosed with prostate cancer. A parish nurse connected him with several others who had the same cancer. Over the next few months they formed a support group. Soon, several neighbors joined the group. They shared stories and research notes, and they met and prayed together regularly. Now when someone receives a diagnosis of prostate cancer, we immediately inform the group and they eagerly respond to help someone with the same knowledge and encouragement that was so helpful to them. I once commented: "If we could form a support group like this one for every disease, we would truly be doing a service for the entire community."

Your Action Ideas:
What are some ways your church can provide encouragement to members, visitors and the community at large?

1. _____

2. _____

3. _____

"I wrote recently about being in hurricane Katrina. I live in Laurel, Mississippi, and we have been the recipients of many love actions. One I would like to tell you about is the day we discovered we had no bread — not even a slice. Lo and behold, three young men came by from Knoxville, Tennessee and guess what they had! Bread! Talk about a miracle. I expressed to them that we needed gas to run our generator and if they could find some, we would really appreciate it. About two hours later they returned with five gallons of gas. Yes, indeed, I know firsthand about God's rich blessings." —Erma

"God is Love. This church is love. Nothing more need be said."—Anon.

WEDNESDAY—Becoming God's Lighthouse

Before we can grow, we must first clean up the mess.

After dark one evening, a Jewish religious leader named Nicodemus,
a Pharisee, came to speak with Jesus. "Teacher," he said, "we all know
that God has sent you to teach us. Your miraculous signs are proof enough
that God is with you."

Jesus replied, "I assure you, unless you are born again,
you can never see the Kingdom of God."

"What do you mean?" exclaimed Nicodemus. "How can an old man
go back into his mother's womb and be born again?"
John 3:1-4

Mention the word audit and most of us cringe. Why? Well, it's like a trip to the dentist office: you dread going, but deep down you know it's necessary. Organizations routinely and voluntarily conduct audits to ensure proper financial procedures are followed. An annual audit of church finances reassures congregations that money donated in good faith is properly accounted for. Then, of course, there is the Internal Revenue Service audit to make sure you have paid what you owe the government.

Like it or not, audits are essential.

But what about a spiritual audit? In other words, how are we doing as followers of God? Are you feeling uncomfortable? So am I. But a regular audit of our relationship with God is necessary to help us improve the relationship and rediscover God's purpose for our earthly lives. Here are six questions you can use to conduct your own spiritual audit:

1. Are you actively pursuing and fulfilling God's purpose?
2. How are you managing the money God entrusted to your care?
3. Where are you utilizing your time and energy? What are your priorities?
4. How is your Christian witness? Do you set a good example for your family? For your church? For your community? For God?
5. What is your influence? Are you respected as a person of faith?
6. How is your relationship with Christ? Are you growing?

A thorough and complete spiritual audit should reveal many excellent qualities about you and your walk with God, but at the same time, you will also discover areas needing improvement.

"OK," you say. "But what does an audit have to do with being, 'born again'?"

Good question. The term "born again" is used by Christians to describe the initial experience of entering into a relationship with Jesus Christ. My own "born again" experience happened in a hotel room in Dallas, Texas, while reading the book *Confessions of a Happy Christian* by Zig Ziglar. Ziglar's book challenged me to radically change from being a part-time, come-to-church, casual Christian to giving everything to Jesus Christ — including my career, my family, my health, my finances and even my attitude.

"So becoming 'born again' is making a major spiritual turnaround in your life?"

Yes. "Born again" became a popular term shortly after a book of the same title was published. In his book, Chuck Colson described his own "born again" experience. Colson made a dramatic character change from being President Nixon's chief hatchet-man to becoming the founder of one of the largest prison ministries in the world. But the term actually comes straight from the mouth of Jesus Christ in the Gospel of John.

"After dark one evening, a Jewish religious leader named Nicodemus, a Pharisee, came to speak with Jesus. 'Teacher,' he said, 'we all know that God has sent you to teach us. Your miraculous signs are proof enough that God is with you.' Jesus replied, 'I assure you, unless you are born again, you can never see the Kingdom of God.'" (John 3:1-3)

"So this person, Nicodemus, made a spiritual turnaround. What does that have to do with me and spiritual audits?"

At this point, many of you who already claim a "born again" experience might stop reading: "I've been there and done that already!" you say. "Why bring up the subject again? This Scripture is for those poor lost sinners who don't know Jesus as their Savior. Let's move on to something more appropriate!"

But don't tune me out yet. There is another significant lesson here and, if you're not careful, you will miss it.

Jesus has a message that revolves around the individual, Nicodemus. We know Nicodemus is a respected religious leader which, by today's standards, would likely mean a pastor. So it seems only natural to follow up with another question: Why would a respected pastor need to be born again? The Scripture goes on to say, *"'What do you mean?' exclaimed Nicodemus. 'How can an old man go back into his mother's womb and be born again?'"* *(John 3:4)*

Maybe Nicodemus struggled with his faith and needed his own spiritual audit. He definitely needed a relationship with Jesus Christ to take the place of simply being a good church person. He needed a change, which is why becoming "born again" is more than just a one-time experience.

So, am I saying that even those of us who are "born again" may need to be *(gulp)* ... "born again" again?

Yes. Suppose you were the owner of a business and given a quota of making a $1 million profit before the month ended.

"Impossible," you scream out. But suppose you reach your quota by the fifth day of the month. Wow! What an achievement. Great news! Let's celebrate! Now suppose you set the same goal for the next month and reach it by day four and you set the same quota for the next month and reach it again by day five? What would you think then?

"Well it sounds like either I will do a lot of celebrating or, more likely, conduct a business audit and learn to set my goals higher."

That's right. You also set your goals too low when you're satisfied with an initial "born again" experience and don't continue regularly auditing, developing and strengthening your relationship with Christ. After all, Jesus did not deliberately die on the cross for you once a long time ago. Christ continues to die for you today, offering you the amazing gift of grace. All Jesus expects in return is an ongoing relationship with you.

Let me put it another way: Suppose you get married, come back from a wonderful honeymoon, and shortly after returning, you go back to your house and your spouse goes to his or her house and both of you go back to living exactly like you were before the wedding? What kind of relationship would that be? Ouch!

So, in other words, becoming "born again" is meant to be more than simply a new birth; it's the beginning of a continually growing relationship with Jesus Christ. This is why the terms, "spiritual audit" and "born again" apply to everyone — even those who claim a "born again" experience. Maybe it's time to look at our audit again, but now more seriously:

1. Are you actively pursuing and fulfilling God's purpose?
2. How are you managing the money God entrusted to your care?

3. Where are you utilizing your time and energy? What are your priorities?
4. How is your Christian witness? Do you set a good example for your family? For your church? For your community? For God?
5. What is your influence? Are you respected as a person of faith?
6. How is your relationship with Christ? Are you growing?

Jesus then said to Nicodemus (and continues to say to us): *"For God so loved the world he gave his only Son, so that everyone who believes in him will not perish but have eternal life. God did not send his Son into the world to condemn it, but to save it."* (John 3:16-17) Are you ready to conduct your own spiritual audit and be "born again?"

SEE THE LIGHT

Maybe Nicodemus struggled with his faith and needed his own spiritual audit. He definitely needed a relationship with Jesus Christ to take the place of simply being a good church person. He needed a change, which is why becoming "born again" is more than just a one-time experience.

SHARE THE LIGHT

1. Using the six questions above, take your own spiritual audit.
2. Did you find your strengths? How can you better apply them?
3. Did you note your weaknesses? How can you improve?
4. How can you apply becoming "born again" to your spiritual audit?
5. Do our churches also need to be "born again?" How?
6. What can you do to share this message with others?

Notes:

LIVE THE LIGHT: The Lighthouse in Action

Even churches need regular spiritual audits. At Timberlake, every year we form at least one task force to examine one area of our church and report back its suggestions. Suggested areas include our vision and mission statement, our membership and leadership process, our missions and ministries and even our church structure. In every case, we appoint the very best people to the task force and allow them to do whatever is necessary to help us see our strengths and weaknesses. The reports are often tough and the suggestions difficult, but most of our church growth and effectiveness can be traced back to those spiritual audits.

Your Action Ideas:
Identify some areas of your church that would benefit from a spiritual audit.

1. _____

2. _____

3. _____

"I wrote you asking for prayer three years ago. I was at a very difficult place in my life. I was hospitalized for depression and, in the process, lost my job, my boyfriend, my beautiful car, my friends, my family and my money. I was so lost. It hurt so bad. I lived in Kenya and just needed to get out and start over as I felt I would surely suffocate. You were there with simple encouraging words: Just there. Thank you. I am now completing my PhD in Australia, I won two prestigious scholarships and even though my boyfriend just broke up with me, I am positive about life, the future and the faithfulness of God, the goodness of people. Thank you." —Beatrice

"The feelings we have for our church are very deep and loving. We have been members for many years and have seen the church grow in size and accomplishments. Our children were baptized here and grew up in these surroundings. We are very proud to call this church our home." —Betty & Frank

THURSDAY—An Attitude that Shines

Growth also means bringing light to the dark areas
of your own life.

*But during the night Jacob got up and sent his two wives, two concubines,
and eleven sons across the Jabbok River. After they were on the other side,
he sent over all his possessions. This left Jacob all alone in the camp,
and a man came and wrestled with him until dawn. When the man saw
that he couldn't win the match, he struck Jacob's hip and knocked it out
of joint at the socket. Then the man said, "Let me go, for it is dawn."*

But Jacob panted, "I will not let you go unless you bless me."

"What is your name?" the man asked.

He replied, "Jacob."
Genesis 32:22-27

Recently I received this e-mail: "I am former Mrs. Abibat Said, a widow
to the late Alhaji Mahi Said. I am 72 years old, suffering from a long
time bout with cancer. My late husband was very wealthy but he died during the Gulf war as well as my only son. I inherited all his business and
wealth. I have now decided to divide part of this wealth by contributing
to the development of philanthropism in Africa, America and Asia. I
selected your organization to receive $10 million. Please immediately get
in touch with my physician and business manager to file for the transfer. I
await your urgent reply."

Imagine receiving this message. "You will receive $10 million!" Wow!
This seems astonishing until you hear the rest of the story. People
responding to the request are told to simply divulge their bank account
numbers and a huge deposit will soon follow. What actually occurs is a
huge withdrawal of every dollar in their accounts.

This is commonly known as the "Nigerian E-mail Scam," named after
the country where it originated. I have received an average of one or two
of these letters a day for the past five years. Authorities estimate victims
have lost billions of dollars. Fortunately I was never one of those sufferers.

Not so fortunately, however, I became a casualty of another internet
scam. An order was placed through the Sowing Seeds Ministry website for

175 copies of one of my books, *Breaking the Peanut Butter Habit,* plus other items. And there was even a donation to our ministry. The shipping address was a remote area of Africa. I was immediately suspicious because the order was so large. And I wondered why would anyone in Africa want so many copies of this particular book. "Maybe the charge card information is no good and the whole thing is a stunt," I thought. Yet the entire order and over $1,000 in shipping charges was approved.

Still suspicious, I called my local banker for advice. He asked, "Did you receive the money?"

"Yes," I answered.

"Then ship it and don't worry," he said. Soon, I discovered my banker was wrong — very wrong.

When you use a charge card in a store and sign a receipt, the credit card company guarantees payment to the merchant even when fraud is involved. But since there is no signature when buying products over the internet, there are few guarantees given to the hapless merchant — who, in this situation, was me.

Several days later, I received a phone call from the fraud division of the credit card company informing me that the order was processed with a stolen credit card and that, within days, all the money would be withdrawn from the Sowing Seeds account. Our little ministry was successfully scammed out of thousands of dollars and 175 copies of my book are now floating around central Africa.

When describing the first e-mail scam, I felt smart and very astute. But succumbing to the lures of the second scam made me feel vulnerable, embarrassed, ashamed and angry. How could I be so stupid and not be more suspicious? Why would someone want to harm our ministry in such a way?

Recently, while preparing for a sermon series on Godly leaders of the Old Testament, I revisited the story of Jacob and his twin brother, Esau, in Genesis. Jacob was the second twin and he was said to have been holding tightly to Esau's heel during birth. The name Jacob literally means grabber and also deceiver. Jacob is the Bible's version of a con artist and his number one mark was his brother Esau.

Jacob grabbed and deceived to get everything he wanted out of life. He grabbed his brother's birthright with what I call, "The World's Most Expensive Stew." Esau was hungry, Jacob had stew and the rest is history.

He also stole Esau's blessing and honor by disguising himself in front of their father, Isaac. Caught in his deceit, Jacob did what comes naturally to any con artist caught in a scam: he ran away. For years Jacob stayed with his Uncle Laban, yet another con artist.

After being deceived and scammed, I'm beginning to understand the rage Esau must have felt when he discovered Jacob's deceit.

Then years later, after living with Laban, we find Jacob wants to pack up his family and return home. All his life, Jacob had been running; but now the con artist was coming home to face Esau, the rest of his family and God.

For years, Jacob escaped the consequences of his deceit and lies. But no more. He would soon face the truth before his brother, who was riding out to greet him — with four hundred armed men. What would they do to him? Fearful, Jacob sent his family across the river to act as shields while he stayed safely behind. Coward!

But during the long night, Jacob experienced a significant turning point which changed his life forever: *"A man came and wrestled with him until dawn."* (Genesis 32:24) Who is this mystery man? Was this a literal wrestling match or a dream? What does it all mean?

"When the man saw that he couldn't win the match, he struck Jacob's hip and knocked it out of joint at the socket. Then the man said, 'Let me go, for it is dawn.' But Jacob panted, 'I will not let you go unless you bless me.' 'What is your name?' the man asked. He replied, 'Jacob.'" (Genesis 25:27)

First, touching the hip or thigh in the Middle East symbolizes where vows are made and life is given. The stranger is deliberately striking at Jacob's weakest point: his integrity.

Second, in those days, Jacob would not ordinarily divulge his name to a stranger because it was believed to reveal your character and surrender power to the person asking. Yet, to this stranger, Jacob the con artist does the unthinkable. He gives him is name. He confesses that he is Jacob, the deceiver, the con artist.

So, first Jacob is struck down for a life of lies and second, by admitting he was Jacob, he was for the first time confessing his true character.

As you have probably guessed, the mystery man is God. So, is Jacob locked in a wrestling match with God? Whether the match was literal or not doesn't matter because God was definitely there. The important part is that Jacob needed to wrestle with the consequences of his life of lies and deceit. So do I. And so do you.

What happens next is one of those significant biblical moments. *"Your name will no longer be Jacob,"* the man told him. *"It is now Israel, because you have struggled with both God and men and have won."* (Genesis 32:28) In one momentous evening, Jacob the "grabber and deceiver" became Israel, who "struggled with God and men and won." But what does it all mean for Jacob and, eventually, for us?

1. There is a Jacob of "grabbing and deceit" within all of us.
2. Someday, we must face our own wrestling match with God.
3. Recognizing who we really are is a necessary step toward divine change.
4. A willingness to change allows God the opportunity to work a miracle within you.

Did Jacob really change? Absolutely! How Do I know? *"Then in the distance, Jacob saw Esau coming with his four hundred men. Jacob now arranged his family in a column ... then Jacob went on ahead."* (Genesis 33:1-3)

The former con artist and coward who hid behind his family and possessions now moved ahead of the line to face his brother and four hundred armed men — alone.

But Jacob wasn't the only one who changed. Esau, the scammed brother, also experienced the miracle of change. *"As he approached his brother, he bowed low seven times before him. Then Esau ran to meet him and embraced him affectionately and kissed him. Both of them were in tears."* (Genesis 33:3-4)

The one with every right to seek revenge instead chose the path of forgiveness and embraced his brother. Is it any wonder that Jacob/Israel would say to Esau: *"To see your friendly smile is like seeing the smile of God!"* (Genesis 33:10) Such is the power of divine grace. Jacob's wrestling match led to a changed life ready for God's service. Esau's willingness to forgive led to the miracle of reconciliation. Wow!

Have you been scammed, taken advantage of? Are you struggling with bitterness, vowing to get even with a relative, coworker or friend? Maybe you are the con artist. Have you scammed others?

Maybe it's time for your own wrestling match with God. Confession leads to change. Change followed by reconciliation is potent medicine for the soul. Do you have the courage to wrestle with God? Like Jacob and Esau, this could be the turning point that will change your life.

SEE THE LIGHT

Jacob was locked in a wrestling match with God. Whether the match was literal or not doesn't matter because God was definitely there. The important part is that Jacob needed to wrestle with the consequences of his life of lies and deceit. So do I. And so do you.

SHARE THE LIGHT

1. Have you ever been scammed? How did you feel?
2. You have very likely also conned someone else. Now what?
3. When is the last time you had a wrestling match with God?
4. Who do you need to forgive?
5. Who needs to forgive you?

Notes:

LIVE THE LIGHT: The Lighthouse in Action

Every church should offer opportunities for someone who seeks forgiveness and a changed life. This is especially appropriate during Holy Communion. At Timberlake, we provide cards for people to write down what troubles them. They bring the cards to the altar and pray, then the cards are gathered and destroyed. Just before Easter, similar cards containing confessions are literally nailed to three large crosses. Can you imagine the impact of literally nailing your sins to a cross? Then, during our Easter sunrise service, those same cards are burned as a part of the Easter celebration.

Your Action Ideas:
How can your church provide opportunities to confess and receive God's grace?

1. _____

2. _____

3. _____

"I feel so ashamed and unworthy for decisions I have made in the past. I was married to my first husband for 12 years and have two grown children. After the divorce I was angry with God and with everyone. I left my church and God. [Eventually] I returned to church looking for solace in God and my new boyfriend asked me to leave. ... I told him that I left God once and wouldn't do it again. He decided to leave. My pastor tried to keep me from marrying him and I did not heed his words. Please include me in your prayers and ask God to forgive me and restore me. I have not waited for the Lord's will and have made mistake after mistake. ... The pastor and congregation have been very loving and kind. ... I just need to grow and get closer to God. I don't want to keep making these mistakes." —Letty

"I enjoy this church because of the people and the service ministries. The people are caring and friendly and we have so many ways to serve the Lord. We also have a wonderful youth ministry where youth can gather with other Christian youth and serve the Lord through missions." —Diane

FRIDAY—Simplify

Growth involves discipline, creativity and something more.

Then Peter called to him, "Lord, if it's really you,
tell me to come to you by walking on water."

"All right, come," Jesus said.

So Peter went over the side of the boat and walked on the water toward Jesus.
But when he looked around at the high waves, he was terrified
and began to sink. "Save me, Lord!" he shouted.

Instantly Jesus reached out his hand and grabbed him.
"You don't have much faith," Jesus said. "Why did you doubt me?"
And when they climbed back into the boat, the wind stopped.

Then the disciples worshiped him.
"You really are the Son of God!" they exclaimed.
Matthew 14:28-33

I have two dumbbells in my office. No, I'm not referring to my coworkers. I'm talking about exercise equipment. The dumbbells symbolize my (eh-hmm) single-minded dedication to exercise, physical fitness, workouts, diets and overall attention to good nutrition. In other words, all of the good stuff I am *supposed* to be doing for a healthy, active life.

The label says, "Executive Dumbbells." What does that mean? I have no idea. What's the difference between executive and regular dumbbells? Probably ten more of my hard-earned dollars.

When is the last time I actually used the dumbbells? Ooh! Did you have to ask? Let me simply say, a very long time. How does the saying go? "I know I have sinned Lord, but I've got really great excuses."

By the way, dumbbells aren't the only unused items I have lying around. If you walk through my house, you will find several pieces of exercise equipment gathering dust. My stair climber is good for hanging dirty shirts. And a quick peek at my library reveals more than a dozen books on diet, exercise and weight control. I can truthfully say that I have read at least the first chapter of each book. But every January, while making New Year's resolutions, I purchase another book. And every February, that same new book lies unread.

So I have a confession to make. When it comes to exercise and weight management, I don't use the dumbbells or the stair climber or follow the advice offered by those books. In other words, I am the dumbbell. No, make that the *executive* dumbbell.

I don't need more exercise equipment or books as much as I need a healthy dose of discipline. For me, discipline is simply the daily willingness to put into practice what I already know to be important steps to a healthier lifestyle: more exercise and better eating habits.

Obviously, I need more discipline in maintaining my physical health: So one way to improve my life is to be more disciplined about exercise and diet. But what about my spiritual health? Yes, discipline is important here, too. Questions to consider:

- Do you have a daily prayer life?
- Do you regularly read the Bible?
- Are you an active member of a local church?
- Are you participating in a small group?
- Do you participate in a ministry serving others?
- Are you actively witnessing your faith?

As we look at the questions above, we need to rate ourselves honestly. How are we doing? I would guess most of us come up short. So another resolution is to practice more discipline maintaining our spiritual health and our relationships with God. Adding discipline to our spiritual lives will improve our walks with God. We must seek to become more disciplined about our spiritual lives as well as our physical health.

But discipline alone is not enough. There are potential hazards with this analogy. Have you ever been around a health and fitness freak? Whoa! Talk about coming on strong; they need to get a life! Unless you practice their extraordinary level of commitment in health and physical fitness, you will be judged unworthy and ignored. People who are serious about spiritual disciplines are often arrogant as well. Dumbbells are a good analogy but we can go too far.

So what do we do now? Maybe, we need another analogy. How about a piano? We have one of those in our house, too. Oh, how fondly I recall the precious memories of sitting at the piano with my chubby little fingers deftly playing Mozart and Beethoven. Well, to me it sounded like Mozart and Beethoven. But to anyone else, it sounded more like *Chopsticks*.

Now, a ten-year old playing *Chopsticks* is cute. My parents were filled with pride as they imagined their musical prodigy in a concert hall, performing for adoring fans. But I couldn't play *Chopsticks* forever. A 40-year-old with years of piano lessons, who can play only one song, is a pathetic waste of talent and a real bore at parties. Eventually I had to learn to play something else — or find a new hobby. (*Or spend the rest of my life hanging around ten-year-olds.*)

To play the piano effectively requires discipline, just like maintaining physical fitness. But now we add a touch of creativity. Discipline is required to learn how to read a musical score and properly stroke white and black keys in proper sequence to play a song. Creativity, however, is adding the personal touch which turns an ordinary song into a listener's delight.

The piano is a reminder of how God challenges us to grow, to experiment, to boldly try new ideas and be creative with our spiritual decisions. He wants us to reach out and discover fresh, innovative ways of getting to know and serve Him. The author of Revelation writes: *"I know all the things you do, that you are neither hot nor cold. I wish you were one or the other! But since you are like lukewarm water, I will spit you out of my mouth!"* (*Revelation 3:15-16*)

Discipline needs the spark of creativity to keep from becoming lukewarm. Creativity adds individuality and passion as we pursue a relationship with God. What's more, others are attracted to creativity.

When someone plays a piano with imagination and passion, people will gather to hear and enjoy the beautiful music. Some will even be inspired to learn to play the piano themselves.

So in addition to discipline, we should seek to become more creative in our walk with God. Now we look at those spiritual questions with a balance of discipline and creativity:

- Do you have a daily prayer life?
- Do you regularly read the Bible?
- Are you an active member of a local church?
- Are you participating in a small group?
- Do you participate in a ministry serving others?
- Are you actively witnessing your faith?

We can ask ourselves these questions and look for innovative ways to improve our spiritual walk with God. How can we add creativity to our daily prayer life, as we read the Bible, while we participate in our local church and small group or as we serve others? How can we witness our faith in a lively, creative way? This may surprise you, but God is never dull.

The piano represents God's gift of creativity. But this, too, is incomplete. Have you ever been around a gifted artist? Many could easily be described as "stuck on themselves." Too much emphasis on creativity alone promotes arrogance and selfishness. We tend to worship our creativity rather than the Creator who provided the gift.

So, if discipline and creativity aren't enough, what do we do? We add one more analogy: a painting.

In my office hangs a painting by Norbert McNulty titled *Peter on the Water*. Surrounded by a dangerous thunderstorm, the disciples are tossed about in their boat, faces flush with fear. With Jesus' permission, Peter timidly steps onto the water. But something goes terribly wrong as he begins to sink into the turbulent sea. There is only one hope as we see Peter desperately reaching for the outstretched hand of Jesus. Amidst the raging storm, Jesus calmly pulls Peter to safety.

We can only go so far on our own. If we are to go farther we must reach for and be willing to accept help.

The Bible goes on to say, "*And when they climbed back into the boat, the wind stopped. Then the disciples worshiped him. 'You really are the Son of God!' they exclaimed.*" (Matthew 14:33)

When we learn to recognize our need for help, God's outstretched arm will be there.

Discipline with a dose of creativity is important in our journey of faith, but we were never supposed to walk alone. This painting stands as a poignant reminder of our constant need for the hand of Jesus to pull us out of the depths. Here is what I learned from the painting:

- Peter was bold to step out of the boat and walk on the water toward Jesus. There is a need for boldness when we reach out for God, but boldness alone is not enough.
- Peter was quickly overwhelmed by the obstacles of wind and high waves. We, too, can quickly become overwhelmed when left to our own devices.
- In the end, Peter could do nothing without Christ's outreached arm. We accomplish nothing without looking and reaching toward Jesus.
- Like the disciples, all we can say is "Truly you are the Son of God."

Now we look at the same spiritual questions again. But this time we are armed with the knowledge that we need help from each other and from God in our turbulent and stormy lives.

- Do you have a daily prayer life?
- Do you regularly read the Bible?
- Are you an active member of a local church?
- Are you participating in a small group?
- Do you participate in a ministry serving others?
- Are you actively witnessing your faith?

So what have we learned? How should we effectively answer the six questions above?

1. We look to God for help in adding more discipline to our spiritual lives. (The Executive Dumbbells)
2. We creatively use our gifts and talents as we walk with God. (The Piano)
3. We recognize our inability to effectively accomplish steps one and two without help. (The Painting)
4. Finally: What else can we say but, "Truly you are the Son of God!"

How can I develop a deeper faith and a closer relationship with God? A great answer is found in two dumbbells, a piano and a painting.

Pray: God, help me to utilize more discipline and creativity in my prayer life and my Bible study. Help me become more active in my local church and in a small group. Help me become more intentional about ministry and witnessing my faith. But Lord, most of all, help me to understand that I am in turbulent waters and I'll surely drown if I don't learn to reach out for Your outstretched hand. I need you Lord. Thank you for being my rescuer in the midst of the storm. Amen

SEE THE LIGHT

Growth involves discipline and creativity, but they will only take you so far. We need to reach out for the already outstretched hand of God.

SHARE THE LIGHT

Remembering your call to discipline, creativity and the need for God's help, how can you answer the following questions?
1. Do you have a daily prayer life?
2. Do you regularly read the Bible?
3. Are you an active member of a local church?
4. Are you participating in a small group?
5. Do you participate in a ministry serving others?
6. Are you actively witnessing your faith?

Notes:

_____

_____

_____

_____

_____

_____

_____

_____

_____

_____

_____

_____

_____

_____

_____

LIVE THE LIGHT: The Lighthouse in Action

A nurse/physical therapist felt our church needed more than covered dish suppers and prayer groups. One morning she started a "Chair Exercise" group to help our retired folks stay more physically fit. I chuckled when she first mentioned chair exercise, but she smiled and invited me to set a good example for the group by participating. I thought to myself: How hard could exercising in a chair possibly be? I would soon find out. Within ten minutes I was gasping for breath and praying for an early end to the class. Over the years this group has grown and become one of the most active groups in our church.

Your Action Ideas:
How can your church create opportunities to improve discipline?

1. _____

2. _____

3. _____

"I really enjoyed today's devotion. The exercise/discipline example is great for my spiritual life. I have one suggestion. I think it is typically American, maybe even human, to think that discipline is solely an individual effort. ... Somehow the aspect of community and support need to be a part of this. Studies have shown that starting an exercise program with a friend or group of friends is more successful than doing it alone. Also think of AA. Overcoming any disease is more effective when done in community, being accountable to others. We rejoice with each other when we succeed and lovingly encourage each other when we fail. I don't know how we miss the "family" and "support group" aspects of the church. Yes, ultimately individuals are responsible for making the decision to make the changes and to discipline themselves, but it sure makes it a better (and more successful) prospect if we know others are there with us." —Andrew

"From the first Sunday we visited, we felt like we belonged. This is a very friendly and welcoming church and I know my spiritual life and my ministry will be strengthened here." —Anonymous

SATURDAY—Start Shining

Sometimes we grow the most when all seems lost.

*One day Jesus said to his disciples, "Let's cross over to the other side
of the lake." So they got into a boat and started out. On the way across,
Jesus lay down for a nap, and while he was sleeping the wind began to rise.
A fierce storm developed that threatened to swamp them,
and they were in real danger.*

*The disciples woke him up, shouting,
"Master, Master, we're going to drown!"*

*So Jesus rebuked the wind and the raging waves. The storm stopped
and all was calm! Then he asked them, "Where is your faith?"*
Luke 8:22-25

One day my grandfather Blacky said, "Larry, we're going shrimping and
fishing early tomorrow morning." As a twelve year old boy, those
words were more precious to me than gold. Of all his grandchildren,
tomorrow was going to be my morning — and mine alone — to be with
grandpa. What a great day it would be.

My older cousin snickered when I told him the news. "So, you're the
new victim. You'll be sorry!"

Every summer our family made the journey from Virginia to a small
fishing town near Panama City, Florida, to visit our grandparents. Blacky
owned a fish house on the bay and every morning he would either escort
fishermen or would go shrimping for bait to be sold in his store. Around
noon he would always return with a happy, joyous group and a boat full of fish.
The younger children, including me, were usually stuck hanging around
waiting for the adults to come home; but not this time. Not tomorrow!

Still, I couldn't help but wonder why my cousin thought it was so
entertaining that I would be chosen.

That night, I carefully arranged my clothes so I would be ready quickly
when Grandpa came. I could hardly sleep, imagining the excitement of
being in the same boat with the greatest fisherman of all time. What life
changing lessons would I learn? I passed the long night hours picturing the
mountainous piles of shrimp and fish we would haul in. I would modestly

smile while acknowledging the envious looks I was sure to receive from everyone on shore wishing they were on that boat instead of me.

Just before dawn, Blacky shook me awake and gently asked "Are you ready for an adventure?"

"You bet, Grandpa!" I replied, leaping out of bed and quickly putting on my clothes. All thoughts of my cousin's snide remarks were quickly forgotten in the excitement of finally going fishing with Blacky.

Within a few minutes we were in the boat heading through the inlet, guided by the slowly rising sun to what we called West Bay. Grandpa pointed out how the buoys floating in the water were really channel markers to guide boats and ships through the deepest and safest part of the bay. "Stay close to those buoys," he shouted over the noise of the outboard motor, "and they will guide you home."

After awhile, Blacky maneuvered away from the buoys to a spot he instinctively knew was the right place, between deep water and shore. Quickly he gathered nets scattered throughout the boat and showed me how to throw them so the attached weights would guide the nets to the bottom where shrimp were waiting. Then, I guided the boat as he showed me how to slowly steer in an ever-widening circle.

After the boat made three or four slow, lazy circles, Blacky motioned for me to stop. Watchfully, we began pulling in the now heavy net and neatly arranging it on the deck. At first we saw nothing but seaweed and an occasional crab. But it wasn't long before we began seeing shrimp. Lots and lots of shrimp. The work was hard, but seeing all those shrimp and working beside my grandpa made it all worthwhile.

We moved the boat to another spot, threw the nets out and once again I guided the boat in ever-widening circles. "You're doing great!" grandpa said, while taking a seat closer to the bow of the boat.

Then Blacky promptly fell asleep — not just a polite snooze mind you, but a symphony filled with snores and wheezes to wake the dead. Try as I might, there was no waking my grandpa. Now what? I was in deep water as well as deep trouble and help seemed many miles away. Now I was beginning to understand my cousin's warning. "So, you're the new victim," he had said. "You'll be sorry!"

A similar situation happened to the disciples as they traveled with Jesus: *"One day Jesus said to his disciples, 'Let's cross over to the other side of the lake.' So they got into a boat and started out. On the way across, Jesus lay down for a nap, and while he was sleeping the wind began to rise. A fierce storm developed that threatened to swamp them, and they were in real danger." (Luke 8:22-23)*

Like the disciples, I was in danger and afraid. My guide and expert wouldn't wake up. I didn't know if he was sick or just very lazy, but either way I needed help from another source.

"The disciples woke him up, shouting, 'Master, Master, we're going to drown!'" (Luke 8:24)

After a moment of panic, I realized something had to change. "Stop and think!" I said to myself. Then, I remembered how grandpa already showed me what to do. I just needed to mentally retrace his lessons.

First, I needed to take in the nets. So I leaned over the side, grabbed the ropes and "Whoa, these nets are heavy!" I thought. Slowly, inch by inch, I began hauling in the heavy nets and placing them on the deck. It wasn't long before I was rewarded with the sight of shrimp — hundreds of shrimp.

Fear turned to wonder as the hold was filled to the brim. I looked over at grandpa with newfound pride, but I could tell by the loud noise coming out of his mouth, he was still fast asleep. My fear returned.

"So Jesus rebuked the wind and the raging waves. The storm stopped and all was calm! Then he asked them, 'Where is your faith?'" (Luke 8:25)

"Stay close to the buoys," grandpa said to me, earlier that morning. "They will guide you safely home."

With a silent prayer I turned the boat toward what I hoped would be where we had come before. Fortunately, it wasn't long before I saw a familiar blue buoy ahead. Soon, I saw the comforting vision of the shoreline in the distance. As the boat glided steadily through the water toward home, I felt a surge of pride. As I glanced at grandpa, he was no longer snoring and there was a trace of a smile on his face. Blacky never admitted it, but others later told me: "It was his way of testing you and you passed."

"And the disciples were filled with awe and amazement." (Luke 8:25)

Occasionally, you may find yourself in deep trouble with help seemingly miles away. You cry out in pain but everyone seems to be asleep. No one answers, at least not right away and not with the response you're looking for. Now what? You can panic. You can abandon ship. Or you can:

1. Stop, think and mentally retrace lessons already learned.
2. Grab hold of the nets with all your strength and pull.
3. Don't stop pulling, don't give up and don't lose faith.

4. Say a prayer and turn the boat in the direction you hope is the right path.
5. Continue looking for the buoys and they will guide you safely home.

Jesus was disappointed in the disciples for allowing a thunderstorm to scare them without trusting in the authority of the One who was already in the boat. The disciples also were being tested, but unfortunately came up short this time. "Where is your faith?" asked Jesus. Later, they would learn their lesson well.

Blacky is in heaven now, but while writing this story, I found new appreciation for the creative way he loved and nurtured me. Through his experience, I discovered valuable lessons. Because of his sleepy test, I discovered newfound strength. And with his loving encouragement, I found courage. Thanks, Grandpa.

SEE THE LIGHT

Occasionally, you may find yourself in deep trouble with help seemingly miles away. You cry out in pain but everyone seems to be asleep. No one answers, at least not right away and not with the response you're looking for. Now what? You can panic or you can abandon ship or you can:

1. Stop, think and mentally retrace lessons already learned.
2. Grab hold of the nets with all your strength and pull.
3. Don't stop pulling, don't give up and don't lose faith.
4. Say a prayer and turn the boat in the direction you hope is the right path.
5. Continue looking for the buoys that will guide you safely home.

SHARE THE LIGHT

1. Who in your family encouraged your growth in creative ways?
2. Have you ever found yourself seemingly lost and those who you depend upon seem to be asleep? How did you find your way back home?
3. How can Christ help you find the way home?

Notes:

_____

_____

_____

_____

_____

_____

_____

_____

_____

_____

_____

_____

_____

_____

_____

_____

_____

_____

LIVE THE LIGHT: The Lighthouse in Action

Lamb's Wool. Do you like to knit? Here is a ministry for you. Lamb's Wool is a non-profit knitting outreach with a mission to provide simple, hand-knit sweaters to needy children all over the world. Anyone who knits or crochets can participate. It's a great project for individuals, church groups, knitting clubs or women's groups. Easy knitting patterns are provided. Check them out for yourself on the web at www.lambswool.org

Your Action Ideas:
Everyone has a talent. How can your church help others turn their talents into ministry?

1. _____

2. _____

3. _____

"I parked my car at the top of a multi-story car park and my son accidentally let go of his [helium] balloon. This balloon went up and up and continued going upwards into the beautiful blue summer sky until just a tiny speck was barely visible. It was then God spoke to me and said, 'I will take you even higher than the balloon you can barely see. I will lift you up and take you to heights you never thought possible.' Often I wondered about this during hardships with my family, in the church and at work thinking what does God mean? I am suffering; does He not care? Then I am reminded of Jesus who suffered on the cross and bore our sins. Life has more meaning than before with Jesus by my side. All worries and anxieties are gone. Death no longer has a hold on me because I have abundant life in Jesus. God is doing amazing things in our lives and He is lifting us every day in His presence." —Judit

"This church has been such a part of our lives. What would we have done without our church? It has been our extended family. The outpouring of love that has been shown to us through the years has helped to mold our lives. Thank the Lord for our church home." —Anonymous

WHAT HAVE WE LEARNED SO FAR?

Monday—We need light
Faith comes from the heart and from committing
to an ongoing relationship with God. We think religious
satisfaction only comes from doing something,
but real faith comes from being something.

Tuesday—Opportunities to Shine
Every experience in your life journey is crafted by God
to mold you. The encouragement of a church
is an invaluable aid toward shaping your future.

Wednesday—Becoming God's Lighthouse
We all need occasional spiritual audits to strengthen
our relationship with Christ. This is why becoming
"born again" is more than just a one-time experience.

Thursday—An Attitude that Shines
Jacob needed to wrestle with the consequences of his
life of deceit. So do I. And so do you.

Friday—Simplify
Growth involves discipline and creativity, but they alone
will only take you so far. We need to reach for
the already outstretched hand of God.

Saturday—Start Shining
You may find yourself in deep trouble with help
seemingly miles away. You can panic or you can stop, think
and mentally retrace lessons already learned.

Now, let's put it all together...

SUNDAY—Live the Light

Win or lose, nothing can keep God away.

And I am convinced that nothing can ever separate us from his love.
Death can't, and life can't. The angels can't, and the demons can't.
Our fears for today, our worries about tomorrow,
and even the powers of hell can't keep God's love away.
Romans 8:38

O nce a year we have our annual "Beach Party" worship service. We dress casual and act a little crazy, but the results are meant to include joyful worship, encouragement and Bible study. One year, the cover of the Sunday bulletin showed a picture of a boy playing baseball with the title: "We're Going to a Ball Game!" One person entering the church looked at the bulletin and sniffed, "Larry's lost his mind."

There is a reason for this particular madness however, so I said to everyone, "Hang in there and trust me!"

The service was designed to resemble an actual baseball game complete with a play-by-play announcer, singing of the National Anthem, popcorn vendors and even a mascot from our own Lynchburg Hillcats.

The Timbretones bell choir dressed up crazy, acted a little wild and provided a lively rendition of baseball music. Everything was designed to recreate a baseball game between our church leaders and the best ball players ever to play the game. Wow! Check out our "All Star" line up:

- First Base: Lou Gehrig, NY Yankees. Iron Man, played 2,130 Games straight.
- Second Base: Rogers Hornsby. Played with several teams but ranked just behind Babe Ruth.
- Third Base: Mike Schmidt, Philadelphia Phillies. Member of the "500 lifetime home runs club."
- Shortstop: Cal Ripken, Jr., Baltimore Orioles. Broke Lou Gehrig's Iron Man streak.
- Catcher: Johnny Bench, Cincinnati Reds. A defensive and offensive powerhouse.
- Pitcher: Sandy Koufax, LA Dodgers. Unofficial Triple Crown Pitching Holder.

- Outfield: Babe Ruth, NY Yankees. Simply the most dominant hitter of his time.
- Outfield: Willie Mays, SF Giants. Famous for the "Basket Catch."
- Outfield: Hank Aaron, Atlanta Braves. Broke Ruth's lifetime home run record.

On the other hand... look at the team our church fielded to play against these "All Stars." (Pretty pathetic!)

- First Base: Dan "the Can" Abrams. Biggest feat: He's been in every jail across three counties.
- Second Base: "Mean" Gene Farley. He's a great hitter. In fact, he hit two umpires, three owners, ...
- Third Base: Lady Fay Turner. Only player called for delay of game for putting on her make up.
- Shortstop: Rappin' Donnie Smith. Signed a recording contract. Sings much better than he plays.
- Catcher: "Big Al" Baughman. He can't catch much but who cares; nobody gets past Big Al.
- Pitcher: Larry "The Mouth" Davies. Teaches pitching classes. Too bad he can't actually pitch.
- Outfield: "Lightning" Larry Spencer. He's not fast but he's been struck by lightening three times.
- Outfield: Betsy "Have Spatula Will Travel" Harkleroad. She can't play, but she makes great snacks.
- Outfield: "Sorry Charlie" Johnson. Charlie can't catch, can't hit and can't throw — but he's so polite.

On paper, our church team looked doomed before the game even started. We didn't stand a chance. Or did we?

Throughout the service our announcer provided the score. Sandy Koufax struck out player after player while Larry the Mouth was under pressure. The Mighty Babe hit a two-run shot over the center field wall. Johnny Bench hit another beautiful home run and Hank Aaron brought in Willie Mays. The church crew struggled, but "Big Al" knocked in two and we hung on to keep the score four-to-three after five innings.

At this point we heard the poem, *Casey at the Bat,* by Ernest Thayer. Everyone knows when Casey comes to the plate there will be victory.

Supremely confident in his unique hitting ability, Casey lets two pitches go and, with two strikes, Casey readies to take a definitive swing for triumph: "And now the air is shattered by the force of Casey's blow." But as we know, the result was not what he planned.

"Oh, somewhere in this favored land the sun is shining bright; the band is playing somewhere, and somewhere hearts are light, And somewhere men are laughing, and somewhere children shout; But there is no joy in Mudville — mighty Casey has struck out."

In sports, we quickly learn the sometimes ugly reality that one team has to win and another must lose. Becoming a follower of God was never meant to be presented as a never ending string of joy, laughter and success. Sometimes losing, tragedy and grief become a part of our journey, too. But either way, I believe we are meant to play on a team and how we play, win or lose, defines who we are.

In the seventh inning, Sandy Koufax found his arm once again and struck out the side. For the church team, Larry The Mouth caught a pop-up ending the inning with the bases loaded — but not before Cal Ripken was brought home with a single by Mike Schmidt. The score stood at All Stars–5, Church Team–3.

Romans 12, slightly altered using baseball terminology, says: And so, fellow teammates, I plead with you to give your team to God. Let them be willing to make a holy sacrifice — the kind deep in the outfield. When you think of what God has done for you, is this too much to ask? Don't copy the behavior and customs of the other team, but let God transform you into a new player by changing the way you think. Then you will know what God wants you to do and you will know how good and pleasing and perfect his coaching really is. (*Romans 12:1-2; New Revised Baseball Version*)

The best baseball teams are full of players who are ever willing and ready to give their all for the good of the team. These are the players we see slamming into the outfield wall or diving to the ground to make the big catch. Their passion and love for the sport is evident whether they are on the field or off. They live, breathe and eat baseball until, at times, we're sick of hearing it; but we admire their passion.

As disciples of Christ, we learn to concentrate on winning in a different way. We have the opportunity to give ourselves totally to God without reservation. This "give it all you've got" attitude will allow God to transform us into new persons by changing the way we think. We will know

God's purpose and how much God wants to guide our lives. Our passion and love for God will become more evident, whether in church or out. We will live and breathe our passion for God until, at times, others will be sick of hearing us; but they will admire our passion. This passion for God will become our witness.

Speaking of passion, in 1927, Jack Norworth wrote a poem about Nelly Kelly, a passionate fan who would rather go to a baseball game than anywhere else. The chorus is routinely sung during the seventh inning. Will you join me?

Take me out to the ball game. Take me out with the crowd. Buy me some peanuts and Cracker Jacks. I don't care if I never get back. Let me root, root, root for the home team. If they don't win it's a shame. For it's one, two, three strikes, you're out, at the old ball game.

Paul goes on to say in Romans (baseball version): As God's player, I give each of you this warning: Be honest in your estimate of yourselves, measuring your value by how much ability God has given you. Just as your team has many players and each player has a special function, so it is with Christ's team. We are all players of his one team, and each of us has different work to do. And since we are all one team in Christ, we belong to each other, and each of us needs the others.

Good baseball players understand their strengths and weaknesses so, when playing together as a team, they know who plays first base, who bats cleanup and who pitches. Paul is challenging us to honestly know our own gifts and talents so that we know what work we are to do. We are needed and wanted and knowing our gifts allows us to contribute in an exceptional way to God's team.

In the eighth inning, Lightening Larry hit a line drive just over the outstretched arms of Willie Mays. Rappin' Donnie Smith ran from second and slid home. Score five-to-four, still in favor of the "All Stars."

In the top of the ninth inning, Iron Man Cal Ripken ran home and collided with our own Big Al, injuring his hand. Big Al had to leave the game and there was no one to substitute for him. What would our church team do now?

Rick Warren, author of two best-selling books, *Purpose Driven Life* and *Purpose Driven Church*, uses a baseball diamond to plot how a church should be a catalyst for spiritual growth. The "Batter's Box" symbolizes newcomers, beginning the process of attending a local church. Will they feel God's presence during worship? Is the message biblically-based and challenging their spiritual perspectives? Will they receive a warm welcome from other church members? If they check the calendar of events, will they find interesting activities, mission projects and groups offering further opportunities for growth?

Hopefully, newcomers return and respond to God's urging to join a church and pledge to support the ministry with their prayers, presence, gifts and service. Jesus' disciple, Simon Peter started the process when he said, *"You are the Messiah, the Son of the Living God."* Jesus replied, *"You are Peter and upon this rock I will build my church."* (Matthew 16:16-18) Congratulations, your newcomers became members. They've hit the ball and reached first base.

Speaking of first base, the score is six-to-four in favor of the All Stars. Big Al is out of the game and there is no one to take his place. "Lend me someone to finish with," said our church team manager. The All Stars manager quickly replied, "No way! We're here to win." Then with a sneer he said, "You'll have to ask someone from the stands. Maybe one of the spectators will volunteer to play." Now the game was getting nasty.

First base is about getting to know Christ better through the church. Many reach first and are satisfied to stay safe; yet God wants us to reach out and enjoy deeper relationships with Christ. First base is exploring opportunities to love and be loved. Paul writes, *"If I could speak in any language in heaven or on earth but didn't love others, I would only be making meaningless noise like a loud gong or a clanging cymbal."* (1 Corinthians 13:1) Loving others is paramount. We could start by joining a Sunday school class, singing in the choir or participating in a small group. Soon, through our increased participation, we reach second base.

Second base is a disciplined desire to strengthen our relationships with Jesus. Many disciples commit to small group Bible studies. Others use special retreats such as "Walk to Emmaus." For two years, while driving 30 minutes to work, I studied by listening to cassettes that offered biblical teaching. Jesus said, *"Yes, I am the vine; you are the branches. Those who remain in me and I in them will produce much fruit. For apart from me you can do nothing."* (John 15:5) Through the church we have many opportunities to nurture our relationships with The Vine and produce fruit. Producing fruit leads us to third base.

Meanwhile, the church manager vowed he would not quit, no matter what. "Will someone volunteer to help us finish the game? We need a good sport."

His plea was met with pained silence from the crowd. Would anyone help out our poor church team?

Third base is a commitment to use the distinctive gifts and talents we possess to serve Christ through ministry within the church. *"God has given each of us the ability to do certain things well."* *(Romans 12:6)* Are you handy with tools? Volunteer to repair rundown houses. Do you enjoy driving? Offer to drive an elderly person to the grocery store or to a doctor's appointment. Are you good at managing money? Become a mentor for someone facing bankruptcy. Utilizing our gifts and talents moves us from third base to home plate.

Home plate should be the culmination of everything we have experienced in church:

- Batter Up! — Welcome
- First Base — Love
- Second Base — Growth
- Third Base — Ministry
- Home Plate — Leadership

Peter wrote *"Care for the flock of God entrusted to you. Watch over it willingly, not grudgingly — not for what you can get out of it, but because you are eager to serve God."* *(1 Peter 5:2)* Now we have the opportunity to re-experience the excitement of running the bases while, at the same time, leading and helping others. When others step into the batter's box, we offer a warm welcome. We enable others to experience the love of God's church as we escort them to first base. We may facilitate the classes that lead to growth and second base. We may establish the ministries that help others serve and reach third base. Finally, we get the added satisfaction of watching someone we nurtured become a spiritual leader for Christ. And God-inspired leadership multiplies home runs into grand slams. Will you accept the challenge of spiritual leadership?

Speaking of challenges, our church team manager was getting nowhere in finding a volunteer. No, wait a minute. Someone came down from the stands. I'd never seen him before. Who was this guy?

The stranger entered the field with a step firm and light. "Give me the mask and mitt," he said. "Let's finish the fight." His hair was sprinkled here and there with streaks of gray. Around his eyes and on his brow a bunch of wrinkles lay. As the stranger picked up the catchers mitt and got into position our manager turned his head and sighed. "Play ball!" shouted the umpire and the game resumed.

Larry the Mouth heaved two strikes at the mighty Babe Ruth. The stranger caught both and did not seem to heed. On the third pitch, Babe took a ferocious swing and found nothing but air. The side was put out and the score still stood six-to-four. Our church team had one more chance.

It was the bottom of the ninth. Mean Gene Farley went out on strikes and Sorry Charlie Johnson was put out at first. But Lady Fay Turner walked and Lightning Larry Spencer smashed a double. With players on first and third, up came the stranger.

Was this how the game was going to end? Everything was in the hands of a mysterious stranger. Is there a lesson here?

Our baseball worship service was fun, but hopefully we also learned several lessons:

1. In sports the thrill of victory and the agony of defeat are both important lessons. Becoming a follower of God was never meant to be a never ending string of joy, laughter and success. Losing, tragedy and grief often represent our journey. Either way, we are meant to be players on God's team and how we play, win or lose, defines who we are.

2. Romans teaches that we are all players on God's team and each of us has different work to do. We belong to each other and we need each other. We especially need God. Good baseball players understand their strengths and weaknesses so when playing together as a team they know who should play where. Paul challenges us to know our gifts and play where we are needed.

3. Using a baseball diamond, we learn how the church should be a catalyst for spiritual growth. We start by making our commitments in the batter's box, then moving to first base and strengthening our relationships with God and the church. Continuing to grow, we round the corner at second base and begin putting our knowledge to use through ministry at third. Home plate is where we practice everything we've learned, becoming spiritual leaders.

Still, something is missing. A critical ingredient is left out. Yes, we play as members of God's team. Yes, we understand our God-given gifts. Yes, we run the bases of spiritual maturity as the church becomes a catalyst for growth — but something of God is simply not there.

The stranger's feet were planted, his face serene, as the pitcher looked his way and grinned before heaving a fast ball. The echo of that fearful swat still lingers. High, fast and far the ball flew as it sailed over the high fence. Three runs came in and victory belonged to our church team. The players gathered to cheer the stranger. "What is your name?" For one brief moment the stranger was still, then he smiled and murmured soft and low: "I'm the mighty Casey who struck out many long years ago." Wow!

Let's look at the passage from Romans again: *"Can anything ever separate us from Christ's love? Does it mean he no longer loves us if we have trouble or calamity?"* Will God stop loving us if we play poorly and lose to the other team? Casey discovered the eternal answer and we can, too: *"No! Our fears for today, our worries about tomorrow and even the powers of hell can't keep God's love away."*

There's the missing ingredient. Whether we win or lose; whether we play or sit in the dugout. Whether or not we are growing in our faith. Whether hitting a home run or striking out. Nothing can keep God away. His grace will accompany us from the moment of acceptance to the forever of eternity.

Now, *that's* a sure thing. Enjoy the game of baseball and life, but always remember: You are already a winner with God.

I owe a special debt of gratitude to Clarence P. MacDonald, author of *Casey – Twenty Years Later*, which inspired the final part of this devotion.

SEE THE LIGHT

Whether we win or lose. Whether we play or sit in the dugout. Whether or not we are growing in our faith. Whether hitting a home run or striking out, nothing can keep God away. God's grace will accompany us from the moment of acceptance to the forever of eternity.

SHARE THE LIGHT

1. If your life could be described as a baseball game, how are you doing?
2. How can your life become more of a witness for God?
3. Paul's letter to the Romans teaches that we are all members of God's team. What position do you play?
4. Using the baseball diamond, how would you describe your spiritual growth?
5. Remembering that nothing can keep you away from God's precious love and grace, can you more fully appreciate that you are already a winner?

Notes:

_____

_____

_____

_____

_____

_____

_____

_____

_____

_____

_____

_____

_____

_____

_____

_____

_____

LIVE THE LIGHT: The Lighthouse in Action

Step one for any church looking to grow in faith and numbers is always prayer. But step two always points to worship. Nowhere is a church more visible than on Sunday morning. Do you have a worship service others will want to attend? How can you revitalize your worship? Two resources I found helpful are *Bore No More*, by Mike and Amy Nappa and *Pastoral Ministry in the 21st Century*, by Brad Lewis (both from Group Publishing).

Your Action Ideas:
What can your church do to enhance worship?

1. _____

2. _____

3. _____

"We were out of town and were not able to bring my mom to church. She seldom comes without us, so I was quite surprised to hear that she came with one of her friends. But my biggest surprise was how much she raved about what a wonderful service it was! Here was my (almost) 90-year-old mother loving it that they were yelling 'Peanuts! Popcorn!' during the middle of offertory, and enjoying all 'nine innings' of the service. What a pleasant surprise to hear her so excited about a service so different from her 'traditional' upbringing! Thanks for stepping outside the [box]!" —Jan

"I met you at the lowest point in my life at a singles retreat. You led a divorce recovery workshop that literally changed my life. You answered tough questions about God's view of divorce. I came to more fully understand that God does not love divorce but does indeed love divorced people. I struggled with how I could be a Sunday school teacher and serve the Lord and be divorced. God helped me through my divorce by sending people like you to guide me through that very difficult time. And then God sent me a good Christian man to spend the rest of my life with. I have been happily married for over four years now. Sometimes we never know how much the things we say can help others." —Rhonda

WEEK FOUR

HELP OTHERS

MONDAY—We Need Light

Most opportunities to help others are right in front of you.

*Dear brothers and sisters, what's the use of saying you have faith
if you don't prove it by your actions? That kind of faith can't save anyone.
Suppose you see a brother or sister who needs food or clothing, and you say,
"Well, good-bye and God bless you; stay warm and eat well" — but then you
don't give that person any food or clothing. What good does that do?
So you see, it isn't enough just to have faith. Faith that doesn't show itself
by good deeds is no faith at all — it is dead and useless.*
James 2:14-17

The checkout at the local grocery store was long and I was in a hurry. Seeing another line nearly empty, I walked over and stood behind the only customer still to make a purchase — a young twenty-something woman holding a small basket with 15 to 20 jars of baby food. There was nothing else in the basket: just baby food.

"This is great," I thought. "She'll only be a minute and I can be on my way."

The clerk took the woman's check for $7.43, efficiently typed in the numbers and slid it into the proper slot on the register. At this point the cash drawer was supposed to open while a receipt was printed, but not this time. A light began to blink: "See Manager." The clerk called on the intercom for the supervisor while running the check through again on her register. The same sign kept flashing: "See Manager."

"Oh no!" I thought. "Not another delay. I'm in a hurry and don't need the cash register to break down."

When the manager arrived, he didn't even look at the cash register, but instead picked up the check and began to talk to the customer. I could feel the muscles in my stomach tighten as the reality of what was happening struck me: The check for $7.43 was no good and the manager was quietly telling the young woman she could not buy her baby food there. The clerk quickly set the groceries aside, closed her account and began to ring up my purchase.

"She should manage her money better!" I tried to convince myself while leaving the store. "She's probably an alcoholic or a drug addict." But my flimsy excuses would not erase the picture in my mind of a grocery basket filled with jars of baby food.

Jesus teaches: *"You are the light of the world ... we don't light a lamp and put it under a bowl. Instead we put it on a stand and it gives light to everyone in the house. In the same way, let your light shine so they may see your good deeds and praise your Father in heaven." (Matthew 5:14-16)*

Every day, we receive opportunities to help someone in need. Our light shines when we use those God-given opportunities to witness our faith by reaching out and getting involved. There is nothing dramatic about these day-to-day encounters, but they emphatically tell the world what kind of Christians we really are.

At this point, I'd like to finish the story by writing that I approached the manager and offered to pay for the purchase of the baby food. It was the right thing to do. I don't have much money, but I can afford $7.43. Instead, hiding my light under a bowl, I turned my head and walked away. There are no acceptable excuses. I had a great opportunity to help someone and walked away. Next time I will do better.

God taught me a valuable lesson that day. What we believe as Christians only works if we turn our faith into action. How about you? How many opportunities have you missed to let your light shine and instead hid it under a bowl?

Next time you are in a check-out line at your local grocery store, instead of worrying about your schedule, look around you. Maybe God will give you the opportunity to help someone who needs $7.43 to buy baby food. Please — let your light shine and give them a helping hand.

$7.43 — Taking Action

A few years later, I was busy republishing the column on $7.43 when the phone rang in my office and a voice on the other end asked: "Do you have church tonight?" Being somewhat of a salesman, I immediately began describing all the exciting services and activities we had. But the caller interrupted me. "My wife and I would like to come. What time?"

After giving him more information, he asked: "Can you pick us up?"

This was not a question I anticipated, so my eagerness changed to concern. "I'm not sure. Where are you?"

The location he described was in another city, miles away. He and his wife were standing in a phone booth just outside a hotel. They had no car and were obviously looking for more than the location of a worship service. We had no transportation available and I was hesitant to commit the life of one of our drivers to a mystery voice on the phone who was sounding increasingly suspicious.

So, I said: "I would love to help you but we have no one available to pick you up. I'm sorry." After a few more minutes of conversation, he thanked me and hung up. At first I was relieved; but I soon felt guilty. A few verses from the Bible singed my conscience.

"Dear brothers and sisters, what's the use of saying you have faith if you don't prove it by your actions? That kind of faith can't save anyone. Suppose you see a brother or sister who needs food or clothing, and you say, 'Well, good-bye and God bless you; stay warm and eat well' — but then you don't give that person any food or clothing. What good does that do? So you see, it isn't enough just to have faith. Faith that doesn't show itself by good deeds is no faith at all — it is dead and useless" (James 2:14-17)

That's strong and clear language: Faith doesn't mean much if not backed up by action. When someone needs food or clothing, we can't just say, "God bless you!" Faith without good deeds is useless and dead.

Had I refused to pick up a couple who genuinely needed help simply because of inconvenience? Could this be another $7.43 opportunity from God to help someone in need? Was I guilty once again of displaying faith with no action? Yet, there was a very real chance the person on the other end of the phone was a con. There was also the risk of picking up strangers who could be dangerous.

There wouldn't be much time to dwell on the situation because later that same evening, while I was teaching a Bible study, in walked the very same couple who called hours before.

Once the others left, we talked. After the earlier phone call, they found someone to give them a ride to our church. Although originally from our area, they had recently moved back after he lost his job. Now they were here with no car, not even a license to drive, virtually no possessions and no where to go.

Once again, I faced a dilemma. Was this a God-given opportunity to help a couple in need or a slick con with me as the mark?

"Suppose you see a brother or sister who needs food or clothing and you say, 'Well good-bye and God bless you; stay warm and eat well' but then you don't give that person any food or clothing. What good does that do?" Now, it was my turn to respond.

But first, I asked our e-mail prayer network for advice. Here is what some of them wrote:

A couple of weeks ago I took my family to see London. As we were coming down the stairs at Westminster Bridge there was a homeless man begging for money. Without thinking I pulled my son near to protect him. Only then I realized that my instant reaction was entirely wrong. I treated that man like he was about to attack rather than needing help. We later tried to find him to offer food but he had gone. I felt even sadder that I missed my opportunity to help. —Muralitharan

My husband and I were like that couple and amazingly we had almost all positive experiences as we "lived by faith" for a year. One couple took us home for a steak dinner. [The wife] opened her closet and told me to take anything I needed. Some churches were incredibly prepared to help those in need. In Salt Lake City, a ministry offered clothes, an opportunity to help feed the homeless on Christmas Day and a job if we stayed there. The only "negative" reaction was when we hadn't bathed for awhile and my husband asked at a church if he could use the washroom. The pastor looked him up and down and said it was not a public washroom. We got cleaned up at a camp nearby. On Sunday, we dressed up for the service. The same pastor came over and told my husband he looked familiar, did they meet before somewhere? —Pat

A guy approached me at a restaurant and asked for food. I told him to sit down and I'd pay for lunch. He seemed hesitant at first, then thanked me and sat down. I had the clerk come over and told him to take the guy's order. The clerk tried to "help" me by refusing, but I insisted. He ordered a hamburger — that's all. I asked if he'd like fries. He said yes. Then I asked about something to drink. He said, "Just water." But I asked if he'd like a soda and he said yes. The manager told the man to leave and not come back after eating lunch. The man thanked me for helping him. I felt that I lunched with God. I've never regretted helping some-one who was hungry. —*Lisa*

Like you, I would've been skeptical. I would've felt terrible seeing them walk in when I doubted their intentions. Sometimes I find myself doing for others less fortunate and I teach my children the importance because we're all "one paycheck away" from needing help. What I need to work on is consistently helping and not judging along the way: that's not my role. —*Tracie*

We should be wise as a serpent and gentle as a dove. It's better to be gullible than cynical. I've given money to someone who was probably a con (but don't regret it). I've offered food to beggars instead of money (and been sworn at). My problem is that I do a mental risk assessment before doing anything. Jesus calls us to lay down our life rather than do a risk assessment. —*Mark*

I met a family who just moved in. When I went to get the kids some food there was little there. The next day after church, my son Max and I went to the store and bought everything from paper towels to peanut butter. We delivered the food and they were surprised! Things were tight and they needed help. Now if a single Mom and five-year-old son can do that, imagine what an entire church could do. Hope this helps others to realize if I can do it so can they. —*Rachael & Max*

I think every opportunity is a way to show forth God's goodness even when you're being taken for a ride. I know situations where people came to cheat and end up being saved. —*Victoria*

Other than money, I guess we could give them jobs to do in church, like cleaning, etc., at the same time monitoring and not forgetting to keep them covered in prayers and teaching the Word of God, and loving them. It's good to be discerning and wise concerning strangers. I understand the difficult decision you have to make. I look forward to hear from you what happened. —*Molly*

$7.43 — Taking Action: My Response

The Bible is very clear about helping others: *"Suppose you see a brother or sister who needs food or clothing and you say, 'Well good-bye and God bless you; stay warm and eat well' but then you don't give that person any food or clothing. What good does that do?" (James 2:15-16)*

I found myself saying to the couple: "Why don't we settle you in for the night in the local motel and tomorrow we'll see what we can do?"

"Thank you," they said, "but our stuff is at a hotel in another town."

So, the three of us left the church late that night to pick up their belongings and transport them to the hotel near us. During the long drive, I learned they both had family in the area but were no longer welcome in either home. Over the last few weeks, they lived in various hotels and shelters supplied by a network of churches and organizations. We were now the church looking after their needs but, in a few days, they would move on to other hotels and other organizations.

We could certainly supply their immediate needs for a day or two, but then what? They needed a job but possessed very few skills. Even if they found employment, how would they get to work? They had no car and could not even legally drive. I was being given a valuable lesson on the difficulty of helping someone climb out of extreme poverty. Providing temporary shelter and a few meals was certainly a nice gesture but it wouldn't begin to solve their ongoing problems. I was offering a band aid for someone in need of open-heart surgery.

The next morning I started making phone calls and found an agency willing to help the couple find work. Another agency promised long-term shelter. Social Services agreed to meet with them and help them find other benefits. Prospects for the couple were looking brighter, so I sent a volunteer to pick them up.

Minutes later, the volunteer called back and told me the couple had bad experiences at the shelter and didn't like the work offered by the agency. In short, they were unwilling to leave the hotel. Now what?

Feeling sorry for their situation, the volunteer paid for them to stay another night in the hotel. I agreed, but asked the volunteer to warn them that we could provide no more help. For several more days, I heard they found other churches to pay their hotel bill and bring food, but I knew it couldn't last.

Proverbs 10:13 reminds me of another painful reality of poverty: *"If you love sleep, you will end in poverty. Keep your eyes open and there will be plenty to eat."* In other words, there is only so much an individual or an institution can do to help someone in need. Critical choices must be made by those seeking help — are you looking for a handout or a helping hand?

Taking full advantage of the creature comforts offered by the hotel, this couple only wanted handouts. But the willingness of people and churches offering aid was fast running out.

A week after our first meeting, at the same Bible study, the couple showed up again. But this time they were truly seeking a helping hand rather than a handout. They talked about making serious choices.

A relative in another state agreed to provide a place to stay and help them find employment if we would get them there. After a meeting with several of our church leaders, we agreed once again to provide help. Later that same evening, both of them boarded a bus with a smile on their faces and hope in their hearts.

Although this particular story had a reasonably hopeful ending, I learned that people dealing with poverty are not so easily helped. As individuals and as churches, we often supply band-aids for people who need major surgery. We as God's people are given a Holy calling to do much more. But I also learned that those who are in poverty must make critical choices to assist themselves before our helping hand can truly be effective. The lesson of $7.43 is that God is calling us to be alert for opportunities to make a difference in the community around us. How will you respond?

$7.43 Continued: A Lesson in Ministry

When I was in sales, I had a boss named Tom Riddle. Tom was a tough but fair boss who always knew how to get the best out of me. Over the years, he became a close personal friend. On a recent trip home, I stopped in to visit him and talk about old times. But instead of small talk, I received a unique lesson on giving and ministry.

At one point Tom said, "I read your book last night and loved your story about $7.43." He looked at me for a moment, smiled and continued: "Well, Larry, what have you done since then?"

"Well, I've helped a few people personally" I replied, not really knowing what he wanted me to say.

"I've got an idea," he said. He picked up the phone and instructed his office manager to bring him a check for $743. Then he handed the check to me and said, "I want you to take this money and put it into 100 different envelopes and give it to 100 people in need."

As I took the check and began to thank him, Mr. Riddle asked me another question. "Larry, this is my gift and I'm happy to do it. Now, the question is — what will you do?"

Again, I didn't know what to say; but I knew he expected me to do something. Mr. Riddle had given something of value and it was now my turn to respond. But how could a preacher give a gift that would make a real difference?

Peter wrote in 1 Peter: "*Each one should use whatever gift they have received to serve others, faithfully administering God's grace in its various forms.*" The message is that all of us have something of great value to give. We simply need to find it and use it.

A voice inside me kept saying: "The best gift you can give is your book."

"But Lord," I weakly replied, "I haven't even paid the printing bill yet!"

Several days later, at a community gathering, I shared the story of Mr. Riddle's gift and passed out 50 envelopes, each containing $7.43, along with 50 copies of my book. The instructions were to give one envelope and one book to someone in need and tell the story of $7.43. The following Sunday morning, 50 people in our church were given the same opportunity.

Two weeks later, Mr. Riddle visited our church and heard stories of lives touched by his special gift:

- One woman who received the gift was experiencing a divorce and used the money to take her kids to a local restaurant. She then read the book for continued devotional support.
- Another gift was sent to a man in prison who used the money for his daughter's Christmas present and passed the book around to fellow inmates.
- A third gift was given to a family struggling through a recent job layoff.
- Another was sent to a missionary family in Sri Lanka.

One person after another stood and told moving stories of gifts given and how they felt compelled to become even more involved in someone else's life. They spoke of the joy of offering something encouraging to a person in need.

Our church was given the opportunity to participate in a miracle. In addition to helping at least 100 people, Mr. Riddle taught all of us a valuable lesson on the importance and the joy of giving — all for only $7.43. Try it for yourself and watch God make your gift grow and grow!

SEE THE LIGHT

The lesson of $7.43 is that God is calling us to be alert for opportunities to make a difference in the lives of the people and the community around us. How will you respond?

SHARE THE LIGHT

1. Virtually every day God provides opportunities to help someone in need. How have you responded so far?
2. Scripture says, "What good is faith without action?" How can you turn faith into action?
3. How can you help your church respond more effectively to those in need?
4. Who could you give $7.43 as a gesture of love and good will?

Notes:

_____

_____

_____

_____

_____

_____

_____

_____

_____

_____

LIVE THE LIGHT: The Lighthouse in Action

$7.43 is a powerful reminder of our God-given responsibility — as individuals and as the church — to be involved in helping people in need. As a church, you could invest $743 and 100 envelopes, along with a favorite devotional book. Challenge 100 families to give the envelopes and books to people in need, then come back and share their stories. My guess is that you will hear about more than one miracle.

Your Action Ideas:
$7.43 is a good start. What are some other ways you or your church can reach out to help people in need?

1. _____

2. _____

3. _____

"I just read your ... devotion and remember you telling this story at an Emmaus gathering and distributing copies of one of your books with $7.43 tucked inside. This story made a huge impression on me, and I remember carrying that book and envelope around looking for [an opportunity] to 'pass it on' as you asked us to do that night. In time I learned of a co-worker who was having financial and family problems, so I quietly slipped it to her. Becoming more aware of the needs for God's light to shine in the darkened moments in other's lives was a great gift given to my spiritual formation, and has repeatedly been a formative story in my own life and ministry. So, if I haven't already, let me offer [my] thanks. Grace and peace." —Bert

"Our church is God's church in action! All of our friends told us to come to this church! One word describes our reaction: overwhelming! They are so involved in so many ministries and so committed to serving; but that is not what kept us here. It was the worship where God's Word is taught and Jesus is Lord." —Anonymous

TUESDAY—Opportunities to Shine

Problems can become opportunities for growth.

"Lord, don't trouble yourself by coming to my home, for I am not worthy.
Just say the word from where you are, and my servant will be healed.
I know because I am under the authority of my superior officers,
and I have authority over my soldiers. I only need to say, 'Go,' and they go."
When Jesus heard this, he was amazed. Turning to the crowd, he said,
"I tell you, I haven't seen faith like this in all the land of Israel!"
And when they returned the slave was healed.
Excerpts from Luke 7:6-10

One unique characteristic of Sowing Seeds of Faith is our prayer ministry. Through our web site, we receive over 100 requests for prayer from around the world every week. Thanks to the dedication of our prayer ministry helpers, three prayer lists are sent each week to several thousand prayer partners who pray and send e-mails offering love and encouragement. Readers often ask: "Larry, where did you get the idea for an e-mail prayer ministry?"

Some say problems have the potential to become opportunities for growth. Well, several years ago, I had a huge problem. I encouraged visitors of the web site to share their concerns through an interactive page entitled "Prayer Needs." Immediately, I received requests for prayer from all around the world. For example:

Alice (Alabama): We are custodial parents of a seven-year-old granddaughter. Now her unfit biological mother is going to file to regain custody and we are devastated.

Stephanie (California): I am a single mother raising a teenage daughter who just turned 13. My church is not offering much support. It's scary and very lonely sometimes.

Larry (Canada): I would like to change but I have a hard time obeying God's Word. I would like to serve him and find happiness. I don't want to fall back to the world.

Allison (South Africa): We have been trying to have a child for almost five years. We have been through many doctors and procedures. We conceived once and lost the baby ten weeks later. We were both devastated.

I personally answered each request with encouragement and prayer; but every day, more e-mails would arrive. Soon the requests for prayer became overwhelming. Increasingly, I was feeling inadequate to meet all the many prayer needs.

Nicole (California): I lost my Mom and have a broken heart. She is with Jesus and I should be rejoicing but some days I hurt so much inside. I want to feel joy again.

Tracy (Peru): I am 33 and the mother of a 12-year-old son. My husband was unfaithful and I must file for a divorce. He has no desire to continue being married to me. I am really struggling with why this happened to me. I don't run around. I've been a good wife.

Patricia (South Carolina): My son is serving a 15-year sentence for something he is innocent of. Please ask God to turn his heart. Pray God's blessings upon him.

Colleen (Colorado): My friend was badly injured in a terrible car accident. He looks well on the outside but he's still having memory loss, fatigue, mood swings, etc. He desperately needs help.

I wanted desperately to suggest words of hope articulating God's love and grace. But at this point, the person needing help and solid scriptural guidance was ... (*gulp*) ... me.

Several respected leaders asked Jesus to come and heal a Roman Officer's slave who was near death. Before Jesus arrived, however, the officer sent friends to tell him *"'Lord, don't trouble yourself by coming to my home, for I am not worthy. Just say the word from where you are, and my servant will be healed. I know because I am under the authority of my superior officers, and I have authority over my soldiers. I only need to say, 'Go,' and they go.' When Jesus heard this, he was amazed. Turning to the crowd, he said, 'I tell you, I haven't seen faith like this in all the land of Israel!' And when they returned the slave was healed. (Excerpts from Luke 7:6-10)*

On the surface, Jesus using a Roman officer as the main character in a lesson about faith makes no sense — unless that is the lesson. You see, it was the Roman Officer, not the religious leaders, who grasped exactly who Jesus was. *"Just say the word from where you are and my servant will be healed."*

While the religious experts — the insiders — were conducting debates, a religious outsider — a Roman officer — went from debates to faith to action.

So here's the bad news: I am the religious insider who neglected to trust in God's authority. The good news is, it's never too late to ask for help. And boy, did I need help. I was at a turning point. Meanwhile, the prayer needs continued to flood in:

Marsha (Minnesota): My 20-year-old twin daughters are leaving home. They both suffer with learning disabilities. I pray their co-workers will be patient and help them succeed.

Holly (Kentucky): My boyfriend has decided to go into the ministry. We are both seeking God's will for our lives and hope to stay close together.

Sharon (Canada): My son and his wife and five children. Their house caught fire and they still have no home, as they are low income. Nearly everything was lost.

Alex (Scotland): My granddaughter has Hodgkin's disease. She has a growth in her chest, near her heart and has spots and holes in her kidneys.

First, I needed to kick myself. Hard. These prayer requests were not burdens; far from it. God was giving me a breathtaking opportunity to minister to others around the world. I needed to learn how to replace worry over what *I* would do with faith in what *God* could do. After all, people were seeking guidance from God, not me. I was simply being asked to pray.

Once again, God provided a turning point in my life. The question was: What would I do with it?

With renewed enthusiasm, I began to pray — really pray. When each request flashed across the computer screen, I learned to bow my head and say a prayer for their situation right then — not later.

In addition, over six thousand volunteers from all over the world have signed on to join me in prayer. Three times each week we send out a list of prayer needs, along with e-mail addresses, so in addition to prayer we can send e-mails of encouragement. We have witnessed miracles!

> Thank you Larry. Because of you and your cause, you have saved my life of pain and torment. I have received so many messages from folks in your prayer group and I am totally overwhelmed! Thank you, thank you, thank you! I now feel foolish for the stupid thoughts of suicide and know there are many who love and care for me! God bless you for your kindness and love! —Flo

A thought kept nagging me: What about the church I serve? Shouldn't they be involved?

Occasionally, during Sunday worship, we distribute copies of e-mail requests from around the world to every member of our congregation. During the following week, we agree to pray for those on the list. Soon everyone in the congregation is praying for someone else. No longer are we simply asking God to be active in national and world events. We are praying for real people around the world and their specific needs.

One worship service ended with Communion. As people moved to the altar to receive the bread and cup symbolizing the body and blood of Jesus Christ, they brought their e-mail prayer requests to the altar and received Communion for themselves and the people on the prayer list.

For us, the time-honored liturgy of Holy Communion took on a new meaning. We prayed: "Pour out your Holy Spirit on us gathered here, and on these gifts of bread and wine. Make them be for us the body and blood of Christ that we may be for the world the body of Christ, redeemed by his blood. By your Spirit make us one with Christ, one with each other and one in ministry to all the world."

What I perceived as a problem was really an opportunity for ministry. Those who asked for prayer are discovering answers. Our church has become an excited partner in a new prayer ministry. And me? I've changed too. When prayer needs flash across the computer, I'm no longer burdened. I know the One who can help is just waiting to be asked. Isn't this what being the church is all about?

William Temple wrote: "When I pray, coincidences happen and when I do not, they don't."

I wish I had the words to express what was in my heart as I read the prayer requests this morning and responded [and] prayed over others. What an eye-opener being part of Sowing Seeds prayer ministry has been and how heavy and anguished I feel after reading so many of them. What a call to prayer! I pray that many will come forward to sponsor Sowing Seeds and pray for others. —*Karen*

SEE THE LIGHT

Clearly, I must learn how to replace worry over what *I* will do with faith in what *God* can do. After all, people are seeking guidance from God, not me. I am simply being asked to pray.

SHARE THE LIGHT

1. We all have problems and burdens. Have you learned to ask for help from relatives, friends ... God?
2. How can we use our prayer lives more effectively for those in need? How can we share our prayer needs more effectively?
3. How can we replace worry with faith?
4. How can our church utilize prayer for others within our worship?

Notes:

_____

_____

_____

_____

_____

_____

LIVE THE LIGHT: The Lighthouse in Action

Sowing Seeds Ministry is making a difference in the lives of people around the world through prayer. You can join our prayer ministry at www.SowingSeedsofFaith.com. Each week you can receive prayer requests that have been received through our web site. You can pray for those requests and, in many cases, respond with an e-mail of love and encouragement if you choose. You may also submit your own request and hundreds of prayer partners around the world will pray for you.

Your Action Ideas:
Are there areas in your church where a perceived problem presents an opportunity for ministry and growth?

1. _____

2. _____

3. _____

"I started some months ago requesting prayers and since have also responded to several prayers. I was going through a divorce and hurt so bad, but I am calming down and able to accept whatever the future holds. God has a plan for me. I know one day I will be healed and better off for having gone through the rejection, abandonment, and betrayal. The Bible says Jesus was a man acquainted with grief and I have been there also." —Eugene

"When I attended your church, I was down because my fiancé left me with no explanation. I spent days and nights crying and questioning why. Then I began reading your book and my eyes were opened. I went to church with my grandfather when I was a little girl. As I got older, I got out of attending. Hanging out with friends until wee hours and sleeping in on Sundays was more important. My grandfather [helped me see] I had given up my faith and lost touch with God. I began attending church again. Things began to turn around for me and I fell in love. Then my old habits kicked in again and I quit going to church. But after reading your book I have decided to ... pull my life together and get back into the church. Thanks for opening my eyes to the One who is always there and can change my life." —Lavinna

WEDNESDAY—Becoming God's Lighthouse

Christmas is a glaring reminder of who receives...
and who does not.

God sent the angel Gabriel to Nazareth, a village in Galilee,
to a virgin named Mary. She was engaged to be married
to a man named Joseph, a descendant of King David.
Gabriel appeared to her and said,
"Greetings, favored woman! The Lord is with you!"
Luke 1:26-28

Just before Christmas one year, I received the following e-mail from a woman named Penny: "I wish for you to pray for my children. I know they will have nothing for Christmas and it's tearing my family apart. I don't know how to tell a child Santa is not coming."

"*God sent the angel Gabriel to Nazareth, a village in Galilee, to a virgin named Mary. She was engaged to be married to a man named Joseph, a descendant of King David. Gabriel appeared to her and said, 'Greetings, favored woman! The Lord is with you!'*" (Luke 1:26-28)

At Christmas, our church regularly receives requests for aid like this one: "I'm sorry to ask for help but I don't know what to do..."

- My husband's been laid off and we have no savings for Christmas presents.
- I'm a single parent and everything I make goes toward paying the bills.
- My daughter has a drug problem and I'm raising her children and doing everything I can but there is no money for Christmas.

They all end their plea with: "Is there anything you can do to help our children have a better Christmas?"

Our church, like others, will do what we can. Several families receive food and gifts for the kids, but it never seems to be enough. I wonder:

1. Why do we get so many pleas for help just before Christmas?
2. Who else is in desperate need but never calls?

"*Confused and disturbed, Mary tried to think what the angel could mean. 'Don't be frightened, Mary,' the angel told her, 'for God has decided to bless you! You will become pregnant and have a son, and you are to name him Jesus. He will be very great and will be called the Son of the Most High. And the Lord God will give him the throne of his ancestor David. And he will reign over Israel forever; his Kingdom will never end!'"(Luke 1:29-33)*

Why do we get so many pleas for help? The answers are as close as your local newspaper. Hundreds of ads scream their slogans: "Make your Holidays Brighter!"; "Catch the Christmas Spirit!"; "Our Gifts Make a Difference!" And my personal favorite: "Beat the After-Thanksgiving, Pre-Christmas Rush with our Pre-Thanksgiving, Pre-Christmas Sale!"

Admit it. Christmas is cleverly advertised as Santa Claus and presents. We talk about giving, but fantasize receiving.

You say it's about family and friends. *(Yeah, right!)* You try to remember the celebration of Christ's birth. *(Watch the kids' eyes glass over as you tell them.)* But turn on the television, visit a department store or pick up a bulky newspaper full of ads and the ugly truth screams its horrific message: The reason for the season is buying lots of gifts! Christmas has become a glaring reminder of who receives generously and who gets little or nothing!

So here's my question: How do you justify all of this to a poorer child who will receive no gifts but is surrounded by children loaded with more toys than they can ever use? How do you politely tell a child that Christmas is for others, but not for him?

"Mary asked the angel, 'But how can I have a baby? I am a virgin.' The angel replied, 'The Holy Spirit will come upon you, and the power of the Most High will overshadow you. So the baby born to you will be holy, and he will be called the Son of God. What's more, your relative Elizabeth has become pregnant in her old age! People used to say she was barren, but she's already in her sixth month. For nothing is impossible with God.'" (Luke 1:34-37)

Christmas was never meant to be this way. Jesus was born in a barn with only farm animals and a few shepherds as witnesses. He grew up the son of a blue-collar worker in a land occupied by Rome. Throughout his earthly life, Jesus had few if any material possessions. How did we get everything so mixed-up? How can we change? How can we truly recapture the Christ in Christmas?

"Mary responded, 'I am the Lord's servant, and I am willing to accept whatever he wants. May everything you have said come true.' And then the angel left." (Luke 1:38)

"When Mary received the gift of God's precious son she responded with praise: 'Oh, how I praise the Lord. How I rejoice in God my Savior! For he took

notice of his lowly servant girl and now generation after generation will call me blessed. For he, the Mighty One, is holy and he has done great things for me. His mercy goes on from generation to generation to all who fear him.'" (Luke 1:46-50)

Christmas presents were meant to be symbolic of God's gift of the Christ child. What Jesus has given to us, we pass on to others as our way of saying "I love you in the name of Christ!" How did we get everything so mixed-up? How can we change? How can we recapture the Christ in Christmas?

The challenge is to broaden our horizons and creatively give to those in need. Our Sowing Seeds readers responded with lively and creative ways to remember the real reason for the season:

> I too, get bothered when people say they can't have Christmas if they don't have money for presents. We deliberately do not put up a tree or give presents because that forces us to stay focused on the real reason we celebrate Christmas. So many people say they wish they could take the stress and commercialism out of Christmas. They could if they wanted to — just stop buying presents! Work in a soup kitchen or collect food for a food bank. —Michael

> A friend gave my children a choice where they wanted a donation sent on their behalf for Christmas. She honored them with a gift. They thought of others and gave as well. —Linda

Mary's song of praise continues: *"His mighty arm does tremendous things! How he scatters the proud and haughty ones! He has taken princes from their thrones and exalted the lowly."* (Luke 1:51-52)

> It is hard to keep the real spirit of Christmas and we're not always successful, but here are things we do to keep the real reason for the season: We watch very little commercial TV and try to attend all the activities our church has to celebrate Christmas. We put up a nativity set, read the 'Christmas story,' and refer to Christmas as 'Jesus' birthday.' We support mission activities and [the kids help by] grocery shopping to buy food for a local pantry. —Kristin

> I am a single parent with four teenagers so I'm always on the lookout for ways to de-commercialize Christmas. We have a 'manger' and

during the month of December, whenever my children do or say something nice, they add a piece of straw. By Christmas Eve, Jesus has a soft place to lay his head. Also, we make a big deal about home made presents." —*Karen*

"He has satisfied the hungry with good things and sent the rich away with empty hands."(Luke 1:52-53)

We have a stocking with Jesus' name on it and each family member writes a note to Jesus and we read it on Christmas day. I bake a birthday cake and we sing *Happy Birthday.* —*Carol*

Together we make an advent wreath, share devotions each week and light the candle(s). It's fun and helps us reinforce the true meaning of the season. —*Christy*

"He has not forgotten his promise to be merciful. For he promised our ancestors — Abraham and his children — to be merciful to them forever."(Luke 1:54-55)

Christmas is a special time for families and particularly kids. I would be more than willing to help the family in Ohio (mentioned last week) with funds to have a good Christmas. I am happy to contribute and you can pass it on. If it can be arranged, I would like to remain anonymous. —*Anonymous in Kuwait*

One of our readers from Canada sent a story to help us all appreciate the true meaning of Christ in Christmas:

"Almost nineteen years ago I loaded up an old car with two children, two cats, a dog and all our possessions packed tightly into an 8x10 U-Haul along with whatever could be stuffed into the covered roof rack and the interior of the already crowded car. Both children were babies in car seats. In the middle of the night, in the midst of a terrible blizzard, we left my home city and all my immediate family because I was running from a bad marriage and an abusive husband.

"The blizzard continued throughout the night and the next day, spanning our home province of Manitoba and the neighboring province of Saskatchewan. Feverishly, I pushed on with very few stops and no sleep, driving endlessly through the whirling, blinding snow. By the time we crossed through Alberta and landed in British Columbia, 38 hours elapsed and, exhausted as I was, I still kept going. We literally ran out of gas in Mission, British Columbia, a town with a rough reputation and the crime rate of a large city; yet they took us in and Mission became our home for 17 years.

"By the time Christmas arrived, the children and I were coming out of a transition house with only a rented, run-down trailer to go home to. I purchased an artificial Christmas tree for a precious $10 but cried night after night as the Christmas season descended upon us. The children looked with hungry eyes at all the wonder of the shopping malls and many gifts. I remember sitting with a heavy heart while they wrote their letters to Santa, looking at the crayon marks and the backward letters lined up in misspelled words. My oldest, a three-year-old, wanted to put the letter in the mailbox himself and so I lifted him high with the precious letter and let him drop it in the box. As we walked home from posting the letter, they kept asking when Santa would send a reply or would he just bring the gifts on the joyous, much-anticipated morning. At this point my heart was breaking and I could think of no answer.

"On Christmas Eve there was a knock at the door. I nervously opened it a crack and saw four big, rough-looking men; but each of them was carrying a huge box filled with food and gifts. My oldest son looked up at the biggest man who was sporting a beard and asked 'Are you Santa?'

"In a deep gruff voice, the man answered 'No, but he sent us — his best elves — to deliver this to your baby brother and you. Santa's only request is that you give thanks for this tonight and every night when you say your prayers. Can you do that?'

"As I type this e-mail, I still get tears in my eyes. The joy and wonderment of that moment will never be forgotten. Someone, somewhere opened that letter and the Salvation Army stepped in along with volunteers from the Rehabilitation Center for Men. I was a single mother with two babies, no job, no home, and I was running out of hope. Yet that Christmas will live on in my heart forever.

"For many years after that, we would go and select two angels off the 'Angel of Hope' Christmas tree. We would spend hours selecting just the perfect gift. My boys are now men, but they still go to pluck an angel from the tree. I also go because I know there are children who may not have a great Christmas and there is also a mother faced with the tears and fears of the day and season.

"Many years have passed and we have since moved from the small town that extended their arms to us. My boys are young men now, but they carry the memories. The kindness and love shown by the unknown people who made our Most Wonderful Christmas will never be forgotten and my love to 'Santa's Elves,' whose quick smiles and twinkling eyes brought it altogether for my family that day. May God's peace and love be there for all — but hopefully it won't stop there! Carry God's love with you always and let your light shine bright." —Joanne

"That night some shepherds were in the fields outside the village, guarding their flocks of sheep. Suddenly, an angel of the Lord appeared among them and the radiance of the Lord's glory surrounded them. They were terribly frightened but the angel reassured them. 'Don't be afraid!' he said. 'I bring you good news of great joy for everyone! The Savior — yes, the Messiah, the Lord — has been born tonight in Bethlehem, the city of David! And this is how you will recognize him: You will find a baby lying in a manger, wrapped snugly in strips of cloth!'"
(Luke 2:8-12)

Once again I asked our many readers to respond with their own ideas on how to put "Christ" back into Christmas.

There were times when I got caught up with the madness of Christmas, the lights, presents, getting into debt, trying to buy everybody a gift. But I have gotten older and the true meaning of Christmas has changed. I don't worry about not having a gift to buy. With so much uncertainly today, we should concentrate more on giving and less on receiving. —Cynthia

I grew up in a rather large and famous church around here. So, I called their office and asked if there was a family that could use some help and fellowship. They had no idea what I was talking about but connected me with the pastor in charge of "that type of thing" and his office didn't know of one single family, student, or elderly person that fit the bill, either. Something is wrong with that picture. I know there are companies working their employees one week on and then a week off. That makes for tight times. I know others have lost their jobs completely and still others have health problems, or are widows ... I still can't believe that a church the size of mine could not help. Have we forgotten how hard the holidays can be on folks? —*Rebecca*

"*Suddenly, the angel was joined by a vast host of others — the armies of heaven — praising God: 'Glory to God in the highest heaven, and peace on earth to all whom God favors.'*" (Luke 2:13-14)

We do food baskets at our church and get toys for children and give them to the needy in our area. I am frequently reminding folks that "Jesus is the Reason for the Season." —*Margaret*

We sponsor a family each year and buy special gifts for the children and the adults. We want to help. —*Buz*

"*When the angels returned to heaven, the shepherds said to each other, 'Come on, let's go to Bethlehem! Let's see this wonderful thing that happened, which the Lord told us about.' They ran to the village and found Mary and Joseph. And there was the baby, lying in the manger.*" (Luke 2:15-16)

One church met with community leaders several years ago and organized "Christmas Parents," which honors "special" parents as examples, then receives donations and presents from others throughout the county providing Christmas for over 500 children every year.

Another church solicits names of needy children from area elementary schools then matches those names with families from their congregation who include those children as part of their Christmas shopping. This church provides Christmas to many needy children every year.

"*Then the shepherds told everyone what happened and what the angel said about this child. All who heard the shepherds' story were astonished but Mary quietly treasured these things in her heart and thought about them often. The shepherds went back to their fields and flocks, glorifying and praising God for what the angels told them and because they had seen the child, just as the angel said.*" (Luke 2:17-20)

A family from Virginia read a Sowing Seeds devotion about a family asking for help and provided Christmas for both the children and parents. A man from the United Arab Emirates sent a donation to Sowing Seeds Ministry, which we used to help two families who had contacted us for assistance.

The third verse from the hymn, *Away in a Manger,* says it best: "Be near me, Lord Jesus, I ask thee to stay, close by me forever, and love me, I pray; bless all the dear children in thy tender care, and fit us for heaven to live with thee there."

What better way to put "Christ" back into your Christmas this year than by helping a child in need. God will bless you for it.

SEE THE LIGHT

Turn on the television, visit a department store or pick up a bulky newspaper full of ads and the ugly truth screams its horrific message: The reason for the season is buying lots of gifts! Christmas has become a glaring reminder of who receives generously and who does not. It was never meant to be this way!

SHARE THE LIGHT

1. How has Christ been left out of Christmas?
2. How can you restore Jesus in Christmas for your family?
3. How can your church help the community better see Christ?
4. What can you do to help the poor enjoy a better Christmas?
5. How can your church become more involved in the needs of the poor?
6. How can you and your church be in partnership with the community at Christmas to help those in need?

Notes:

_____

_____

_____

_____

_____

_____

LIVE THE LIGHT: The Lighthouse in Action

There are many organizations devoted to helping the poor and most of them are bombarded with requests for help during the Christmas season. Challenge your small group or church to pick one organization and provide support. In addition, your family can provide Christmas for a local family in need. Involve the children in the shopping and let them hear the story of the family you are helping. Add Christmas cards with notes of encouragement and include a devotional book or two.

Your Action Ideas:
What organizations that help the poor could your church support?

1. _____

2. _____

3. _____

"Thank you for giving so many people, including myself, a place to share our heartaches and triumphs. I came upon this site during one of the hardest periods of my life: Finding myself divorced, with two young children, after seventeen years of marriage. Everyday was a struggle. After reaching out, which was something I had not been able to do before, comfort was sent to me in the form of Sowing Seeds angels. Many days since that dark period, I have tried to reach out and help others as I was helped. Thank you again, for giving me this place of refuge." —Marie

"I've been in three churches in my lifetime and this church is the first one where people don't seem to have personal agendas. It seems that everyone has the same desire: 'What is God calling us to do and what is best for the people we serve.'" —Anonymous

THURSDAY—An Attitude that Shines

The best way to beat stress is to put God in control.

Now there are different kinds of spiritual gifts but it is the same Holy Spirit who is the source of them all. There are different kinds of service in the church but it is the same Lord we are serving. There are different ways God works in our lives but it is the same God who does the work through all of us. A spiritual gift is given to each of us as a means of helping the entire church.
1 Corinthians 12:4-7

I don't mean to complain, but the last few weeks have been pretty stressful. My daughter is having minor surgery and my wife is experiencing numbness in her feet and hands. There have been many changes as a result of a rapidly growing congregation and I can't keep up. So many people are visiting our church, I can't get around to meeting all of them. Several church members have experienced tragedies and I must be there for them. Our church has a bigger budget than ever and I am responsible for managing it. Our family has a new puppy with lots of energy and she's driving me nuts. My computer has been in the shop, which keeps me from doing my work. ... Moan and groan!

Have you noticed all the emphasis on me? Me, Me, Me! Everything is about me!

When stress becomes intolerable, we can often trace the root cause to a dreaded disease known as "Me, Myself and I." You know you're afflicted when you think or say things like: "I must do everything myself if it's to be done right!"; "You just can't find good help now!"; "No one ever volunteers but me!"

Are you catching on to the problem?

The "Me, Myself and I" disease infects most of us occasionally, but if we don't seek treatment, we will suffer immeasurable pain — not to mention losing a few friends. Fortunately, God has a prescription for what ails us: quiet reflection, a measure of prayer and a solid dose of Bible study. One Scripture reference I think is helpful is found in 1 Corinthians:

"Now there are different kinds of spiritual gifts but it is the same Holy Spirit who is the source of them all. There are different kinds of service in the church but it is the same Lord we are serving. There are different ways God works in our lives but it is the same God who does the work through all of us. A spiritual gift is

given to each of us as a means of helping the entire church." (1 Corinthians 12:4-7)

The common interpretation of this passage is, "All of us are blessed with various talents and abilities." But recently I noticed another lesson. Look at the second part of each sentence:

- different kinds of spiritual gifts ... *but the same Holy Spirit*
- different kinds of service ... *but the same Lord*
- different ways God works ... *but it is the same God*

The emphasis was never meant to be on our gifts, however good. Three times the author makes the point: *it is the same Holy Spirit, the same Lord and the same God.* In other words, we all have different gifts, but we are all coordinated and encouraged by the same Lord.

It is God who is ultimately in control, not me.

When I put the emphasis on me, myself and I, the result is always the same: chaos and stress. But with God in control, there is always another way. Look at my complaints again:

- My daughter is having minor surgery and my wife is experiencing numbness in her feet and hands. *Yet, hundreds of people are offering comfort and praying for our family.*
- There have been many changes as a result of a rapidly growing congregation and I can't keep up. *Every change has resulted in good things for our church and for me.*
- So many people are visiting our church, I can't get around to meeting all of them. *This is supposed to be a problem? Come on Larry, get real!*
- Several church members have experienced tragedies and I must be there for them. *Yet in the midst of those tragedies, I found God giving comfort in so many ways.*
- Our church has a bigger budget than ever and I am responsible for managing it. *Each time the budget grows we are touching more lives for God.*
- The family puppy has too much energy and she's driving me crazy. *But thanks to my constant walking of her, I've lost weight and I feel better.*
- My computer has been in the shop which has kept me from doing my work. *Maybe this is God's way of giving me extra time for family and prayer.*

As Paul promised, *"A spiritual gift is given to each of us as a means of helping the entire church."* Our church functions more smoothly and my stress level goes down considerably when I learn to stop thinking everything revolves around me and trust God to provide the people and resources we need.

Lord, please replace my stress with faith in You! Now, if God would only help our puppy calm down.

SEE THE LIGHT

Our church functions more smoothly and my stress level goes down considerably when I learn to stop thinking everything revolves around me and trust God to provide the people and resources we need.

SHARE THE LIGHT

1.   Everyone struggles with the stress disease. Describe yours.
2.   What are your spiritual gifts? How are you using them?
3.   How is God in control of your spiritual gifts and your life?
4.   Look at your sources of stress again. How can you put God in control?

Notes:

_____

_____

_____

_____

_____

_____

_____

_____

_____

_____

LIVE THE LIGHT: The Lighthouse in Action

Churches offer a variety of options for stress relief: Prayer groups can help you turn worry into faith. Worship helps you find God in the midst of your troubles. Ministry opportunities get you involved beyond yourself. Sports and activities provide fun, companionship and exercise. Social events offer opportunities for relaxation and encouragement.

Your Action Ideas:
What can your church do to provide stress relief?

1. _____

2. _____

3. _____

"You and your church family, prayer group and readers of your web site have made a difference in my life. God has worked miracles and opened the windows of heaven and showered me with blessings, more then I could dream of. Just to labor in His field is such a blessing. I have been touched physically and spiritually and I am busy ministering for His glory. Thanks for all the prayers and e-mail." —Nancy

"I've been teaching high school youth in Sunday school now for 11 years and have fought the literature. My group hates just about every lesson series I have tried because the literature treats them as if they were middle school students or it is 'boring' and does not address their lives. On a whim, I started using 'Sowing Seeds of Faith' [columns]. We read it, discuss it, and look more closely at the scriptures in the text. They absolutely love it and have asked that we continue to use this book and then move on to your other devotions. It is still too early to tell, but it looks as though attendance is picking up as well. ... I thought you'd appreciate knowing that your seeds are sprouting in the lives of 22 teenagers." —Deborah

FRIDAY—Simplify

Sometimes leaps of faith start with small steps.

After a long time their master returned from his trip and called them
to give an account of how they had used his money.
The servant to whom he had entrusted the five bags of gold said,
'Sir, you gave me five bags of gold to invest, and I have doubled the amount.'
The master was full of praise. 'Well done, my good and faithful servant.
You have been faithful in handling this small amount, so now I will give you
many more responsibilities. Let's celebrate together!'
Matthew 25:19-21

A t a church board meeting, I asked: "What if our church gave $10 to every family in our congregation and challenged them to use their creative abilities to multiply the money for God? Then in two months we can hold a celebration Sunday where everyone can share how they handled the $10 challenge." I was answered with a long, uncomfortable silence.

Jesus once said: "The Master called together his servants and gave them money to invest for him while he was gone. He gave five bags of gold to one, two bags of gold to another, and one bag of gold to the last — dividing it in proportion to their abilities — and then left on his trip." (Matthew 25:14-15)

I sensed mental calculators throughout the room working overtime, adding up the total cost of my crazy scheme—approximately $4,000. Why should we give church members money? The church board response was less than enthusiastic but, taking a leap of faith (backed by my personal guarantee to make up any money lost), they reluctantly granted approval.

Days later, a few leaders quietly pulled me aside and asked again: "Are you sure about this, Larry?"

I honestly wasn't sure how the "$10 Challenge" would work, but I knew God wanted us to do it.

"The servant who received the five bags of gold began immediately to invest the money and soon doubled it. The servant with two bags of gold also went right to work and doubled the money. But the servant who received the one bag of gold dug a hole in the ground and hid the master's money for safekeeping." (Matthew 25:16-18)

Weeks later, near the end of Sunday worship, every family in our church received an envelope with $10 and instructions: "You have just been handed a $10 bill with a challenge to multiply and use it for God. What will you do?"

The Bible has a story about three servants who were given various amounts of money and told to manage it. Two servants invested wisely and returned a profit. One buried the money until time to give it back. The two wise servants were rewarded and the lazy servant was punished. The lesson: We are to invest God's resources wisely. *(from Matthew 25:14-30)*

The instructions went on: "You are limited only by your talent and imagination:

- Buy ingredients and bake bread or cookies.
- Offer to cook dinner for a busy family.
- Buy gasoline for your lawn mower and cut someone's grass.
- Instead of going out for lunch, brown bag and apply the savings.

"Pray for guidance and have faith God will supply an idea. In two months, we'll have a celebration service to share what happened. We are going to have a great time and hear exciting stories. I pray you will have a story of your own."

As people filed out of the sanctuary, their reactions seemed mixed. A few were excited, but many were concerned. "What can I do with $10? I don't have any talents," said one woman.

Another member laughed and said, "This is the only church that has ever handed me money."

Another, with a somber look, said, "Larry, I come to church to escape stress not receive more. I don't know what to do."

"Pray!" I responded. "Pray."

The responses to the $10 challenge were immediate:

What talents do I possess? I understand you don't want me to hold the money. You want me to use it to help others and multiply my resources so many would benefit. Maybe our pastor is just plain crazy and it is a dumb idea, but I know in my heart God is teaching me a valuable lesson. I am stressed out over what to do. I called a friend and told her about the $10 challenge. "What a great idea!" she said. "You're a great cook so make cakes and sell them." —*Sue*

I was stumped for a few days. But after careful thought about what to do with the $10 challenge, I kept going back to the Scripture of the talents and couldn't help but take the word "talent" literally. God has blessed and given me abilities and talents which I use to help others. I've been sewing since I was 12 and put "many miles" on my sewing machine. I designed and constructed clothes for the Dance Academy for years. I used my $10 to purchase thread and supplies for ballet costumes for 10 dancers and am happy to share my reward. —*Joan*

Our families will never forget how the "Ten Dollar Challenge" began. Our daughters opened the envelopes and were they ever surprised to find *real* ten dollar bills inside. Immediately they both said, "Let's have a Bake Sale!" The girls asked a few more friends from four other families if they would like to join in. Everyone wanted to bake together, but no one had a kitchen big enough, so we decided to use the church. Through it all, a great time was had by the whole crew. The day of the sale finally came. The children were so excited; we all got to church early, which is a rarity. It was a huge success! Please use this money for God's work. It is given by many cheerful hearts! —*Six Happy Families*

Two other families put on a Sunday night concert. Another family clipped coupons and donated the savings. Our youth leader sponsored a basketball tournament.

"After a long time their master returned from his trip and called them to give an account of how they had used his money. The servant to whom he had entrusted the five bags of gold said, 'Sir, you gave me five bags of gold to invest, and I have doubled the amount.' The master was full of praise. 'Well done, my good and faithful servant. You have been faithful in handling this small amount, so now I will give you many more responsibilities. Let's celebrate together!'" (Matthew 25:19-21)

Our three families took a combined $30 and, along with the help of fellow employees, we put on a luncheon to benefit our local Free Clinic. This small seed planted, resulted in over $800 in contributions. The only word to describe it is *awesome!* —*Anonymous*

One Sunday school class organized a bus trip and donated the profits. A local artist offered to provide an oil painting or portrait for a raffle winner and raised $1,000. Many families used the money to buy supplies and sold crafts or baked goods.

> I am an amateur herpetologist and spend my spare time raising and breeding reptiles. My idea is to buy feeders with the $10 for my animals. As they begin to breed, lay eggs and have babies, I will take the money made from a clutch of babies and give it back to the church. —*Anonymous*

Several taught special classes on finance or donated computer expertise. A group of children made and sold snow cones. Two families purchased baby chickens to send to an underdeveloped country.

> *"Next came the servant who had received the two bags of gold, with the report, 'Sir, you gave me two bags of gold to invest, and I have doubled the amount.' The master said, 'Well done, my good and faithful servant. You have been faithful in handling this small amount, so now I will give you many more responsibilities. Let's celebrate together!'" (Matthew 25:22-23)*

> I interpreted the $10 challenge in a different way. I thought of how many people might be reached with a total cost of only $10. I teach college students and we are not allowed to witness in words, but actions are okay so here's what I did. I took my $10 and bought 60 rolls of sweet 'n sour candy that had wrappers with verses from the Bible on them. Any student would have to at least see and read the words in order to open the wrapper. I also passed out several contemporary Christian CDs. Those two actions allowed me to silently witness to 62 different college students. I was so happy! —*Sharon*

One family gave up fancy coffee and another gave up fast food breakfasts then donated the savings. Another group pooled their money and sold goods at a flea market. Several groups sponsored and cooked dinners or breakfasts.

The biggest surprise came when a contractor announced during our celebration service: "I feel led by God to build a church for my $10!" Two years prior, Lawyers Missionary Baptist Church was devastated by a tornado.

During that time, they had been meeting in our church. At first, we didn't really believe it could be done. But donations poured in and, less than two years later, there was a new church building to celebrate.

What were the results?

- Thousands of dollars were raised for church ministries and other charitable organizations,
- A brand new building for a church desperately in need.

But the best part was the enthusiasm and joy on the faces of hundreds of people as we all used our gifts and talents in unusual and creative ways to serve God. We all walked away with a new appreciation for each other and for God.

Wow! Not a bad lesson for $10.

SEE THE LIGHT

Our church took a leap of faith, investing $4,000 in the $10 Challenge. The best part was the enthusiasm and joy on the faces of hundreds of people as well all used our gifts and talents in unusual and creative ways to serve God. We all walked away with a new appreciation for each other and for God.

SHARE THE LIGHT

1. If you were handed $10 and instructed to use it for God, what would you do? Why don't you take $10 and give it a try?
2. You are given extraordinary gifts and talents from God. How can you better use them for your church and for God?
3. How can your church better use the resources and talents given by God to be in ministry to the community? To the world?

Notes:

LIVE THE LIGHT: The Lighthouse in Action

Take the $10 Challenge for yourself and see what happens. You are limited only by your talent and imagination. Review the ideas in the list on page 167 and the stories from people in our church. Pray for guidance and have faith that God will supply an idea. In two months, have a celebration service to share what happened. We had a great time and heard exciting stories. I pray you will have a story too.

Your Action Ideas:
How can your church put the $10 Challenge into practice?

1. _____

2. _____

3. _____

"I feel like I am needed and I can serve the Lord in so many different ways at this church. I am blessed for being a part of the fellowship and I feel like I can be a blessing to others in the world, the local community and in God's church. I guess the most important reason I like being a part of my church is I know that in every program, meeting and worship service, God is there; I feel his mighty presence." —Sue

"What does my church mean to me? There are so many words that come to mind but I believe comfort would be my top word. My church has been a comfort to me in a time of life when I felt out of place in the 'church world.' This church has been a comfort to my children, giving them a safe place to grow and learn. This church has been a comfort to me and the 36 girls in our Girl Scout troops by giving us a safe place to meet. My church has been a comfort to my family when my husband was sick and we had no clue as to what was wrong. Whenever we enter for church service, pre-school or Girl Scouts, it's like we are wrapped in a warm blanket of God's love and there is no greater comfort than that." —Krista

SATURDAY—Start Shining

Helping others starts one-on-one by simply showing you care.

All praise to the God and Father of our Lord Jesus Christ.
He is the source of every mercy and the God who comforts us.
He comforts us in all our troubles so that we can comfort others.
When others are troubled, we will be able to give them the same comfort
God has given us. You can be sure that the more we suffer for Christ,
the more God will shower us with his comfort through Christ.
So when we are weighed down with troubles, it is for your benefit
and salvation! For when God comforts us, it is so that we, in turn,
can be an encouragement to you. Then you can patiently endure
the same things we suffer. We are confident that as you share in suffering,
you will also share God's comfort.

2 Corinthians 1:3-7

One of my first hospital visits as a minister was to Rosa, a woman reportedly dying of complications related to emphysema. Rosa was a sweet lady who worked hard all her life as a waitress in a local restaurant. "Smoking was a bad habit, but it helped to calm my nerves," she admitted. Then she grabbed my hand and pleaded "Will you pray for God to heal me?"

I hesitated, not knowing how to respond. Should I pray for healing when someone is expected to die? Suppose I ask God for healing and nothing happens? Maybe I should just pray for God to provide comfort and ease her pain — but wouldn't that be a cop out? After all, I claim to believe in miracles, so who am I to say God won't provide one now? What would a more experienced pastor do? If there were instructions on what to say in a situation like this, I hadn't read them yet.

With a look of concern, Rosa quietly asked, "Are you okay, Larry?"

"Yes, yes I'm fine," I replied. Gently taking her hand and the hand of Willie, her husband, I said, "Let us pray." With all the fervency I could muster, I prayed for God to give Rosa a miracle of healing and provide her the opportunity to spend more time with her husband and family. After the prayer, they thanked me for the visit and asked me to come again soon. Despite the prayer, I left the hospital room convinced Rosa would not make it through the day. I was wrong.

Rosa came home from the hospital several days later, very much alive and bubbling with enthusiasm and energy. That Sunday, she and her husband appeared at our worship service for the first time in years. Rosa told everyone how she was on the verge of death, but God, and a prayer by her preacher, miraculously healed her.

Wow! It was pretty exciting stuff. Maybe I did have a healing touch. In fact, I was feeling pretty cocky for a struggling young preacher. "Billy Graham better look out!" I thought I was something.

Several months later, Rosa went into the hospital again. She recovered but was noticeably weaker. Once again, I began to pray in earnest, confidently expecting God to provide yet another miracle; but it would not happen this time. Within a few days, Rosa slipped into a coma and died.

"What happened to my healing ministry?" I cried out to God. "Why was this time so different? Why did Rosa have to die? What a waste! What did I do wrong?"

Obviously I needed a few tough lessons on humility. But I also needed to understand something even more important: God does not promise to heal just because we ask. Healing is meant to be an extraordinary miracle, not simply reduced to an everyday occurrence. What God does promise is something I never really understood until much later: God is always ready to offer *comfort*.

The Apostle Paul said it best: *"All praise to the God and Father of our Lord Jesus Christ. He is the source of every mercy and the God who comforts us."* (2 Corinthians 1:3) This statement is meant to actually define who God is: God is the source of every mercy and the God who comforts us.

Shortly after the funeral Rosa's husband, Willie, came by to thank me. I was visibly surprised and embarrassed, but before I could apologize for failing Rosa so miserably, he went on to say: "Larry, Rosa and I were never as happy as we were these last few months. We both rediscovered our faith in God and we fell in love with each other all over again. We were blessed with a miracle!"

Lost in my foolish and selfish pride, I missed God's real miracle of healing through comfort. A family was given the precious gift of extra time and they wisely took advantage of every moment.

I vowed never again to forget that the real "healing touch" belonged to God. He may not always provide healing, which is why, when He does, it is called a miracle. God can — and always will — provide comfort.

But wait, Paul has more to say: *"He comforts us in all our troubles so that* we can comfort others. When others are troubled, we will be able to give them the same comfort God has given us." (2 Corinthians 1:4) Not only are we promised comfort, but also, somehow we are meant to share the comfort we receive with others.

Joni

A diving accident when she was a teenager left Joni Eareckson Tada completely paralyzed from the neck down. In the early years after the accident, Joni was griped with the dull, lonely ache of total despair. In her book, *Joni*, she writes:

> Here I was, trapped in this canvas cocoon. I couldn't move anything except my head. Physically, I was little more than a corpse. I had no hope of ever walking again. I could never lead a normal life. ... I had absolutely no idea of how I could find purpose or meaning in just existing day after day — waking, eating, watching TV, sleeping.

Joni begged God for healing but didn't get it. Then she begged God to let her die. No way. Instead, God provided healing comfort. Joni wrote:

> I'm alive. I can at least still feel in my neck and tops of my shoulders. I can see the moon through the hospital window. My friends are coming to see me and the doughnuts they bring taste good. And like holding on to a thin kite string, I have hope that it might get better. I see it in the eyes and smiles of my family, my friends and a few of the nurses. Oh, and one more positive thing — they might find a cure for spinal cord injury!

"You can be sure that the more we suffer for Christ, the more God will shower us with his comfort through Christ." (2 Corinthians 1:5)

God provided comfort for Joni Eareckson Tada and then He provided a ministry. With God's help, Joni began the process of learning to live with her disability. As part of her therapy, she started painting by holding a brush in her mouth. She discovered her artwork was quite good and provided a unique opportunity to appear before groups and share how God helped her cope successfully with her disability. Speaking soon led to writing devotions.

After writing her autobiography, Joni received thousands of letters. To better respond to the needs and questions, Joni formed a Christian organization, "Joni and Friends," dedicated to extending the love of Christ to people who are affected by disability. Now, Joni has literally touched lives all over the world.

"So when we are weighed down with troubles, it is for your benefit and salvation! For when God comforts us, it is so that we, in turn, can be an encouragement to you. Then you can patiently endure the same things we suffer." (2 Corinthians 1:6) Few have suffered more than Joni Eareckson Tada, yet even fewer have achieved the same world-wide impact of helping so many through her inspiring life.

In her book, *Ordinary People, Extraordinary Faith,* Joni writes:

When a person is suddenly disadvantaged — whether through disability, death or deep disappointment — a new element is introduced. The hero has become hobbled, so he or she has much less chance of winning. No one would blame the story's hero if he gave up. But if he overcomes in spite of the odds and by the grace God, well … that's what makes the story powerful, important and truly worth reading.

"We are confident that as you share in suffering, you will also share God's comfort." (2 Corinthians 1:7) Joni has certainly suffered, but she also has received and shared God's blessed and healing comfort.

A woman dying of emphysema taught me that God will not often physically heal someone just because they ask; rather, healing is an extraordinary miracle which should never be reduced to an everyday occurrence. However, God does promise and is always offering healing comfort. As Paul wrote, *"God is the source of every mercy and the God who comforts us."* (2 Corinthians 1:3)

Through Joni Eareckson Tada and her struggle as a quadriplegic, I learned how God's healing comfort turns into an opportunity for ministry. Joni's transition from wanting to die to becoming a painter, author and founder of "Joni and Friends," has allowed her to witness her faith worldwide. *"He comforts us in all our troubles so we can comfort others. When others are troubled, we will be able to give them the same comfort God has given us."* (2 Corinthians 1:4)

Me

My personal encounter with divorce taught me the greatest lesson of all: God will allow us to feel pain, disappointment and heartbreak, but in the midst of the crisis, God stands ready to offer healing comfort and then provides an opportunity for us to offer that same comfort to others.

When my marriage was disintegrating, I begged God to heal our relationship. He didn't.

"I'm leaving you. I don't like this town or this life and I don't love you!" The conversation took longer, but that was what she meant. Within days, my wife of 15 years packed her clothes, half our furniture and many of our memories in a borrowed pickup truck and moved away to start over. Left behind were two crying children, an emotionally wrecked husband and a confused church.

So many questions come to mind during an experience like this and I remember asking them all: Why is she leaving me? Am I really that hard to live with? How will I care for my children? Will she come back? What about my career as a minister? How can I stand in front of a congregation and admit to being a failure? Will they let me continue as pastor? Do I even want to continue? Is this what God had in mind when I changed careers to serve the church?

"Oh, Lord! Why me?"

Divorce explodes the perfect pastoral image. In addition to the excruciating personal pain of a marital break-up, there is also the public humiliation of having your leadership abilities challenged before church and community. So clergy divorce becomes a dual tragedy — personally and professionally — causing severe emotional damage to the pastor, his or her family and the church.

God did not heal our marriage but I soon received healing comfort.

Within hours I was surrounded by friends, church members and pastors. No one knew what to say but it didn't matter. They offered reassurance that I was loved. Their gestures touched me in ways I will always cherish.

A neighbor listened quietly while I talked, cried, rambled and even cursed. He lovingly allowed me the opportunity to be angry, to say stupid things, to be human, to release years of pent-up frustration and to grieve. Through him and others, God provided healing comfort.

Over the next few months, I discovered other people facing similar difficulties. Eventually we formed a divorce support group and began meeting regularly. We all needed a chance to talk freely in the company of those who understood the unique problems of separation and divorce.

One session would be about anger, then a Bible study on divorce or possibly a discussion on how to raise children as single parents. I soon began preaching and writing on those experiences.

Divorce is a sin against the sacred covenant of marriage. Yet in the midst of my sin, I rediscovered the precious gift of God's amazing grace. I found healing comfort in the midst of my crisis. Then God unveiled a vital new ministry. I was broken, received comfort and was transformed by God.

"He comforts us in all our troubles so that we can comfort others. When others are troubled, we will be able to give them the same comfort God has given us." (2 Corinthians 1:4) Thank you, God.

Rosa, Joni and Me: Healing, Comfort & Ministry

A woman dying of emphysema taught me that God will not often physically heal just because we ask. Rather, healing is a miracle never to be reduced to an everyday occurrence. However, God always provides healing comfort if we are alert to recognize and accept what is offered.

"Peter and John went to the Temple one afternoon to take part in a prayer service. As they approached the Temple, a man lame from birth was being carried in. Each day he was put beside the Temple gate so he could beg from people going into the Temple. When he saw Peter and John about to enter, he asked them for some money." (Acts 3:1-3)

The man in the Scripture, lame from birth, asked for money not knowing that God had so much more in mind. For me, healing means being alert to God's intention for me as well as for those I come in contact with.

Joni Eareckson Tada's struggle as a quadriplegic showed how God's healing comfort became an opportunity for ministry. Joni eventually became a painter, author and founder of the Christian organization, "Joni and Friends," allowing her the opportunity to become God's witness worldwide.

"Peter and John looked at him intently, and Peter said, 'Look at us!' The lame man looked at them eagerly, expecting a gift. But Peter said, 'I don't have any money for you. But I'll give you what I have. In the name of Jesus Christ of Nazareth, get up and walk!'" (Acts 3:4-6)

Sometimes God uses our weakness to be a witness to others. We must be ready to give our strengths and our weaknesses willingly to God. The lame man had a purpose far beyond anything he ever imagined. So do you.

My personal encounter with divorce, taught me that God will allow us to go through pain, disappointment and heartbreak, but in the midst of the crisis, God stands ready to offer healing comfort and then provides an opportunity for us to offer that same comfort to others.

"Then Peter took the lame man by the right hand and helped him up. And as he did, the man's feet and anklebones were healed and strengthened. He jumped up, stood on his feet, and began to walk! Then, walking, leaping, and praising God, he went into the Temple with them." (Acts 3:7-8)

The lame man received a precious miracle from God, but so did Peter. By using his gifts, combined with God's extraordinary healing grace, Peter accomplished a healing far beyond what any human could ever imagine. Our response should be as the lame man: *"Then walking, leaping and praising God, he went into the Temple."*

Over the years these three stories helped me understand and believe in the miracle of God's healing and healing comfort. This revelation was a critical turning point in my life and ministry.

- Healing is a loving act of God's compassion and mercy not a performance or act.
- Healing involves spiritual, emotional and physical wholeness more than physical deeds.
- Healing occurs in God's way and God's time, not simply because of what we say or do.
- Healing can include responses such as nursing care, counseling and acts of friendship.
- Healing may mean courage to endure suffering and hardship, not an instant reprieve.
- Healing ultimately trumpets our earthly death as victory, ensuring eternal life in heaven.
- Healing comfort always results in ministry if you are willing to share your pain and lessons learned with others who are suffering in the same way you have.

"All the people saw him walking and heard him praising God. When they realized he was the lame beggar they had seen so often at the Beautiful Gate, they were absolutely astounded! They all rushed out to Solomon's Colonnade, where he was holding tightly to Peter and John. Everyone stood there in awe of the wonderful thing that had happened." (Acts 3:9-11)

During one worship service, I shared our intention as a church to expand our healing ministry in several spiritual and practical directions. That afternoon we offered our first healing service. After sharing Scripture and appropriate prayers our parish nurses and pastors stood at the altar and offered an opportunity for people in the congregation to receive prayers of healing.

For the longest moment, nothing happened. Then the miracle of God's healing began. First one woman needed help in dealing with a death. Right behind her was another suffering from chronic back problems. One man confessed an addiction and asked for help. While a musician quietly played in the background, others patiently waited their turns as we prayed for one person after another for over an hour. I never before witnessed such a spiritual and emotional outpouring.

The Scripture illustrates a chance encounter between Peter and a man born lame. One is looking for a handout while another plans to attend a prayer service. Yet, somehow God turns this ordinary event into a miracle of healing. What should be our response? We can only stand in awe.

SEE THE LIGHT

Over the years these three stories helped me understand and believe in the miracle of God's healing and comfort. This revelation was a critical turning point in my life and ministry.

- Healing is a loving act of God's compassion and mercy not a performance or act.
- Healing involves spiritual, emotional and physical wholeness more than physical deeds.
- Healing occurs in God's way and God's time, not simply because of what we say or do.
- Healing can include responses such as nursing care, counseling and acts of friendship.
- Healing may mean courage to endure suffering and hardship, not an instant reprieve.
- Healing ultimately trumpets our earthly death as victory, ensuring eternal life in heaven.

continued...

- Healing comfort always results in ministry if you are willing to share your pain and lessons learned with others who are suffering in the same way you have.

SHARE THE LIGHT

1. Rosa teaches the meaning of healing comfort. How does that help you deal with your suffering? How does it help you help others?
2. Joni and her struggle with being a quadriplegic teaches us how God's healing comfort turns into an opportunity for ministry. How can you turn your struggles into ministry?
3. My encounter with divorce taught me that God offers healing comfort and then provides an opportunity to offer the same comfort to others. How can you share this lesson with others who suffer?
4. How has this day's devotion helped you better understand healing? How can you and your church become more involved in a healing ministry?

Notes:

_____

_____

_____

_____

_____

_____

_____

_____

_____

_____

LIVE THE LIGHT: The Lighthouse in Action

A healing ministry can involve many ministries you currently do well. Regularly visiting the sick is a healing ministry. Delivering communion to shut-ins is a healing ministry. Worship services offering prayers for those in need is a healing ministry. Celebrate the healing ministry you already have.

Parish nursing is an excellent option for any church, especially if a nurse or retired nurse already attends. Many local college campuses and teaching hospitals offer training or you can search the internet for "parish nursing" web sites.

Your Action Ideas:
How can your church be more involved in a ministry of healing?

1. _____

2. _____

3. _____

"Thank you so much for writing to me. I cried when I read 2 Corinthians 1:3-7. I knew then I wasn't feeling this way for nothing. God bless you for your prayers and support; your ministry is like God speaking to me through earthly angels. Thank you again!" —Sharon

"Today's story on the healing comfort of God was so right on. Both my husband and I suffer from chronic illnesses that God has chosen not to heal, at least not yet. ... Having fibromyalgia for over 30 years can get me down, but one thing I know is God sends his healing hand of comfort to me 24/7 so that I can give that touch to someone else. God bless you as you continue to be used through this ministry. 'Look to the Lord and His strength. Seek His face always.' (Psalm 105:4)." —Teri

WHAT HAVE WE LEARNED SO FAR?

Monday—We need light
God is calling us to be alert for opportunities to make
a difference in the community around us.

Tuesday—Opportunities to Shine
We must learn to replace worry over what *we* will do
with faith in what *God* can do.

Wednesday—Becoming God's Lighthouse
Put Christ back into Christmas by helping
a child or family in need.

Thursday—An Attitude that Shines
We function more smoothly and our stress levels go down
when we stop thinking everything revolves around us
and we trust God to provide.

Friday—Simplify
The best part of the $10 Challenge was the opportunity
to use our gifts and talents in unusual and creative ways
to serve God.

Saturday—Start Shining
Healing comfort always results in ministry if you are willing
to share your pain and the lessons you have learned
with others who are suffering in the same way you have.

Now, let's put it all together...

SUNDAY—Live the Light

God chose you. The church needs you.

"Oh that you would bless me indeed and enlarge my territory,
that your hand would be with me and that you would keep me from evil."
And God granted him his request.
1 Chronicles 4:10

My Uncle James was head of parks and recreation for one of the largest cities in the country, a demanding job managing thousands of employees. Several years ago, feeling the need to do more for God, he asked the leaders of his local church how he could become more involved. So, they asked him to serve on several important committees including the pastor-parish relations committee and the building committee. He even became a trustee. As we talked, I noticed the church never seemed interested in the job my uncle managed most every day of his life — a job which impacted several million people. Uncle James was seeking a ministry, but the church put him on a committee.

James is not unusual. One recent trend in America is called "Halftime," named after the book of the same name, by Bob Buford. *Halftimer* is a term that describes people who desire something more in their lives to enable them to move from financial and career success to achieve new goals which are more significant and more spiritually motivated.

The issue is not whether people want something more significant in their lives. We already know they do. The real question is how the church will respond. Will we help them find and develop a meaningful ministry or will we take the easy way out, plug a hole and put them on a committee?

What about you? God called you for a ministry. Do you know what it is? How should the church help? Committee work is important, but there is so much more. As a minister, I emphasize two themes:

1. A church should provide an atmosphere of encouragement and love for you to improve your relationship with God through worship, prayer, Bible study and small group participation.
2. A church should help you discover your unique gifts and talents and use them toward a ministry of serving and helping others within your family, at work, at church, in your community and around the world.

"*The Lord now chose seventy-two other disciples and sent them ahead in pairs to all the towns and villages he planned to visit. These were his instructions to them: 'The harvest is so great and the workers are so few. Pray to the Lord who is in charge of the harvest and ask Him to send out more workers for his fields. Go now and remember that I am sending you out as lambs among wolves. Don't take along any money or a traveler's bag or even an extra pair of sandals.'*" (*Luke 10:1-4*) I found at least five major lessons in this passage:

1. **The Lord chose you.** You don't just decide to serve God. You were chosen long before you were born. The questions you should ask are "What task was I chosen for?" and "Am I doing it?"
2. **Travel in pairs.** God knows it is very difficult to work alone. We all need encouragement either from a friend, a pastor, a church group or family. Ministry always needs a partner.
3. **Pray for more workers.** Your life of prayer is just as important as your willingness to work. Praying and asking for God's help is an important part of your ministry.
4. **Lambs among wolves.** You are receiving a divine warning to be careful. Remember wolves see lambs as only one thing — supper. Serving God always involves risk. Be prepared.
5. **Travel light.** The ad says, "less filling — tastes great!" Too much stuff, no matter how good, can become a burden and weigh down your ministry. Keep your message and your faith simple.

How are churches doing with following these basic lessons? Actually, the church is not doing very well. A survey taken among active Christians found startling news: 70 percent never encourage someone to believe in Christ; 45 percent never talk about their faith; 64 percent rarely pray; and 77 percent rarely read the Bible.

Why? There are many reasons. We are afraid of controversy. Churches tend to seek members rather than disciples. We're busy and preoccupied. We fear rejection. We face too many choices of how to spend our time.

I found surprising answers in a prayer buried in 1 Chronicles and, strangely enough, a children's game called *Mousetrap*.

First: *Mousetrap*. If you walked by my office several years ago, you might have been concerned about my sanity or at least my work habits. Why would a preacher take time out from a hectic schedule to play *Mousetrap*? But it's so exciting!

Watch. This is the crank that turns the shoe … that kicks the marble back and forth down the stairs … then rolls down the chute … that moves the hand … that drops the marble through the thing-a-mi-jig into the tub … that flips the diver into the pool … that triggers the cage … that traps the mouse! Isn't this fun?

No, I'm not crazy! (*Well, maybe a little.*) *Mousetrap* is an interesting way to explain how a church functions. (*You are crazy!*) No, I'm serious.

The game is a fascinating mixture of cranks, marbles, stairs, chutes, tubs, divers and pools — all designed to trigger a cage that traps a mouse. But if you remove even one piece from the formula, the trap no longer works and the mouse goes free.

How is that like a church? Well, a church is an interesting mixture of preachers, teachers, musicians, secretaries, youth, children, single adults, families, new Christians, old Christians, laborers and sales people all designed to trigger an atmosphere of encouragement that will help you deepen your relationship with God, discover your spiritual gifts and use them to reach out to others. But if you remove even one piece from the formula, the church weakens and others remain unreached.

But pieces have been removed from the formula. The church is not doing well. Halftimers like my uncle are given little chance to make a difference.

A survey taken among active Christians discovered that most of us never or rarely encourage someone to believe in God, seldom talk about our faith and rarely pray or read the Bible. If this is true then how can the church change?

Now, we look at the *Prayer of Jabez*.

There is a virtually unknown Bible character hidden in 1 Chronicles whose name is Jabez — which means "pain." What a name! After giving birth, his mother named him *Pain*. Yet, Jabez apparently overcame his painful background, because he alone is singled out as being blessed by God. Why? Because Jabez said a prayer and God granted his request. Obviously, this was a very special prayer.

I discovered the prayer through a wonderful and now famous book written by Bruce Wilkinson, *The Prayer of Jabez: Breaking through to the Blessed Life*. Let's examine the prayer:

"*Oh that you would bless me indeed and enlarge my territory, that your hand would be with me and that you would keep me from evil.*" And God granted him his request. (*1 Chronicles 4:10*)

1. **Oh, that you would bless me indeed...** sounds selfish at first, but Bruce Wilkinson describes blessings as "supernatural favors from God." Asking for a blessing is seeking the power of God to flow through you. You are requesting miracles so don't be surprised when God provides.

2. **And enlarge my territory...** challenges you to go beyond what is comfortable. Today as you begin your day, ask God to look for some-one or something new in your life. Take risks for God.

3. **That your hand would be with me...** Stepping beyond what is com-fortable can be dangerous. You are in uncharted territory. Ask for God's hand to look after you.

4. **And that you would keep me from evil...** is simple recognition that you will be tempted in many ways. Your success with this prayer can cause feelings of no longer needing God. There are more distractions and more temptations. This is a reminder that you always need God.

Here is the Prayer of Jabez challenge: Every day, for thirty days, use this prayer as often as possible. Paste copies wherever you can easily see it. *Oh, that you would bless me indeed and enlarge my territory, that your hand would be with me and that you would keep me from evil.* Then simply be alert for the opportunities God sends your way. Will you take the challenge with me?

Now, I'm excited! I anticipate a *Mousetrap* church coming together. As you and your church begin to pray, God starts the miracle: The crank is turning and the shoe kicks the marble down the stairs, then rolls down the chute that moves the hand that drops another marble through the thing-a-mi-jig into the tub that flips the diver into the pool that triggers the cage that traps the... well, that's the exciting part!

Maybe this is the answer for my Uncle James and his need to do more for God. My uncle was seeking a ministry, but the church he served never caught on and simply put him on a committee.

So what have we learned so far?

1. A church should provide an atmosphere of encouragement and love.

2. A church should help you discover your unique gifts and talents and use them toward a ministry.

In the book of Luke, we learn valuable lessons from Jesus:

1. The Lord chose you… What task were you chosen for?
2. Travel in pairs… We all need encouragement.
3. Pray for more workers… Ask for God's help.
4. Lambs among wolves… Be careful. Be prepared.
5. Travel light… Don't let too much stuff weigh you down.

From *Mousetrap* we learn this about the church:

1. A church is an interesting mixture of people.
2. All of them are necessary in order to reach out to others.
3. When they all work together, the church is a wonder of God.
4. Churches are not using their people effectively.

From the prayer of Jabez we learn:

1. Oh, that you would bless me… Boldly ask for blessings.
2. Enlarge my territory… Take risks for God.
3. That your hand would be with me… Ask for God's help.
4. Keep me from evil… You will always need God.

I mentioned earlier about "Halftime," a recent trend in America named after Bob Buford's book describing people who desire something more in their lives. The issue is not whether people want something more significant in their lives, but how the church should respond. Will we help them find and develop a meaningful ministry or will we simply plug a hole and put them on another committee?

One person described it this way: "Life is like a dog race. You are forever chasing the rabbit. One day the rabbit breaks down and stops in the middle of the race. Now what? There is instant bedlam as dogs begin yelping and biting each other. "

Is this how we are? Running to achieve success but, upon catching the rabbit, not knowing what to do next? If this describes you, welcome to halftime. Maybe it's time to step out of the dog race and look for something more significant. Here are some examples of halftimers within our own church:

- Al owns a successful insurance business but also leads a ministry team at his church and is actively involved with the Salvation Army.
- Betsy, a retired school guidance counselor, now works for the church as a volunteer coordinator, helping others become more involved in ministry.
- Polly retired from college administration and joined mission work teams helping to rebuild houses in Mississippi and filling care packages destined for Russia.
- Vance recently sold his communication business and is now using many of those same skills to help the church explore new ways of communicating the message of Jesus Christ.

Now what? Maybe you are beginning to see yourself as a potential halftimer. Something likely triggered this reaction: success or failure in your career; maybe a divorce; the death of a parent; or your grown children leaving the nest. Maybe your life has been too calm and you are looking for opportunities to get involved in something more meaningful. Lloyd Reeb, author of *From Success to Significance*, offers some questions to consider:

- I've been relatively successful. Is there more to life than my current situation?
- What do I consider eternally significant?
- What is my real purpose on earth? What would give my life more meaning?
- Was my first-half experience a foundation for something more meaningful?

Rodney is not a television show I normally watch, but while channel-surfing one night, I noticed the action of the show was taking place inside a church during worship. Curious, I watched to see what would happen.

The preacher was pacing the floor, shouting: "You must straighten up and get right with God now. Because if you don't, do you know where you're going? Well, do you?"

The congregation as one voice began to shout: "Hell!"

"Where?"

"Hell!"

"What did you say?"

"Hell!"

Everyone was enthusiastically shouting — except for poor Rodney, who was quietly sinking deeper into the pew looking more and more lost.

Later that same day, a now panic-stricken Rodney drove to the preacher's house. But the Reverend was trying to watch a ball game and was obviously annoyed at the interruption.

"Please help me," Rodney pleaded. "Don't let my family go to heaven without me. What should I do to be saved?"

Noticeably annoyed, the preacher first said, "Can you come back later?" Finding that didn't work, he asked: "You'll do anything?"

When Rodney nodded his head, the preacher said: "You could cut my grass."

Ouch! Rodney was searching for an answer to one of life's deepest questions: "What can I do to have a restored relationship with God? How can I be forgiven for my past and receive hope for the future?"

And the preacher, the representative of God's church, responded: "You could cut my grass." ... Just like what happened to my Uncle James who was looking for a significant ministry and found himself assigned to a committee.

Jesus showed the right way to handle a Rodney or an Uncle James in the way he dealt with a man named Zacchaeus: *"He was one of the most influential Jews in the Roman tax-collecting business, and he became rich. Zacchaeus tried to get a look at Jesus, but he was too short to see over the crowds. So he ran ahead and climbed a sycamore tree beside the road, so he could watch from there."* (Luke 19:2-4)

Zacchaeus was one of the most hated and despised persons in all of Jerusalem. Yet when Jesus saw Zacchaeus, He "called him by name, 'Zacchaeus!' he said. 'Quick, come down! For I must be a guest in your home today.'"

To everyone, including church folks, Zacchaeus was worse than Rodney. He was a crook and a traitor, yet Jesus took the time to invite him to lunch. Why? What's the point? Here is the rest of the story:

"Zacchaeus climbed down and took Jesus to his house in great excitement and joy. But the crowds were displeased. 'He has gone to be the guest of a notorious sinner,' they grumbled. Meanwhile, Zacchaeus stood there and said to the Lord, 'I will give half my wealth to the poor, Lord, and if I have overcharged people on their taxes, I will give them back four times as much!' Jesus responded, 'Salvation has come to this home today, for this man has shown himself to be a son of Abraham. And I, the Son of Man, have come to seek and save those like him who are lost.'" (Luke 19:6-10)

Zacchaeus was a dishonest thief, but he was ready to make serious changes. The church of that day offered nothing but rejection and scorn. Jesus, however, sensed a changed heart and offered the hand of fellowship and forgiveness. In response, Zacchaeus became a blessed child of God.

If you are considering making serious changes in your life, remember how Jesus called Zacchaeus by name and offered the hand of forgiveness and fellowship. He will do the same for you.

So what about Rodney? Rodney cut the grass for the preacher, then the church grass. He would have cut anyone's grass if it would help, but it wasn't enough.

The preacher then asked Rodney to speak to a group of youth about sin. So he described his own sins — in graphic detail. The parents were horrified, the pastor was angry, the church was ready to throw him out and poor Rodney was humiliated and more confused than ever.

Finally, the preacher pulled him aside and, rather than scold Rodney, he pleaded: "Can you please forgive me? You came looking for help and instead of listening, I gave you meaningless chores. Let's go to lunch and talk about how to have a real relationship with God and what you can do next."

Maybe the church my Uncle James attended should consider saying the same thing: "James, can you forgive me? You came looking for a significant ministry and instead of listening, we put you on committees. Let's go to lunch and talk about how God is leading you."

Maybe all of us should take the 30-day prayer challenge. What a miracle that would be. *Oh, that you would bless me indeed and enlarge my territory, that your hand would be with me and that you would keep me from evil.* Then simply be alert for the opportunities God sends our way. Will you take the challenge with me?

SEE THE LIGHT

The issue is not whether people want something more significant in their lives, but how the church will respond. Will we help them find and develop a meaningful ministry or will we simply plug a hole and put them on another committee?

SHARE THE LIGHT

1. What are you searching for? Are you trying to follow God's plan for your life?
2. Is your church providing an atmosphere of love and encouragement for people to improve their relationships with God?
3. Is your church helping you discover your unique gifts and talents and then providing a way for you to use them in ministry?
4. How can your church find the missing pieces that will help the "mousetrap" work more effectively?
5. Could you be a halftimer? Are you at that point in life where you can consider something more significant?
6. Will you take the 30-day Prayer of Jabez challenge?

Notes:

_____

_____

_____

_____

_____

_____

_____

_____

_____

_____

_____

_____

LIVE THE LIGHT: The Lighthouse in Action

Oh that you would bless me indeed and enlarge my territory, that your hand would be with me and that you would keep me from evil.

Take the 30-Day Challenge: Pray this prayer each morning and watch what God does next for you and your church.

Your Action Ideas:
How can you encourage your church or small group to take the 30-day challenge?

1. _____

2. _____

3. _____

"I came to this church as a last resort. I'd gone all my life, but in the last few years had encountered people in church who were contentious, fought over everything and even tried to run off the pastor. I'd changed churches, trying to find a better one where people wanted to serve the Lord, but found another church with people in positions of power who were trying to put forth their own agendas instead of God's. I decided to look one more time for a church.

"At the time I started to look, you had an article in the paper in which you were speaking about the many exciting things going on [in your church]. I was intrigued and decided to visit. I found it to be just as you described. The people spoke to me and smiled and were welcoming. When they asked visitors to raise their hands in the service, I did and was surprised to receive a red gift bag full of information and even a book written by you! You preached and were such a good speaker. Hard to believe that someone who could write well could also deliver an excellent sermon in an interesting way that kept my eyes riveted to the front. After the early service, there was a full breakfast served in the Breakfast Café. Biscuits and gravy will always get me! My experience at church was so positive, I returned the next week and the next week. After a number of weeks, I felt God leading me to join and I did. I've been very happy. I sing in the choir, help with special projects and serve on our Mission and Outreach Team." —Lisa

WEEK FIVE

TO LIVE LIKE CHRIST

MONDAY—We Need Light

Sometimes we need a Godly wake-up call.

You are the light of the world — like a city on a mountain,
glowing in the night for all to see. Don't hide your light under a basket!
Instead, put it on a stand and let it shine for all.
In the same way, let your good deeds shine out for all to see,
so that everyone will praise your heavenly Father.
Matthew 5:14-16

As you read in Week Three, at least once a year we act a little crazy at Timberlake. One Sunday we even had an Elvis sighting! That day, the bulletin featured a picture of Elvis and the title: "Elvis in Concert: A Rock & Roll Worship!" Now *everyone* was convinced I had lost my mind!

Charles Wade, an Elvis historian wrote: "Elvis had an abiding love of gospel music. For him it was not an affectation, nor a passing fancy. He returned to this part of his music over and over again — a music that helped to define his style, his career and the complex personality that changed the face of American culture."

Peter Guralnick, author of *The Unmaking of Elvis Presley: Careless Love* wrote, "This is a story of fame. It is a story of celebrity and its consequences. It is, I think, a tragedy. Elvis Presley may well be the most written-about figure of our time. He is also in many ways the most misunderstood. 'It's very hard,' Elvis declared without facetiousness at a 1972 press conference, 'to live up to an image.'"

The worship service was designed to resemble an Elvis concert. There were various opening acts performed by our music ministry: *Just a Closer*

Walk with Thee by our handbell group, and *Crying in the Chapel* and *Precious Lord* by our choirs. We even had a "young Elvis" who sang several early hits. Everything was designed to lead up to the appearance of "Elvis" himself.

Periodically, someone would announce the whereabouts of the King of Rock and Roll: "Elvis has left the hotel." … "Elvis is in the limousine!" Several young girls shrieked. You could feel the anticipation!

In addition, HBN-TV — our fictitious "Heavenly Broadcast Network" — sponsored "Elvis in Concert" and was allowed to videotape the worship service. As part of the arrangement, Elvis agreed to a live interview.

Maintaining the concert atmosphere, we titled our prayer time "Love Me Tender," with the words subtly changed to better reflect an offering of love and praise to God: "Love me tender, love me sweet; never let me go. You have made my life complete and I love you so. Love me tender, love me true, all my dreams fulfill. For my dear Lord, I love you and I always will."

Our children's story was based on the song *Don't Be Cruel*. I told the children, "Sometimes we can all be cruel to each other. Brothers hit sisters; sisters slap brothers. We tell lies about our friends. We make cruel and hurtful remarks. Do you think God meant for us to be cruel?"

The children quickly shouted "No!"

The Bible says *"Always be full of joy in the Lord. I say it again —rejoice! Let everyone see that you are considerate in all you do."* (Philippians 4:4-5)

How can we be full of joy and more considerate in all that we do? Elvis sang a song describing how we should treat others: "I don't want to be your tiger, 'cause tigers play too rough. I don't want to be your lion 'cause lions ain't the kind you love enough. I just wanna be your teddy bear." There is something so loveable and huggable about a teddy bear. Maybe Elvis' version of Philippians 4:4-5 would sound something like this:

"So, Don't be Cruel to your friends or to your Hound Dog, because you might get us All Shook Up, break our Wooden Hearts and send us Crying in the Chapel or to the Heartbreak Hotel, where we'd be singing Jailhouse Rock. Instead, follow Jesus, read the Bible and learn to Love Me Tender in order to Let me be your Teddy Bear. Because when it comes to being nice, It's Now or Never before someone gets mad and says to you… Return to Sender." *(I know it's corny, but it was fun!)*

As the kids went back to their seats, the announcer's voice boomed: "The limousine has just pulled in! … Elvis is here! … Elvis Presley has entered the building!"

It had been many years, but Elvis was back. What would he say? Or sing? More importantly — what does Elvis have to do with me and my relationship with God?

Maybe I should let Elvis answer for himself.

With *2001: A Space Odyssey* playing in the background, as in many concerts, the announcer proclaimed: "He's been gone for many years but now he's back! The king of rock and roll ... the one and only ... Elvis!"

As the crowd screamed, "Elvis Presley," accompanied by three mean-looking body guards and followed by a wave of screaming youth, came running down the center aisle of the sanctuary. His suit was black with a full cape and loaded with sequins. He sure looked like Elvis, but would he sing like Elvis?

The fist song was *That's Alright Mamma*, and he sang like only Elvis can sing. Then, accompanied only by his faithful guitarist, Charlie Hodges, Elvis began the song that convinced us all: "Wise men say only fools rush in, but I can't help falling in love with you." And the congregation knew — only Elvis could sing like that. It really was Elvis Presley!

As the applause slowly died down, a voice came over the loud speaker: "Elvis, I'm with HBN — Heavenly Broadcast Network — and I would like to ask you a few questions. Of course all of us would like to know: Where have you been?"

Elvis replied: "Well, for the last month I've been on a diet so I could fit in this suit. I've been eating a few too many fried peanut butter and banana sandwiches. As far as what I've been doing ... For awhile, I was sitting out back of the pool house at Graceland watching everyone go by.

"I took a ride on my Harley through Washington State and ran into 'Bigfoot.' He scared me half to death and I ain't been back since. I've been to a lot of 7-11 stores and McDonald's. My favorite is in Kalamazoo, Michigan. You know it's hard work making sure I show up at all those places."

The voice continued: "That's funny, Elvis. Now we know where all those Elvis sightings came from. What about your beginnings? How did you get started singing and what were the early years like?"

"They say when I was 3 years old," Elvis continued. "I got away from my parents in church and walked in front of the choir and started beating time on my leg. I loved gospel music from the beginning. I sang with quartets like the Blackwoods, who were members of our church. I wanted to be a gospel singer but they told me I couldn't harmonize. Can you believe that?

As a teenager, I would sneak into the blues clubs on Beale Street in Memphis.

"My first recording was *That's Alright Mamma*, a gift for my mama. Sam Phillips at Sun Records heard me and persuaded me to record *Heartbreak Hotel*, and the rest is history. Gospel music will always hold a special place in my heart. After we finished our show, I would have the boys stay up until dawn singing gospel songs. I'd call out a title and see who could hang with me. One of my favorites is *Where Could I Go But to the Lord*. Why don't I sing it for you?"

After Elvis finished, the voice from the booth asked another question: "How important was your mother in your life?"

"My mama was the world to me. Everything I did was for her. She was the driving force in our family. There's not a day goes by that I don't think of her. Mama stood up for me when everyone said I was evil and was a bad influence on young kids. I had a twin brother, Jesse, who died at birth. She worried that something would happen to me, too. I think my going in the military really affected her."

"Elvis, you served in the military when you didn't have to. Why?"

"I'm very proud of my time with the boys in the Army. I love my country and felt the right way to serve was to do what everyone else had to do. They wanted me to go into Special Services and sing, but I just wanted to be another soldier. I was an engineer in a tank battalion. Man it was cold, and I hated being away from Graceland. I was a sergeant when I got out. I'm proud to say this will always be one of my greatest achievements. Of course, the best thing that happened was I met my future wife, Priscilla."

The tone of the interview was about to change.

"Is this when you became a drug addict?" the interviewer asked. Presley's face burned beet red in obvious irritation, for he was not used to being challenged by anyone. The interview was not going as expected. Who did this HBN guy think he was?

Regaining his composure, Elvis replied; "I was never a drug addict. President Richard Nixon awarded me a badge to serve our country as a narcotics agent. He felt I could help guide children away from street drugs. Yes, I take sleeping pills; you can't imagine what it's like after a concert. It's hard to come down from the high energy level I need on stage for my fans. During the day I take Dexedrine to wake up and get going again. But, everything is prescribed by my doctor, Dr. Nick."

There was a brief moment of silence before the interviewer continued: "You're a famous rock and roll star, Elvis, yet you still sing a lot of gospel in addition to your other material. Why?"

"Well sir, my faith in God has always been strong and I've never been afraid to share that faith with my fans. Gospel music is a part of my heritage and tells a story like no other music. Gospel music is ..."

Before he could finish, the interviewer cut in: "Elvis, your faith and your lifestyle do not reflect the gospel music you claim to love. You live a wild life of nonstop parties. Despite what you say, you are hopelessly addicted to prescription drugs! You've also been unfaithful to the very wife you claim to love."

"Who are you and just who do you think you're talking to!" Elvis screamed. He gestured to a body guard: "Find that Heavenly Broadcast idiot in the sound booth and bring him here."

Long, agonizingly silent minutes passed before the body guard appeared in the sound booth and shouted down to Elvis: "There's no one in the booth but technicians!"

Elvis was stunned. "Well, where is he?" He looked around frantically. "Where are you?"

"I'm still here, Elvis."

"Where is here? Who is here?" Suddenly, he realized the obvious answer. "Are you trying to tell me that you are ... God?"

"Yes. And I'm very disappointed in you, Elvis. You could have influenced millions to follow me through your gift of music. Instead, you did everything to suit only yourself. What do you have to say?"

There was a long pause as the "King of Rock and Roll" gathered his thoughts.

Slowly, Elvis began to talk: "God, I've always known there had to be a purpose for my life. I read the Bible and sang gospel music with passion. I guess the true meaning was right in front of me. I needed faith that comes from the heart. I have to drop my ego and make room for You. I sinned deeply and missed a great opportunity to serve and witness to millions. If only I could live my life over again. Can you ever forgive me?"

God replied, "Elvis, I've already forgiven you. You are a wonderful person, blessed with many unique talents. But I put you on this earth to use those talents wisely. What's important is what you will do now."

Elvis said, "Lord, I always loved *You'll Never Walk Alone*, but I haven't sung it in a while. The words are simple and short but the meaning seems appropriate now. I know that faith is truly one of the greatest gifts you offer. With faith I know that I'll never have to walk alone again. Thank you, God!"

There was a pause before God spoke: "Elvis, sing so the others will see me through your talents."

With passion born anew by restored faith in almighty God, Elvis sang as only he can:

When you walk through a storm,
hold your head up high and don't be afraid of the dark.
At the end of the storm is a golden sky
and the sweet silver song of a lark.
Walk on through the wind.
Walk on through the rain
though your dreams be tossed and blown.
Walk on.
Walk on with hope in your heart and you'll never walk alone.
You'll never walk alone.

Thank you Elvis, for helping us see God through your struggles.

SEE THE LIGHT

Elvis was blessed by God with extraordinary gifts. Yet, instead of using his gifts and influence to serve and point people to God, he did everything to suit himself. The results were disastrous. We can learn from his mistakes.

Special thanks to David Baldree for writing much of the dialogue between Elvis and God for our special service — and for being such a believable "Elvis impersonator."

SHARE THE LIGHT

1. Elvis may be a famous example of ignoring God's will and going your own way, but we all do it. What is your story?
2. To live like Christ calls for important decisions about our careers, our lifestyles and even the ways we spend our time. What decisions do you need to make to "live the light?"
3. God is willing to forgive all our sinful mistakes just as soon as we recognize the importance of always living our lives for Him. Have you confessed your sinful mistakes to God lately?
4. "When you walk through a storm, hold your head up high and don't be afraid." Remember "you'll never walk alone."

Notes:

_____

_____

_____

_____

_____

_____

_____

_____

_____

_____

_____

_____

_____

_____

_____

_____

_____

LIVE THE LIGHT: The Lighthouse in Action

Godly encouragement. These words should guide the mission of any sports, music or other ministry. If God comes first, then those who want to play or sing will be welcomed, regardless of their skills. Of course excellence should be honored, but not above the power of being a Godly encourager for others. The biggest mistake any ministry will ever make is valuing work over Godly encouragement.

Betty was a member of our choir for many years. Her hearing was bad, her voice was off-key and, occasionally, she fell asleep during rehearsal. But she had a radiant smile and loved being in the choir. When she was no longer able to drive, choir members picked her up.

Was Betty a nuisance? Yes. Did she add to the excellence of the choir? No. But Betty did add something unique and special. When she died, the funeral was packed and one choir member after another spoke of Betty's smile and her warm personality. Young ones spoke of her encouragement when times were hard. Older members recalled her continued enthusiasm. If you ask who had the greatest influence on them in choir and even in life, many will mention Betty.

Your Action Ideas:
How can you or your church follow Betty's example and offer Godly encouragement?

1. _____

2. _____

3. _____

"I received a special blessing from your supportive e-mails. Things are actually looking good around here lately. I know the power of prayer and I praise the Lord for his intervention ... and thank you [and] the others who prayed for me when I was unable to pray for myself. ... After coming out of this slump, I am happier and more at peace than I was before." —Sherry

"This is a Spirit-filled church with loving and caring people. You definitely show the 'light of the world.'" —Debbie

TUESDAY—Opportunities to Shine

If you will take one step toward God,
God will take two steps toward you.

You see, this is what can happen: Weak Christians who think it is wrong
to eat this food will see you eating in the temple of an idol.
You know there's nothing wrong with it, but they will be encouraged
to violate their conscience by eating food that has been dedicated to the idol.
So because of your superior knowledge, a weak Christian,
for whom Christ died, will be destroyed.
1 Corinthians 8:10-11

Alex Haley, author of *Roots*, first gained fame for writing the autobiography of Malcolm X, a famous black radical who lived in the early 1960s. In the book, *Autobiography of Malcolm X*, Haley told the story of Malcolm's change from jail-house criminal to Black Muslim religious leader. It seems Malcolm was in prison during his younger years for dealing drugs. During his incarceration, he received a letter from his brother, talking of something new and exciting. His brother promised he would soon send more information, but in the meantime, he instructed Malcolm: "Don't smoke cigarettes or eat any pork."

Malcolm figured this would be a new scam to get out of prison. So at the next meal, as prisoners lunged for the pork, Malcolm calmly handed his portion to the next prisoner.

This simply was not done in prison. Caught by surprise, the other prisoner stopped, stared and finally asked: "Why aren't you having any pork?" Malcolm replied, "I don't eat pork!"

Malcolm X would later refer to this incident as his "conversion experience," even though, at the time, he was insincere. When he said, "I don't eat pork!" he took a first step toward God. And, as he told Haley: "If you will take one step toward God, God will take two steps toward you."

Think about that: *If you will take one step toward God. God will take two steps toward you.*

As sincere and committed Christians we, too, must be prepared to stand up and say to the world, "I don't eat pork!" Our priorities should change. We claim to love the Lord with our whole heart, with our very soul and with our entire mind. We say we love others as much as we do ourselves. So, we should act different and think different. Shouldn't we?

This noticeable change in attitude becomes our witness to the outside world.

Speaking of pork, the Apostle Paul had something to say about food. He wrote: *"So now, what about it? Should we eat meat that has been sacrificed to idols? Well, we all know that an idol is not really a god and there is only one God and no other."* (*1 Corinthians* 8:4)

Have you been tempted to eat idol food lately? No? Me neither. At first glance, this scripture doesn't make much sense, so let me share a more appropriate example: Let's talk about alcohol.

First, let me confess: I don't drink.

"Big deal," you say. "You're a preacher! Most preachers don't drink. Now, if you actually admitted to drinking, then you would grab my attention!"

Yet, long before becoming a minister, I did drink alcohol in moderation. My fellow business owners and managers met frequently, and these meetings often included an open bar.

Now, you may be thinking "Is that so wrong?" Not really. I don't know of any verses in the Bible that specifically say, "Thou shalt not drink." I wasn't drinking heavily so what's the problem? Let's look further at what Paul wrote:

"You see, this is what can happen: Weak Christians who think it is wrong to eat this food will see you eating in the temple of an idol. You know there's nothing wrong with it but they will be encouraged to violate their conscience by eating food that has been dedicated to the idol. So because of your superior knowledge, a weak Christian for whom Christ died will be destroyed." (*1 Corinthians* 8:10-11)

One way to interpret the scripture is this: It may not be wrong for me to drink alcohol in moderation, but someone who has a drinking problem could see me enjoying a drink and be encouraged to join in. And of course, for them, it would be a big mistake. And I would be responsible for hurting someone else. I certainly don't want that on my conscience.

As an added benefit, others might notice I was no longer drinking and ask, "Why?" This would offer an opportunity to share my newfound faith in Christ.

So, at the next business meeting I summoned up my courage and ordered grapefruit juice — nothing else —just grapefruit juice. It wasn't long before someone asked what I was drinking, and when I told him grapefruit juice, he replied: "Why just grapefruit juice?"

Wow! This was exactly the opportunity I prayed for! Here was my chance to say loudly and clearly to someone: "I don't eat pork!" This was my opening to be a witness for Christ — to share my faith.

So what was my response to this God-given opportunity?

"I'm not drinking because … I'm on a diet."

What?

I'm on a diet. *I'm on a diet?* Is that lame or what? God offered a golden opportunity and I said, "I'm on a diet?"

Here was my chance to be a witness for God and say to the world, "I don't eat pork." But instead I said, "I'm on a diet?" What was wrong with me? Was I ashamed, afraid of taking a stand? I was not off to a good start as God's witness.

Eventually, I did gather the courage to tell others how my life had changed and I used those opportunities to share my faith.

In many ways, this was my first, hesitating step toward God. And it wasn't long before God took many steps toward me.

But, this story is not as much about drinking or not drinking as it is about being a more effective witness. There are many other ways we can say to the world, "I don't eat pork!"

For example, I also had a bad habit of occasionally entertaining my friends with off-color stories and jokes. My newfound faith demanded better.

At first, I simply walked away from the crowd when the jokes turned spicy, but that only made me look judgmental and cold. So, I discovered a better way — by not walking away from the crowd and learning to tell new stories with a more spiritual message.

Maybe this was my preparation for ministry. (*Just kidding!*)

"Disciple Bible Study" is taught at our church every year and requires a daily habit of Scripture reading. Students frequently take their Bibles to work so they can read during breaks. Before the course ends, at least one student will mention someone from work approaching their desk asking, "Why are you reading the Bible so much?" This produces a golden opportunity to share their faith.

A large family met for lunch after church every Sunday and spent the entire meal criticizing their pastor and church. One woman in the family was deeply concerned but didn't know what to say. She tried being quiet. She tried making more positive statements. Nothing seemed to work.

"Maybe I should just tell them off, get up from the table and leave!" she said. "But they're my family. I love them. What should I do?"

Several weeks later, she approached me with a smile and said, "The Lord answered my prayers. Last Sunday during lunch, when the conversation began to sour, I suggested we try saying a prayer for our pastor and church.

"There was a long silence, but my uncle finally said, 'I think it's a great idea.' The next thing I knew, we were praying together and afterward, the criticism miraculously stopped."

Every day, God gives you a chance to say to the world, "I don't eat pork."

Ask yourself this question: If you were arrested for being a Christian, would they have enough evidence to convict you?

Paul goes on to say, "*Anyone who claims to know all the answers doesn't really know very much. But the person who loves God is the one God knows and cares for.*" (*1 Corinthians* 8:2-3) Actions speak louder than words.

John was trying to leave for the long journey home. But a snowstorm developed and traffic advisories urged everyone to stay off the roads. "It's all interstate. I can make it," he thought. Within an hour, John regretted his decision. The snow was coming so thick he could hardly move. Finally pulling off beneath an overpass, John tried to decide what to do.

Then, he heard a tapping on his window. "Sorry to bother you," the stranger said. I saw you leave earlier, so I figured you knew what to do and I followed you."

I figured you knew what to do and followed you. Like it or not, we are all watched and followed. The question is: Are we leading ourselves and others in the right direction?

SEE THE LIGHT

Every day, God gives you a chance to say to the world, "I don't eat pork." Others are watching and probably following. So ask yourself this: If you were arrested for being a Christian, would there be enough evidence to convict you?

SHARE THE LIGHT

1. What could you change in your life that would say to others who come in contact with you, "I don't eat pork?"
2. I messed up my first opportunity to be a witness for Christ by making the excuse, "I'm on a diet." What excuses have you used?
3. Faith is not as much about having answers as it is about loving God and being willing to stand up for that love. How can you more fully love God and stand up for that love?
4. How can you share this story with a friend, a small group or your church?

Notes:

_____

_____

_____

_____

_____

_____

_____

_____

_____

_____

_____

_____

_____

_____

_____

_____

_____

LIVE THE LIGHT: The Lighthouse in Action

Local churches offer wonderful opportunities to say to the community, "I don't eat pork." One church gives ballroom dancing lessons every Friday night. Single adults and couples can enjoy themselves in an atmosphere that is safe and encouraging. Youth groups sponsor "coffee houses" with an environment that encourages fun in a wholesome way. On Halloween, churches provide safe alternatives for kids to gather and experience a message that counteracts the culture of "witches, goblins and ghouls."

Your Action Ideas:
How can your church become more active in your community?

1. _____

2. _____

3. _____

"I just have to tell you all what a great God we serve! Some of you will remember my very suicidal prayer requests. About eight months ago my Mum and Dad were going to file for a divorce; my sister and I were very suicidal. (It's a miracle in itself that we are all still alive!) Well now the whole family is founded in a wonderful church. Mum and Dad are more happily married than they have been for years. We are not the same family — even the neighbors mentioned how they can't hear us fighting anymore! What a great witness, huh!? God told me to encourage as many Christians as I could because, although we can't always see what our effort is doing, it is always doing something! Thanks for all those prayers you made for me. They changed my life." —Katherine

"I look forward to the prayer requests from around the world every week. The devotions are uplifting and when I get stressed out they always make me feel better. I talk with people across the world through the prayer chain and it's nice to know that so many people take the time to read and pray for each request. I hope to keep enjoying this ministry for many years." —Alison

WEDNESDAY—Becoming God's Lighthouse

To truly live like Christ involves taking risks.

The servant returned and told his master what they said.
His master was angry and said, "Go quickly into the streets and alleys
of the city and invite the poor, the crippled, the lame, and the blind."
After the servant had done this, he reported, "there is still room for more."
So his master said, "Go out into the country lanes and behind the hedges
and urge anyone you find to come, so that the house will be full.
For none of those I invited first will get even the smallest taste
of what I had prepared for them."
Luke 14:21-24

Frequently, in meetings with other church leaders, I'm told: "There is little hope for our church to have any influence in even our community, much less the world. We are small and only getting smaller, so we can hardly pay our pastor, much less effectively help anyone else. We have very few young people to give us energy. We have no money to pay additional staff salaries. Our volunteers are faithful, but they are old and tired. What are we to do?"

Having served churches just like this for many years, I have discovered helpful answers.

1. Don't allow yourself to get discouraged and quit.
2. Pray to God right now for guidance and wisdom.
3. Find something you can do and start doing it.
4. Expect God to challenge you to think bigger.

Jesus told a parable that provides solid answers: *"A man prepared a great feast and sent out many invitations. When all was ready, he sent his servant around to notify the guests that it was time for them to come. But they all began making excuses. One said he had just bought a field and wanted to inspect it. Another said he had just bought five pair of oxen and wanted to try them out. Another had just been married, so he said he couldn't come." (Luke 14:16-20)*

God seems to be the "man" in the parable, inviting us, the church, to a great feast; so great, that nothing else should take precedence. The invitations come at first to the guests we would expect to attend any great feast.

They are the so-called "good" people of the community: land owners, shopkeepers and those commonly described as successful and influential — the same people who would also proudly claim membership in a church. In other words, God is inviting the church first.

Yet, these very same people — "good" people who receive gold-embossed invitations from God — are the ones who, for one reason or another, are simply unable to attend the most important event of all time. They claim to be busy buying land, tending to other business necessities or they are too busy with personal matters.

Excuses! Good excuses, but excuses just the same. However, don't judge them too quickly. Remember the excuses given by our own church leaders? "We are so small. We have very few young people. We have no money. Our members are old and tired." Do they sound familiar?

What is God's response? *"The servant returned and told his master what they had said. His master was angry and said, 'Go quickly into the streets and alleys of the city and invite the poor, the crippled, the lame, and the blind.' After the servant had done this, he reported, 'there is still room for more.' So his master said, 'Go out into the country lanes and behind the hedges and urge anyone you find to come, so that the house will be full. For none of those I invited first will get even the smallest taste of what I had prepared for them.'"* (Luke 14:21-24)

Ouch!

As the church, we apparently receive the first invitation to God's feast. But then we are expected to respond. If we don't, the implication is that God will be angry with us; He will invite others and we will miss out.

How are we to respond when we are so limited? What does God expect us to do? Do you remember my suggestions?

1. Don't allow yourself to get discouraged and quit.
2. Pray to God right now for guidance and wisdom.
3. Find something you can do and start doing it.
4. Expect God to challenge you to think bigger.

Obviously the "feast" describes God"s opportunity to be the church in a big way. Our response should be to say *yes* to the invitation with faith, knowing that serving God is more important than our occupations, our families or even our very lives. We say *yes*, trusting God for answers, resources and courage to enable us to do far more than we ever imagined possible.

Can it really be that simple? A few years ago, I would have sincerely struggled to give you a good answer. Our church was growing and active in the community, but we were not really a mission-oriented church. What we didn't know was that we were about to be challenged by God.

Several of our members traveled to Jamaica to offer medical aid and church construction help. Their stories, and the enthusiastic change God brought into their lives, affected us all. At this point we were eager for more opportunities.

Then, we stepped out in faith to provide a home for Lawyers Missionary Baptist Church after a tornado destroyed their building. In response to a church-wide $10 challenge, one of our members led a community-wide effort to help rebuild their church.

Today, their beautiful new church still stands as a testimony to what one individual, one church and one community can do to help others. But wait — God was not finished. This was just the beginning.

On December 26, 2004, a massive Tsunami swept the Indian Ocean. More than eleven countries were struck by the enormous waves, with a loss of life estimated at more than 300,000 people.

Like most churches, we raised money. But we found ourselves asking what else we could do. How could we become more directly involved? As we searched for answers, God once again began to move within us.

We visited "Gleaning for the World," a local humanitarian agency that specializes in getting equipment and supplies to the poorest countries in the world. Their CEO, Rev. Ron Davidson, offered two projects.

The first project involved receiving and sorting large bales of used hospital linens which we then boxed to be shipped to third-world countries. Within a matter of days, a large truck unloaded huge, tightly-packed bales of linens that, when unpacked, literally expanded and filled our gymnasium.

Hundreds of volunteers, from toddlers to the elderly, converged upon our church. For the next few days we sorted, folded and boxed literally thousands of hospital gowns and sheets.

The second project from Gleaning for the World involved using the money we raised to ship 40,000 pounds of rice from Vietnam to Sri Lanka — enough to feed at least 150,000 people several meals.

Now, remember those four suggestions?

1. Don't allow yourself to get discouraged and quit.
2. Pray to God right now for guidance and wisdom.

3. Find something you can do and start doing it.
4. Expect God to challenge you to think bigger.

Well, God was about to challenge *us* to think bigger.

Rev. Davidson called and asked: "Would you like to go to the tsunami zone and see the rice being delivered, assess the damage and look for other opportunities to help?"

I thought we would just be visiting another aid agency nearby, so I said, "Sure! Where are we going?"

"Sri Lanka," he replied.

What could I say but "Yes!" Ten days later, I secured a passport, received my shots and began a series of flights that would last over thirty-six hours and take us literally half-way around the world.

Four of us made the trip: Rev. Ray Buchanan with "Stop Hunger Now," Rev. Ron Davidson with "Gleaning for the World," Len Stevens, anchor of our local news television station WSET-TV, and me.

A guidebook describes Sri Lanka as, "The Teardrop of India: a tear of sheer joy frozen in mid-air." Others describe it as the original Garden of Eden and proudly point to places named after Adam, the first man. How could such a beautiful country face such massive destruction? We were about to find out.

SEE THE LIGHT

Our response should be to say *yes* to God's invitation, with faith, knowing that serving our Lord is more important than our occupations, our families and even our very lives. We say *yes*, trusting God for answers, resources and courage to enable us to do far more than we ever imagined possible. It's important to remember:

1. Don't allow yourself to get discouraged and quit.
2. Pray to God right now for guidance and wisdom.
3. Find something you can do and start doing it.
4. Expect God to challenge you to think bigger.

SHARE THE LIGHT

1. The temptation for churches is to say "We are too small to make a difference." Yet God teaches differently. How can we make a difference in our communities and the world?
2. How can you discover the needs in your community?
3. How can community needs be matched with your gifts and talents and those of your family or church?
4. Don't get discouraged. Pray. Find something. Keep thinking bigger. If you had nothing to lose, what would you do? How can you take the first step?

Notes:

_____

_____

_____

_____

_____

_____

_____

_____

_____

_____

_____

_____

_____

_____

_____

_____

_____

_____

_____

_____

LIVE THE LIGHT: The Lighthouse in Action

A local school principal approached his Sunday school and asked for help. Some students were coming to school with no winter coats. "Can't we do something to help?" he asked.

"I sell winter coats," volunteered one person. "I could purchase a quantity of coats wholesale." Another member who worked at a local car dealership volunteered to lead the fund raising. Others volunteered to contact local schools and develop a list of children who needed coats. Before long, the coat project was launched. Now every school in the county receives help from this Sunday school class and more than 150 coats are purchased and distributed every year.

Your Action Ideas:
Don't limit yourself. Pray. Think bigger. How can your church reach out to the community? The world?

1. _____

2. _____

3. _____

"It is difficult to say what my church means to me. I first realized it when my husband was sick and passed away ten years ago. At the time, I had no family [nearby] other than my one daughter and her family. We had only been coming [to church] for about five years, but every one was so supportive. ... At [the] memorial service my cousin said, 'These people are so friendly. They treat you like an old-time Southerner!' They couldn't do enough for me. Most friends I made are through the church. ... They really practice their faith when out in the community and the world." —Betty

"I loved your column [about] acts of kindness. One thing I do is hand out Windex and paper towels to my youth choir. We go to the local supermarket (with permission) and clean windshields. We leave a card that says: 'Your windshield just got cleaned by a bunch of teenagers. We hope you see your way clear to attend the church of your choice Sunday.'" —SIGHT Youth Choir, Central United Methodist Church, Rogers, Arkansas

THURSDAY—An Attitude that Shines

In order to live like Christ,
you have to respond to God's challenges.

The thought of my suffering and homelessness is bitter beyond words.
I will never forget this awful time as I grieve over my loss.
Yet I still dare to hope when I remember this: The unfailing love
of the Lord never ends! By his mercies we have been
kept from complete destruction. Great is his faithfulness;
his mercies begin afresh each day. I say to myself,
"The Lord is my inheritance; therefore, I will hope in him."
Lamentations 3:19-24

We landed in the capital city of Colombo, location of the only international airport in Sri Lanka. This is where I discovered my first lesson about living in Sri Lanka: there is traffic. Lots of traffic. The small, narrow roads were jammed with bicycles, motor bikes, cars, rickshaws, cows, dogs, pedestrians and trucks. Everyone drove fast, monitored the many mirrors around their vehicles and kept one hand constantly on the horn: beep, beep! There are two rules: the largest vehicle always wins and you better beep before you swerve.

Colombo was on the other side of the island, away from the tsunami zone, but everyone seemed to know someone affected by the waves. Amazingly, just a few miles away, a train jammed with hundreds of passengers was destroyed as the waves literally curved around the island.

Len Stevens, news anchor for our local station WSET-TV, visited the area and was told that, as the water approached, someone or maybe several people in a state of panic pulled the emergency stop cord. The train was moving away from the oncoming wave but, instead, stopped and received the full blow.

After the train tipped over, local residents told Len, you could hear the cries of the wounded and dying for hours; but because of the very real fear of another Tsunami, no potential rescuers approached the train.

The next day, we flew to the other side of Sri Lanka to visit the tsunami-ravaged beaches. Even the news reports could not prepare us for what we were about to witness.

Demolished hulks once used as fishing boats littered the beach area of

Kalmunai. Piles of brick and rubble, scattered among the palm trees, represented what used to be houses and small businesses.

The desolation and destruction caused by the tsunami stretched for miles along the beach and for at least a mile inland. We witnessed an endless array of destruction, despair and hopelessness.

Flapping in the breeze by one house was a large white flag. Residents said, "The white flag represents our enormous sadness and grief." In other areas near the beach, clusters of the same white flags were used to mark mass graves.

Despite the overwhelming tragedy, young children were the first to greet us and appeared remarkably exuberant as they scrambled to pose for pictures. There were giggles and laughter as we distributed kits filled with household necessities, school supplies, games and frisbees. Yet, when we mentioned the word tsunami, their faces became more somber. One little girl spoke of losing her entire family, including her mother and father, three brothers and one sister.

Two images on the beach I will never forget: First, a little child's flip flop, buried near a pile of bricks that once formed a house. Holding the shoe, I could only imagine what must have happened to the little girl who once played on this beach.

Second, is the image of a woman's yellow blouse billowing gently in the breeze, caught on a tree limb approximately ten feet off the ground. How did a blouse become lodged so high? How could one wave cause so much destruction?

We were told the tsunami was actually made up of three consecutive waves. Each one would sweep through the area, enveloping everything in it's path for miles, but then the water would quickly recede with a powerful suction that literally swept everything back out to sea.

Women and children were especially vulnerable to being washed away. Hours or even days later, the bodies of the victims washed back ashore. But many have never been found.

Now imagine this: We witnessed the destruction on one beach in one village of Sri Lanka. The Tsunami struck 11 different countries all around the Indian Ocean. Within Sri Lanka there were 500 miles of shoreline, all hit by the gigantic waves. Yet in this one area, Kalmunai, nearly 3,000 people died. An elementary school near the beach enrolled 62 students — 57 died. A church claimed 350 members; 61 were gone.

A woman approached me with a plastic bag clutched in her hands.

She reached inside and handed me a type-written piece of paper describing how she lost all seven of her children to the tsunami. Then she handed over a white card containing the name, age and description of each child. Through an interpreter, she said to us, "Please pray for my family. I have lost them all."

All I could do was exclaim, "I am so sorry!" and cry.

Yet, while walking through town, we were frequently greeted with warm smiles and urged to stop for a moment and visit a tent or other place of shelter. Noticeably polite, everyone was eager to offer hospitality. They all asked one question: "From where did you come?"

A few asked for handouts, but only a few. Most simply wanted to share their stories and thank us for visiting. When asked what we could do to help them, the answer was nearly always the same: "We are fishers of the sea. We want to fish again?"

There was one tense incident. We were surrounded by a crowd led by a large man we later discovered was the town leader. They seemed upset. Not knowing their intentions, we were getting scared.

Through an interpreter we heard, "You people come to our town with your cameras, take pictures and make many promises. Then you go home and give us no help. Others receive aid but because we are Muslim and you are Christian, we get nothing."

"Suppose you see someone who needs food or clothing and you say, 'Well, good-bye and God bless you; stay warm and eat well' — but then you don't give that person any food or clothing. What good does that do?" (James 2:15-16)

We made a promise to the crowd and the town of Kalmunai that we would not abandon them. Our group had traveled a long way to do something good. We were about to have our opportunity.

Amidst the rubble, I picked up a cluster of fishing net and showed it to several men as they described their desire to go back to work. "We must fish to survive!" they emphasized.

Our guide told us that for approximately $3,000, a new fishing boat equipped with a motor and nets could be built in Sri Lanka. With each new boat, four families could go back to work.

Before leaving Kalmunai, we stopped at the home of our guide, R.K. Jeyakumaran, to visit his family and enjoy dinner. While there, we noticed a six-foot-high, dark line on every wall in the house.

Mr. Jeyakumaran described how the waves swept through, leaving the watermark. Both, he and his wife sought safety on the roof, only to watch helplessly as their son and daughter were swept away. Both children were later found alive, but the reality and the horror of the tsunami was evident on his tear-filled face.

Still, despite the tragedy, we were beginning to find signs of God's presence. Through the eyes of this godly family, we witnessed hope mixed with grief and we saw — in them and others — a strong determination to rebuild and start anew.

In the Bible, the book of Lamentations is written for a community facing tragedy: *"The thought of my suffering and homelessness is bitter beyond words. I will never forget this awful time as I grieve over my loss. Yet I still dare to hope when I remember this: The unfailing love of the Lord never ends! By his mercies we have been kept from complete destruction. Great is his faithfulness; his mercies begin afresh each day. I say to myself, 'The Lord is my inheritance; therefore, I will hope in him.'"* (Lamentations 3:19-24)

God never guaranteed a life free from suffering and tragedy. What He did promise is this: *"The unfailing love of the Lord never ends."* This is the assurance we must cherish, especially in the midst of unspeakable suffering. *"The Lord is my inheritance; therefore, I will hope in him."*

As the church, we are called by God to respond to suffering and tragedy wherever and whenever we find it. As we step out in faith, we not only discover the joy of helping others, but also experience the very presence of God.

In just three short days in Sri Lanka, we discovered tragedy beyond comprehension. But we also found practical needs we could meet:

1. The Kalmunai community needed fishing boats. The cost would be only $3,000 each if built in Sri Lanka. Each boat would provide four families a living income.
2. Funds distributed through reliable local contacts will stretch considerably farther than supplies purchased and shipped. We established connections and knew we could make a difference.

I left Kalmunai, forever saddened by the horrific tragedy we witnessed. Yet, I also left Sri Lanka hopeful, discovering a strong sense of familial love and a hardy determination to survive. God seemed to give our little group a unique opportunity for ministry which could make a real difference in Kalmunai, Sri Lanka. *"Great is his faithfulness; his mercies begin afresh each day."*

During the long, 36-hour flight home, the four of us made plans to share pictures and stories. We vowed to work together to raise funds throughout the community in order to purchase as many fishing boats as possible for Kalmunai. We set our goal at 10 to 15 fishing boats, but at the time we wondered if it would be possible.

Our Community Reaches Out to Kalmunai

Within days of our return, people throughout the area responded. Money was raised by various churches to purchase boats, but groups and families also adopted the fishing boat idea as projects.

- One family in the real estate business donated the proceeds from the sale of a house toward a boat.
- A local bank board pooled their resources after their annual meeting and donated enough to purchase a boat.
- Sunday school classes, youth groups and women's groups throughout the area worked to purchase boats.

By the end of the campaign, our community far surpassed our goal of 10 to 15 boats, eventually purchasing 33 boats for the people of Kalmunai. In addition, other donations were funneled directly to contacts made in Sri Lanka, preventing unnecessary confusion and expenses. But perhaps more importantly, a sense of hope was restored to Kalmunai as one community aided another.

Despite heroic efforts to provide fishing boats, there were complications even after the new boats arrived. Rev. Davidson, CEO of Gleaning For The World, told us that, as the first fishing boats arrived in Kalmunai, nothing happened; no one would actually venture out to sea to fish.

We discovered through interpreters that all of the fishermen were afraid to go back out to sea. They were afraid of the possible return of the tsunami, but even more tragically, afraid of catching fish in the same water that contained lost loved ones who were washed out to sea. They told the interpreter: "The possibility of eating fish that ate our relatives is just too much to bear."

Finally, to satisfy our need for photographs, several volunteers agreed to take the new boats out. They immediately caught a record number of fish! This was interpreted as a positive omen from God so families from all over Kalmunai once again could return to their livelihood.

Four people left a small city in Virginia to travel half way around the world to Sri Lanka. At one point, I wondered if we were doing the right thing spending money to travel that could be better used to help those in need. Once we arrived however, we knew God brought the four of us together for a divine purpose.

- Ray Buchanan was our ever-present guide. His extensive experience traveling throughout the world, offering aid to those in need, helped the rest of us quickly go where we were needed most.
- Len Stevens, through his TV news reports, told the story of our trip and what happened so effectively that our entire community was motivated to take the action needed to help Kalmunai.
- Rev. Ron Davidson became the coordinator for the distribution of aid when we returned to lynchburg. Through his efforts and contacts, the money that was raised made a huge difference.
- I was the church contact. The involvement of our church set an example and encouraged other churches to join our efforts.

Len Stevens remarked, "Normally, as a media person, my job is to present the news without bias or getting personally involved. But this time was different. I could tell the story and know that I was also encouraging the people of Lynchburg to make a difference for the people of Kalmunai."

Still there was one thing we all missed out on: We never got the opportunity to see the looks on the faces of the leader and the people in Kalmunai when those 33 boats arrived. Someday, we hope to go back and revisit our newfound friends. Who knows — maybe we can do a little fishing.

SEE THE LIGHT

In a country that is primarily Hindu and Muslim, the Christian church is making a difference and has become a significant source of aid and relief. Although it was outside our comfort zone, we accepted God's challenge and he gave our little group an opportunity for ministry that will have a real impact. *"Great is his faithfulness; his mercies begin afresh each day."*

SHARE THE LIGHT

1. Tragedy can strike individuals, families and whole communities. What has been the most recent tragedy in your life?
2. How has the tragedy in your life shaped your faith in God?
3. How can you or your church become better prepared to offer help to others in times of crisis?
4. Sri Lanka has been involved in a bitter civil war for many years. There was a temporary lull in the fighting shortly after the tsunami, but the war has resumed. Many of the people we helped are once again victims. Please join me in praying for the village of Kalmunai and the people of Sri Lanka.

Notes:

_____

_____

_____

_____

_____

_____

_____

_____

_____

_____

_____

_____

_____

_____

_____

LIVE THE LIGHT: The Lighthouse in Action

Every church should have "hands-on" involvement with at least one humanitarian aid agency or denominational mission agency. Here are two that have helped our church stay involved in areas outside our own community:

- **Gleaning for the World** secures medical supplies (new), furniture and other necessities that otherwise would be disposed of or destroyed in this country and provides them to impoverished or devastated areas both in the U.S. and around the world. (www.gftw.org)
- **Stop Hunger Now** works to send food where it is needed most, both on an emergency basis and by coordinating food and medical aid projects around the globe. (www.stophungernow.org)

Your Action Ideas:
What agencies in your community can you and your church become more involved with?

1. _____

2. _____

3. _____

"I just returned from a mission trip to Venezuela where I was asked to speak at the English-speaking Baptist church in Maracaibo. This was a spur-of-the-moment request and I was rescued by your weekly devotionals. The volunteer mission group held devotions each morning, and I had taken my copies of your weekly series. What a blessing! Thank you for your work and your commitment to serving God. It is amazing how God can use our everyday activity to spread the Gospel. Sowing Seeds of Faith is presented in such down-to-earth fashion that it truly reaches people. You don't have to be a theologian to understand the message." —Your sister in Christ, Jean

FRIDAY—Simplify

Your church cannot do as much until you decide to do more!

Jesus called out to them, "Come, be my disciples,
and I will show you how to fish for people!"
And they left their nets at once and went with him.
Matthew 4:19-20

People often ask: "Larry am I doing what God wants me to do?" Since I often ask this question of myself, I use ten questions to regularly guide my ministry and spiritual life. Recently, I shared them in church and several people asked for a copy. *(Well, actually it was just my mom, but she seemed genuinely interested.)* Maybe you will find these questions helpful, too. But first, a word of caution: Don't think you have to check off everything or feel guilty about what you are not doing. These questions are simply meant to be a practical guide for you and your church.

1. **Do you pray regularly?** It sounds simple, yet nothing happens without prayer. Personal struggles often seem magnified when your prayer life slacks off. Does your church emphasize prayer as a regular and critical part of ministry? Prayer is always step one.
2. **Do you have a vision?** It is difficult to shoot an arrow if there is no target. So how can you function without a vision from God and goals to help you fulfill the vision? What talents and resources are available to you? To your church? What is needed in your community?
3. **Are you growing in faith?** Spiritual formation is a continuous journey of learning, experiencing and sharing the Word of God. Young and old are discovering a passion for God's Word but don't always know where to begin. Bible studies and small groups play a key role in spiritual development. Start a Bible study, participate in Sunday school or join a prayer group.
4. **Are you caring for others?** What are you doing to maintain loving contact with friends and family? Do you regularly offer encouragement? What is your church doing to care for each other? Most offer shepherd groups, support ministries or prayer chains. Perhaps you can help. The simple gesture of sending a card is a ministry that often works miracles.

5. **Do you cultivate friendships above and below your own age?** If you don't, why not? Maybe you need to get a life! Just kidding ... but it's important that you reach beyond your comfort level and seek to understand other age groups. You will learn a lot and probably have a great time. Young and old alike have so much to offer, but they both need our love and respect.

6. **Are you involved in a community ministry?** Is there a Habitat for Humanity near by? Am I doing anything for children at Christmas? Are groups fixing broken down houses for people too poor or sickly to make their own repairs? Is there a Meals on Wheels? Every community has needs. To meet those needs, God has given us all unique talents. What are you doing with yours? It's usually not that hard to find out what's needed and ask: "How can I help?"

7. **Are you a witness?** Do people really know what you believe? How can you talk about God without others feeling intimidated or offended? Do coworkers look upon you as someone they can trust? Will you listen to their concerns with respect and love? Are you praying for opportunities to share your faith? The best definition for being a witness is the willingness to make a sincere and honest attempt to be a friend in the name of God.

8. **What about men?** Sixty-one percent of those not attending church are men. Maybe you can help by starting a ministry for them. Mission trips, building projects and sports have all proven to be successful ways to include guys. Many come back to participate in other church activities.

9. **Are you reaching single adults?** More than 56 percent of the unchurched population is single. Surveys indicate that many single adults believe in God but feel isolated from the church. We can start recognizing their needs by changing our language. "Family Night" supper implies that one must be married to attend. Instead, call it a "Fellowship and Fun" supper. Ministry ideas could include divorce and grief recovery workshops or single parent programs.

10. **What about children?** Parents are struggling to provide a wholesome environment for their children. It usually starts at Sunday school and they often need your help as a teacher or volunteer. There are other ideas such as: after-school ministry, Parent's Day Out or MOPS.

"I can't possibly do all that!" True, but you can do something. My prayer is for these questions to stimulate your thinking. Then, let God guide you. We all face a challenge to reach out in ministry in creative ways. The most important thing is to be open-minded, be in prayer and celebrate the victories.

In the last few years, I have witnessed many people inspired by God to become involved in ministry. It has been the biggest joy of my life. The excitement of doing something worthwhile for God is more contagious than a flu epidemic and the results are far more lasting and satisfying.

So, what are you waiting for? Find your ministry today and may God be with you! Whether your church is big or small, God can create miracles. But don't take my word for it... read on.

The Little Church that Could!

Do you remember the famous children's book by Watty Piper, *The Little Engine that Could?* A train full of toy animals, dolls and every kind of thing boys or girls could want was stranded and could not get over the mountain to the village of children on the other side. What would they do?

A shiny new engine, when asked by the dolls and toys to help, replied, "I pull the likes of *you?* I am a passenger engine. Indeed not!"

A big engine, stopped by the toy clown waving a flag said, "I am a freight engine. I am a very important engine indeed. I won't pull the likes of you!"

A rusty old engine, when asked, replied: "I am so tired. I must rest. I can not. I can not. I can not."

The dolls and toys next asked a very little engine. Seeing the tears in their eyes, he replied, "I'm not very big, but I think I can. I think I can. I think I can."

"Puff, puff, chug, chug, went the Little Blue Engine. 'I think I can... I think I can... I think I can... I think I can...'"

We all know the end of the story. "'Hurray, hurray,' cried the funny little clown and all the dolls and toys. 'The good little boys and girls in the city will be happy because you helped us, kind, little blue engine.' And the little blue engine smiled and seemed to say as she puffed steadily down the mountain: 'I thought I could. I thought I could. I thought I could. I thought I could.'"

There are plenty of churches who behave much like the engines in the story. There is the shiny new church that says to people in need: "I'm too busy paying for my new building!" There are large, mega-churches who reply: "I'm too busy with my own ministries." Then, there are far too many established churches struggling to survive who say: "I'm too tired and discouraged to help you!"

Meanwhile, there are people all around them who desperately need to hear the hope of God that only the church can offer.

There was one very little church, however, which had once been vibrant and full of life, but now was struggling. On a typical Sunday morning there would only be 10 or 12 people in attendance. But they prayed about the needs of their community and two from their church joined a year-long intensive Bible study. During one class, both people felt the need to open their very little church to an after-school ministry for local school children.

"With God's help," they both said, "I think I can ... I think I can ... I think I can!"

Within a few weeks, 30 children were being dropped off at that very little church. They were greeted with cookies and began an hour-and-a-half of fun, music, games and Bible study. Over the next few months and years, some of those children, along with their parents, began attending that little church.

"With God's help, I think I can ... I think I can ... I think I can!"

One man in the same community had a heart attack and nearly died. While in the hospital, he made a vow to serve God more faithfully and come to this same very little church. Another man, discouraged with church life brought his whole family, looking for a fresh start. Both men became a source of inspiration and motivation for others.

"With God's help, I think I can ... I think I can ... I think I can!"

A new, year-long Bible study was ready to start, but this time the very little church had its own class full of people who were looking for answers and seeking ways to serve God. One woman in the class persuaded her whole family to join the Bible study, while another woman began teaching youth in the Sunday school. A couple living together repented of their sin and ask to be married in the little church. The class even formed a choir.

"With God's help, I think I can ... I think I can ... I think I can!"

"Hurray, hurray," cried the preacher and people everywhere as this very little church — now much bigger — smiled and puffed steadily on in the service of God: "With God's help, we thought we could ... we thought we could ... we thought we could!" And God replied: "Well done, good and faithful servant."

With God's help, you can too! It all starts with becoming a disciple.

Disciples

Our message one Sunday morning introduced the twelve disciples who followed Jesus. Interestingly enough, twelve young people happened to be joining our church that same Sunday. So, twelve empty chairs were placed up front and, as the name of each disciple was read, one child came quietly forward to sit in an empty chair.

The message was simple but profound. Jesus said to the disciples and says to each of us: "Follow me!" As the names were called and children took their seats, they symbolized real disciples. I also remembered several recent and vivid examples of real disciples within our own congregation.

Friday night, I was called to the home of a woman facing more chemotherapy because cancer, which she had battled twice successfully, had returned. She cried, talked to her family, gathered strength and then after a prayer announced with a steely look of determination: "Larry, I'm ready! I'll see you Sunday and I'm coming with a smile."

The next morning, I visited a family caring for their son who was dying of cancer. It was a sad situation, but no one was complaining as they rallied their resources and gave him the best possible care they could. They also continued to come to church, secure in the knowledge they would receive strength to carry on.

"One day as Jesus was walking along the shore beside the Sea of Galilee, he saw two brothers ..."

Rain now covered the windshield as I drove to check on a house that needed roof repairs. The woman inside was too poor to have it fixed, so two churches, including ours, worked together to put up her roof. Jim, the foreman of the project wrote: "I had visions of many youth scurrying around picking up discarded old shingles. What really happened was a total surprise. Our church only provided a couple of folks, but the other church showed up with many volunteers, none of them under 60 years old.

"An 89-year-old lady discarded her walking cane and, for over an hour, stooped to pick up roofing nails, raked shingles and inspired others to do the same. Other elder members of the church would load them into trash cans and cart them over to the dumpster. Not only was this an inspiration, but the work was followed by a delicious lunch served by the same older people. The fellowship was wonderful and the conversations, mixed in with the pounding of roofing nails, served to replenish friendships."

"... he saw two brothers — Simon, also called Peter, and Andrew — fishing with a net, for they were commercial fishermen."

Coming back to prepare for Sunday worship, I noticed a familiar truck in the parking lot. Wallace was busy, working in the garden. For months, he and a dedicated crew of volunteers had been patiently planting, weeding and watering to turn a newly-finished construction project into a place of beauty.

Later in the afternoon, I joined Percy and Shirley to celebrate their 50th wedding anniversary. Included with their friends and family was a Sunday school class formed only three years ago. This class bonded in a very short time and learned to support each other through crisis as well as celebration.

"Jesus called out to them, 'Come, be my disciples, and I will show you how to fish for people!'"

On Saturday evening, staff and volunteers came together to serve dinner to 20 of our youth before they left for various school proms. The idea actually came from the youth, who wanted to share this special time together and with their church. So, they received a wonderful meal served personally by the church staff and were treated like royalty.

"We have a surprise," I announced. "Your limousine has arrived." There were squeals of delight from the youth until they peeked outside and saw the limo was actually our old church van driven by Donnie, the youth pastor. "Maybe next time."

"And they left their nets at once and went with him." (from Matthew 4:18-20)

One by one, children playing the 12 disciples continued taking their places. But we still had a problem. Who would be Judas Iscariot? No one wanted to be the person who betrayed Jesus. So we left one chair empty, signifying our hope there would be no Judas at our church. Yet, this also meant one child would not go up front. Who would be left out?

Without hesitation, someone generously volunteered and we promptly gave her another role. Our newest members received Holy Communion, the sacred gift of Christ's body and blood, and then helped us serve the congregation. What an extraordinary moment!

You don't have to be special to be God's Church or Christ's disciple. You simply have to say *yes* to God when He calls, "Follow me!"

SEE THE LIGHT

The little church said, "With God's help, we thought we could ... We thought we could ... We thought we could!" And God replied, "Well done, good and faithful servant." With God's help, you can too! It all starts with becoming a disciple.

SHARE THE LIGHT

1. Are you doing what God wants you to do? Have you found your purpose?
2. How are you helping your church become more active in reaching out to others?
3. How can the ten questions on pages 223-224 guide you and your church?
4. How are we like the disciples Jesus called into ministry?
5. Have you said *yes* to the call of Christ: "Follow Me?"

Notes:

_____

_____

_____

_____

_____

_____

_____

_____

_____

_____

_____

_____

_____

_____

LIVE THE LIGHT: The Lighthouse in Action

Pre-Thanksgiving Meal. It started as a meal for our divorce recovery group, so they could be with each other just before Thanksgiving. Then we discovered that many other single adults and families who were too far from home were looking for an opportunity to be with friends. Now our Pre-Thanksgiving meal is one of the most-attended meals of the year.

Advent Wreath Night. One person asked for help in making an Advent wreath and soon we had a class. We discovered this is a great opportunity to learn a new craft skill and make new friends. Family Craft Night started for the same reason but continues all year long.

Scrapbook Club. This has become a cottage industry, but in our church it is a great opportunity for moms to get together.

Free Child Care. This is a must for any church trying to start new ministries or groups. We deliberately schedule many of our ministries and small groups to meet at the same time and provide child care so that child care is not an issue for anyone interested in attending.

Your Action Ideas:
Look again at all the ideas presented today. Which ones can you or your church do?

1. _____

2. _____

3. _____

"Often the church is referred to as light. Like a moth, I am drawn to the light. Sometimes I fly close and enjoy the warmth. Other times I stray into the dimly-lit area and fly my own way. God allows me to dart out into the dark, but I am always drawn back to the light of the church." —Jim

SATURDAY—Start Shining

In order to start shining, you must first turn on the light.

"If any of you wants to be my follower," he told them, "you must
put aside your selfish ambition, shoulder your cross, and follow me.
If you try to keep your life for yourself, you will lose it.
But if you give up your life for my sake
and for the sake of the Good News, you will find true life."
Mark 8:34-35

There is a parable about a wild goose shot down by a local hunter. Only wounded in one wing, the goose landed safely in a barnyard. Naturally, the local turkeys and chickens were quite startled by this sudden visitor from the sky. As they became more comfortable with the stranger, however, it was only natural to ask about what they had seen but never experienced: "Tell us what it's like to fly!"

"It's wonderful!" said the Goose, who told story after story of his flights. "It's so beautiful to soar out in the wild blue yonder! Why this barn looks only an inch high and all of you look like tiny specks from such a distance. First you fly high and then you can glide and enjoy the astonishing scenery."

All the birds were quite impressed by the goose and his stories. Later they asked him to tell more about his high-flying adventures. Soon, it became a weekly event for the goose to entertain all the barnyard birds. They even provided a little box for him to stand on so everyone could see him better.

But the strangest thing happened; or maybe I should say *never* happened. While the domestic birds very much enjoyed hearing about the glories of flight, they never tried to fly themselves. And the wild goose, even though his wing had healed, continued to talk about flying but never actually flew again.

As a church pastor, I find this parable frightening. Why? Because it hits too close to home. How easy it is to talk about being a Christian without acting like one. How easy to stand in church and say, "Jesus is Lord," without actually turning our lives over to His direction. How easy for us to sit in our comfortable seats and ignore a world in desperate need of our witness. How easy for us to talk ministry without actually doing anything.

Talk is easy; we must flex our muscles and really flap our wings to actually *fly*.

Jesus spoke to his disciples about what it takes to fly: *"'If any of you wants to be my follower,' he told them, 'you must put aside your selfish ambition, shoulder your cross, and follow me. If you try to keep your life for yourself, you will lose it. But if you give up your life for my sake and for the sake of the Good News, you will find true life.'"* (Mark 8:34-35)

"Shoulder your cross and follow me." Other versions of the Bible quote: *"Take up your cross and follow me."* I used to think the cross stood for the pain of being a Christian. In other words: If you really want to follow me, you must be willing to endure pain and suffering. This is not very exciting; nor is it completely true. Although pain strikes us all, it's not what Jesus had in mind. If this were about pain, we would all keep "pain diaries" to see which one suffers the most and "pain winners" would go to heaven.

So, what does it truly mean to shoulder your cross and follow Christ?

Well, you're not going to believe this, but I think Jesus is talking about flying. *(What, Larry? Have you lost your mind? Where is flying mentioned in the Bible?)*

Jesus is talking about being committed to our mission. Jesus accepted suffering because that was his purpose. The cross was his ultimate assignment and he was committed to seeing it through to the end. A bird's purpose is to fly; but he must first be committed to the work and effort of flapping his wings over and over again. Our decision to take up the cross of Christ and follow God regardless of the cost is our commitment to "flap our wings" and to keep flapping until we finally fly.

And make no mistake: Flying is the best part. It may be safer to stay in the barnyard, but look at what we miss. Imagine the beauty of soaring as we ride the air currents. If we always live carefully, protecting and watching our own self-interests; if we make no effort for anyone but ourselves, we will miss the very best part of life — knowing our God-given mission and having the satisfaction of carrying it out to the best of our ability.

A song from the musical *Godspell* said it best: "Day by day, day by day: Oh, dear Lord, three things I pray: To see thee more clearly; Love thee more dearly; Follow thee more nearly, day by day." If we learn from God to see more clearly, love more dearly and follow more nearly, we will take up our crosses and *fly!*

SEE THE LIGHT

In Mark 8, Jesus is talking about being committed to your mission. Jesus accepted suffering because that was his purpose. The cross was his ultimate assignment and he was committed to seeing it through to the end. If we want to fly, we must determine our purpose — and then flap like crazy!

SHARE THE LIGHT

1. The goose told great stories but never did fly again. Why?
2. The other birds were impressed but also never flew. Why?
3. How can we go from talking to flapping our wings?
4. The song says it best: "See thee more clearly; Love thee more dearly; Follow thee more nearly, day by day."

Notes:

LIVE THE LIGHT: The Lighthouse in Action

Speaking of flapping your wings… One church in our area was faced with declining membership and attendance. Their location is near downtown, in one of the poorer sections of the city. Rather than give up, several members banded together to start a feeding mission on Wednesday nights. Determined to offer more than food, however, this church also organizes a time of spiritual devotion complete with music. Approximately 100 people come every Wednesday night to eat and share in the worship and fellowship. Churches from all around now join in to make this one of the area's most successful ministries.

Your Action Ideas:
How can you or your church partner with another church to be in ministry to those in need?

1. _____

2. _____

3. _____

"I read the article, 'If You're Going to Fly … You've Got to Flap Your Wings!' I thought about giving up my ministry. God knows my heart. It never ceases to amaze me on how He gently leads me back to where I should be serving. You wrote: 'Jesus is talking about being committed to your mission. Jesus accepted the suffering because that was his mission. The cross was Jesus Christ's ultimate mission and he was committed to seeing it through to the end. A bird's mission is to fly, but you must first be committed to the work and effort of flapping your wings over and over until you learn to fly.' Wow! What timing. God wants me to complete my mission. God wants me to keep flapping my wings. I appreciate your Sowing Seeds Ministry because, through you flapping your wings, others begin to fly in their areas of mission too." —Sue

WHAT HAVE WE LEARNED SO FAR?

Monday—We need light
We need light. Even someone as famous as Elvis Presley
needs a Godly wake-up call. "You could have influenced
millions to follow me. ... What do you have to say?"

Tuesday—Opportunities to Shine
Every day, God gives us a chance to say to the world,
"I don't eat pork."

Wednesday—Becoming God's Lighthouse
Our response should be to say *yes* to God's invitation,
with faith, knowing that serving our Lord is more important
than our occupations, our families and even our very lives.
We say *yes*, trusting God for answers.

Thursday—An Attitude that Shines
God will often give you an opportunity for ministry
which will make a real difference.

Friday—Simplify
With God's help, we thought we could ...
We thought we could ... We thought we could.
And guess what? ... We could!

Saturday—Start Shining
Jesus is talking about being committed to your mission.
Jesus accepted suffering because that was His purpose.

Now, let's put it all together...

SUNDAY—Live the Light

Be the right place at the right time with the right stuff.

God has given gifts to each of you from his great variety of spiritual gifts.
Manage them well so that God's generosity can flow through you.
1 Peter 4:10

Hurricane Katrina ripped through southern Mississippi and Louisiana with a fury like no other storm in history. At first, we were deceived. Television reports showed weather forecasters hunched over in the wind and rain, holding their microphones and hats. There was wind damage, but once the storm blew through, my first thought was: "Maybe it wasn't too bad." But I was wrong. Katrina was a devastating tragedy!

I didn't immediately notice the storm surge — the 20-plus foot wall of water that submerged cities and towns throughout the coastal area. I didn't know about the gaps in the protective levy encircling New Orleans, a city already eight feet below sea level.

I had traveled around the world to Sri Lanka to see damage caused by a tsunami. I never expected to see similar carnage in my own country.

For days, an anxious world watched the plight of thousands trapped in the New Orleans Astrodome and wondered when help would finally arrive. Where was our crisis response team? Where was our leadership?

There were gruesome stories about people fighting each other for survival, and deep down I wondered what my response would be to the horror they were forced to endure.

Yet, for every horror story, there were many more acts of compassion and heroism:

- The helicopter rescue of thousands stranded on rooftops.
- Prayer meetings and acts of sharing in the coliseum.
- Neighbors banded together to help each other.
- Police, medical personnel and rescue workers helping others in the midst of their own losses.

Around the country, people and churches responded quickly with generosity and compassion. Our church set up a display outside of a department store and within four days received enough supplies to completely fill a large tractor trailer. Literally thousands of people brought supplies and donations. Many were going to multiple locations, looking for any opportunity to contribute to the relief effort.

One mother commented: "We were at church when you asked for help receiving relief supplies. The kids were so excited and ready to go. Several people stopped to thank us as they had family in the Katrina-ravaged area. "

Then, one family pulled up and asked if we were collecting for the survivors of the hurricane. They were newly-arrived from New Orleans. They saw what we were doing and wanted to thank us. Well, the goose bumps were rising at this point and I was holding back the tears as one man said, "We will go back soon and rebuild."

A biblical sufferer named Paul wrote: *"I think you ought to know about the trouble we went through. ... We were crushed and completely overwhelmed and thought we would never live through it. In fact, we expected to die. But as a result, we learned not to rely on ourselves, but on God who can raise the dead. And he did deliver us from mortal danger. And we are confident that he will continue to deliver us. He will rescue us because you are helping by praying for us. As a result, many will give thanks to God because so many people's prayers for our safety have been answered."* (2 Corinthians 1:8-11)

In this passage, Paul provides several helpful lessons in how to respond to suffering and tragedy:

1. Overwhelming, crushing trouble could happen to anyone.
2. As a result we learn to rely not just on ourselves, but on God.
3. God will deliver us and continue to deliver us.
4. Our help and prayers are an important part of God's response.
5. We give thanks because so many prayers have been answered.

Two women came out of a store with two full shopping carts and headed toward our donation area. We expected them to hand us one or two items but, instead, one lady reached into the cart, pulled out a book and handed over everything else saying, "They need these items more than we do. Please hurry!"

It was exciting to see the tremendous amount of supplies and money our community raised, but I knew that God wanted more.

My mother was born and raised within five blocks of the beach at Gulfport, Miss., the city nearest to the full fury of Katrina. None of her immediate family lives there now, but we still have personal ties to the area.

One of our church members also had family in the area and helped us make contact with a local church in Pascagoula, Miss., just a few miles away. Rev. Jim Fisher invited our church to send a team to the area to assess the damage and deliver our supplies.

So, within a few days following Katrina, amidst fears of a gas shortage and rumors of looting, we prepared a team to go check out the damage and see what we could do to help.

Seventeen people volunteered: two from the local newspaper, two from our television station, plus two nurses, two pharmacists, one mission building trip coordinator, a deputy sheriff, two truck drivers, four all-purpose folks and me. Later, I would find out how urgently each of them and their various gifts and talents were needed.

We took a 54-foot tractor trailer loaded with water, baby supplies, cleaning materials, flood buckets, medicine and food. We also carried cash for agencies or anyone who needed immediate help, and delivered two police cars donated by our sheriff's department.

The Apostle Peter wrote: *"God has given gifts to each of you from his great variety of spiritual gifts. Manage them well so that God's generosity can flow through you. Are you called to be a speaker? Then speak as though God himself were speaking through you. Are you called to help others? Do it with all the strength and energy that God supplies. Then God will be given glory in everything through Jesus Christ. All glory and power belong to him forever and ever. Amen."* (1 Peter 4:10-11)

God provides gifts and abilities so that his generosity can flow through each of us. For me, as leader, this meant using my gifts and those of our team to trust God's will and do His work. Our team was being sent to bring help and hope to the people of Coastal Mississippi. If we were willing to take risks and make the journey, God would do the rest.

Where were we going? ... I wasn't sure. What would we do? ... I didn't really know. How would we get back? ... I had no idea. But we did know that we must go and trust in God to guide us.

One person suggested we purchase beds to replace the thousands ruined in the flooding. Calling a local retailer, I received a special price on 20 complete twin bed sets. After we purchased them, employees of the store pooled their money and bought sheet and pillow sets for all 20 beds.

But, while driving to Mississippi, I admit that I questioned the wisdom of spending so much money and taking up so much space on the truck for beds when Katrina victims seemed to need food and water. I began to think my decision in this area was a mistake.

We drove all night and arrived early the next morning at a Mobile, Ala., distribution site co-managed by the Red Cross and various churches. We were there early and, as we stood around waiting for something to happen, we began to get a little testy and impatient. This was when I began learning why God provided other members of our team.

Randy, one of our drivers, jumped on a fork lift and started unloading our supplies himself. Within minutes other fork lift operators who had been standing around suddenly began moving.

Ishmael LaBiosa and Danner Evans, our two television reporters, broke out their cameras and started interviewing people in the building. Thinking we were from the national network, the Red Cross manager who ignored us at first, suddenly appeared and began directing everyone to move quickly and get us unloaded.

One of the church leaders pulled me aside and whispered: "Can you guys stay awhile? I haven't seen the Red Cross move this fast since we arrived."

While others were unloading, I began looking for places to send our supplies. A church in Pascagoula needed cleaning supplies and the pastor mentioned another church in Biloxi. After giving me the cell phone number, he cautioned that phone lines were down and I might not reach him. But this would be the first of many miracles. When I called, he answered immediately. "This phone hasn't worked in days," he exclaimed. "How in the world did you get through?"

By now, the team was gathering around, listening to our conversation. I asked the pastor: "What does your church need right now?" And I'll never ever forget his answer:

"We have plenty of water and food for now. This may sound strange, but we actually need beds for the relief workers who will be coming."

Looking up at the team, almost choking with emotion, I asked: "How many beds do you need?"

"I'm not sure ... maybe twenty?"

Twenty beds! The exact number we packed on the truck. Twenty beds ... the number we were urged to procure but had no idea why. Twenty beds! The sign from God we needed in order to know that we were in the right place, at the right time, with the right stuff.

My exhaustion vanished, replaced by newfound hope and enthusiasm as I excitedly shared the story with the rest of our group. Within hours, the 20 beds and other materials were loaded onto another truck. Later that afternoon, we visited the church and pastor and helped unload those beds!

While we were there, Rev. David Cumbest, the pastor, gave us a tour of his church which had been converted to an aid station. The kitchen and halls were used for storage and feeding areas. Sunday school classes became dorm rooms. Even in the sanctuary, pews were moved to the back wall so beds could be set up for tired relief workers.

During the tour, Rev. Cumbest told us how their church suffered: "More than forty percent of our congregation lost their homes. Many more lost their jobs at least temporarily." But at the same time, he talked excitedly about helping literally thousands of people receive supplies and comfort.

I knew we were at the right place. This church was busy making a difference in the midst of tragedy. This would be the first place we would provide cash in addition to supplies. "Use this money to purchase whatever you need. When we go back to Lynchburg we will work with you to continue helping others in this area."

Afterward, several of us started wandering around the church. At the front entrance we met a lady responsible for greeting those needing aid and helping them fill out paper work. Many in this position simply do their job, but this lady considered herself a missionary of comfort.

Each person was greeted with a tender, "Hi sweetie! May I give you a hug? While you're filling out the forms, please tell me what happened and how you're doing." She would listen to each story carefully, with tender compassion — as if that particular family was her most important job. She would then escort each family to the back of the church to receive aid and then help them carry the supplies back to their car.

We discovered later that her home had been destroyed by Katrina but, refusing to give in to discouragement, she worked nearly every day at the church giving aid and comfort to others.

In just one short day, we saw God's miraculous hand at work, bringing beds exactly where they were needed and showing us a church on the front lines helping others despite their own losses. And we witnessed the tender testimony of a woman offering God's encouragement and love.

Later that afternoon, we drove to the waterfront area of Biloxi, Miss., to witness the damage firsthand. At first we were stopped by National

Guard troops stationed all around the beach area. After seeing we were aid workers with members of the press, we were allowed to enter the heavily damaged beach area. It was as if we were entering a war zone. Military vehicles were everywhere and groups of helicopters flew overhead continuously.

No words can describe the enormity of the destruction we saw for miles all around us. The few trees still standing were strewn with paper and plastic over 15 feet high. Looking up, you had to wonder how trash could possibly end up so high in the air. Then you realized: that was the water level. How could it possibly be? Realizing the enormity of so much water sent cold chills through us all.

Houses and businesses along the shore were ripped apart. We would see buildings minus one or two walls, stripped bare of any furnishings. Automobiles were buried in the sand or stacked on top of each other. Virtually everything was destroyed. Yet in the front yard of one house was an ominous sign: "You loot, we shoot." The owner stood guard with his gun cocked and his car parked in the yard.

On one street where an antique store once stood, the owners gathered and reorganized what merchandise they could find and displayed it across the ground where the store once stood. Propped up, standing freely with no walls anywhere was the front door and alongside was a sign: "We Buy, Sell or Trade." Within the door frame was another sign: "No Trespassing." I didn't know whether to laugh or cry at such a strange sight.

But, we also witnessed signs of hope amidst the ruins. While we were there, several people drove by to offer food, clothing and other assistance to those still living in the area. One man unloaded several boxes of canned food and bottled water. He said: "I have more than I need and just want to share."

There is a letter in the Bible that speaks eloquently of our need to share: *"Dear brothers and sisters, what's the use of saying you have faith if you don't prove it by your actions? That kind of faith can't save anyone. Suppose you see a brother or sister who needs food or clothing, and you say, 'Well, good-bye and God bless you; stay warm and eat well' — but then you don't give that person any food or clothing. What good does that do? So you see, it isn't enough just to have faith. Faith that doesn't show itself by good deeds is no faith at all — it is dead and useless." (James 2:14-17)*

Hurricane Katrina was a disaster that cried out for a nationwide response. We do not deserve the name Christian if we ignore their needs.

All of us on the team knew we were brought there by God to bring help. We would not fail to hear God's call.

All the sermons in the world will never adequately show our love to the people affected by hurricane Katrina. Our actions speak so much louder than our words. What we saw in Coastal Mississippi was devastation beyond imagination; yet we also witnessed so many gestures of God's amazing love.

As we returned later in the evening and crossed the bridge from Biloxi into Pascagoula, we noticed yet another powerful example of the remarkable power within Hurricane Katrina. There was a huge barge with a giant crane lying by a section of the bridge. It looked like the crane was there to repair bridge damage, but actually the barge and crane *caused* the damage. Originally the barge was on the beach nearly a mile away. Somehow the storm blew this multi-ton barge across nearly a mile of land, where it smashed into the bridge causing major damage which will take months or even years to repair.

That evening, after driving all night and working all day, we returned to our host church exhausted, expecting to eat our packaged meals and get some rest. However, we were surprised with some wonderful Mississippi hospitality. Several members of the church prepared Jambalaya, a tasty rice dish popular in the area and filled with chicken and sausage. This was church fellowship at its delicious best.

While everyone slept, I printed photographs taken of the damage. One picture was of a lighthouse standing on the beach of Biloxi. Underneath was a pile of rubble from the storm. It was as if the lighthouse stood against the fury of the storm to provide all of us a symbol of hope.

Our church uses a lighthouse as our symbol along with our mission statement: "A light to guide you safely home." We wanted to be a lighthouse for the people affected by Hurricane Katrina.

That photo of a lighthouse standing strong against the storm reinforced and revitalized our own mission of hope and has become a symbol of hope amidst the tragedy of Katrina.

The next morning we traveled to Gulfport, Miss., and I visited the church where my mother attended as a young girl and I was baptized. Unfortunately, no one was there, but another miracle happened that illustrates how God works in the midst of tragedy. Just like David's powerful Psalm of the Shepherd protecting the sheep, God provides guidance and help when we need it most.

"The Lord is my shepherd; I have everything I need." (Psalm 23)

"Can I help you?" said the young man as he strolled across the street toward our mission group. He didn't look dangerous so much as as quirky, with his red goatee and loose-fitting beach shirt. Oh yeah — did I forget to mention he was eating cold spaghetti right out of the can? Quirky is definitely the right word.

"He let me rest in green meadows; he leads me beside peaceful streams. He renews my strength."

"Where are you all from?" Maybe to him, our group of twelve appeared out of the ordinary, standing around an abandoned church in the midst of the damage left behind by Hurricane Katrina in downtown Gulfport. We were supposed to be meeting the pastor, but communications were all but impossible. On the front door someone had nailed several large sheets of paper for members to write messages, letting others know where they were and how they were doing: crude but effective.

"He guides me along right paths, bringing honor to His name."

Our group was frozen in place and rapidly becoming frustrated. We quickly discovered excellent contacts in Pascagoula and Biloxi, Miss., who would enable our church to send future supplies and teams of workers to help them rebuild. We needed someone in Gulfport, too; but instead we found ourselves standing around talking to a guy eating cold spaghetti out of a can. Now what would we do?

"Even when I walk through the valley of death, I will not be afraid, for you are close beside me."

Sensing our frustration the young man again asked: "Can I help you?" Figuring there was nothing to lose, others gathered around and I began telling him of our journey from Lynchburg, Va., and our need for a contact in Gulfport. Others also excitedly chimed in. He listened intently, occasionally interrupting to ask questions. Then he looked at each of us and said, "Let me show you something."

"Your rod and staff protect and comfort me. You prepare a feast for me in the presence of enemies."

We followed him across the street toward a typical downtown structure marked only by a dingy, gray-colored brick wall and a door with a sign overhead: "The Extreme Teen Center." Inside we discovered the ultimate teen hangout, complete with wild posters, strobe lights and even a stage for the rock band. In this quirky young man who quite obviously had a heart for youth ministry, we found our third contact.

"You welcome me as a guest anointing my head with oil. My cup overflows with blessings."

"My name is Brad Holt with Coastal Mississippi Youth for Christ. We provide youth ministry for hundreds of churches and faith groups in the area. God must have sent your group to us because our ministry is to support volunteer work teams and provide a place to sleep. If you can give us cots and bedding materials, we'll supply the rest."

"Surely your goodness and unfailing love will pursue me all the days of my life ..."

Immediately, our group gathered and we pooled our resources to provide funds for the cots. Then we continued talking with him to make plans for future work teams.

Later, while walking the debris-covered streets of Gulfport and surveying the damage, we marveled at how, even in the midst of the chaos and tragedy of Katrina, God delivered exactly the answer we needed.

"... and I will live in the house of the Lord forever." (Psalm 23)

All too soon, it was time to leave Mississippi for the long trip home. While saying goodbye to our hosts and new friends, we sensed a mission which will keep us working together for months, even years, to come. Mostly, we rediscovered God as our loving shepherd, even in the midst of disaster.

Looking Back

Because we were there quickly and returned with much-needed information, we were able to provide even more help for Mississippi than we did for Sri Lanka. Contacts made in Pascagoula, Biloxi, and Gulfport, helped us to send thousands of people and tons of supplies from churches and communities all over Virginia. Most of the teams stayed with the church led by Rev. David Cumbest in Biloxi.

Later, Rev. Cumbest visited our church in Lynchburg, Va., to personally say thank you. He also urged us not to forget what happened. "Rebuilding will take years, not months," he reminded. "We need all the help you can provide. More than that, we need the godly hope you bring with you."

Later, Rev. Ron Davidson, my Sri Lanka buddy with Gleaning For The World, once again played a major role in the relief effort, sending hundreds of truckloads of supplies wherever they were needed. Then, thanks to a generous furniture manufacturer, Gleaning For The World also sent dozens of tractor trailer loads of new furniture that had been donated to help families rebuild. Our media people, including the newspaper and TV, were able to provide a steady stream of pictures and stories to keep our community informed and involved.

Danner Evans, a reporter with WSET-TV wrote: "I lived on the Gulf Coast for two years [and] spent time in Louisiana, Mississippi and Alabama. When Katrina hit, my friends were evacuating. When you've lived there and know the people affected, you feel like it's happening to you, too. How could I sit in the comfort of my Virginia home, far away from a place that I loved [that was] writhing in pain?

"I think we all looked within and said 'What can I do?' I've been blessed with a job in the media. I have the ability to reach thousands of viewers in this region of Virginia. So, the answer was easy: Use the airwaves to tell stories and raise money to help.

"When we got there it was something; I couldn't put my arms around it all. I wasn't prepared. It was hard not to stare. It was hard not to cry. It was hard to sit down because there was so much to do. I went with a microphone, but often ended up unloading relief supplies, holding hands and giving hugs. It was impossible for me to remain an objective observer. I don't think you cover a tragedy or event of this proportion and remain the same person you were before.

"I didn't see God in the destruction. I saw God in the relief and the love that spread over the Gulf region after Katrina. The churches were the places where everyone ran for help, the places that organized and fulfilled the needs. The federal government couldn't do it. The states couldn't do it. God's church, the congregations across the country and around the world [stepped] in and filled the extreme gaps. How could you not see God all over the place?"

Ismael LaBiosa added: "Working with ABC-13 News officially brought me to the affected area from Hurricane Katrina. As a Christian, I had another obligation to give hope and lend a hand. I'll never forget driving through Biloxi. It was astonishing to see only foundations where historic homes and hotels once stood. It looked like an atomic bomb went off. I also flew in a blackhawk helicopter over the damaged area. It was unbelievable to see enormous shrimp boats sitting on highways and giant floating casinos crashed into tall hotels. Even the smell so far up in the air was unbearable. The smell was even worse on the ground.

"It was hard retelling folks back home what I saw. I think our community stepped up in time of need. I know many donations were made from our area. This experience made me realize how we depend on each other for even simple supplies used everyday. I think it's so important to love each other and to lend a hand anywhere when someone needs it.

"I see God everywhere. He is there with the hurricane victims now. He was there when the hurricane came. I know we need to trust Him and know He won't give us more than we can handle. I only hope that I would have their strength and faith to make it through tough times."

SEE THE LIGHT

Twenty beds. The exact number we packed on the truck. The number we were urged to procure with no idea why. Twenty beds. The sign from God we needed in order to know that we were in the right place, at the right time, with the right stuff.

A biblical sufferer named Paul wrote: "*I think you ought to know about the trouble we went through ... We were crushed and completely overwhelmed and thought we would never live through it. ... But as a result, we learned not to rely on ourselves, but on God. ...And he did deliver us from mortal danger. And we are confident that he will continue to deliver us.*" (*excerpts from 2 Corinthians 1:8-11*)

When we answer *yes* to the call of God, He will give us the answers, resources and courage to do far more than we ever imagined possible. In short, He will put us in the right place, at the right time, with the right stuff. And we will witness miracles.

SHARE THE LIGHT

1. Hurricane Katrina brought amazing responses from people, groups and churches all over the country. How did your church respond?
2. Suffering can happen to any of us at any time. Where is God when we suffer?
3. As Christians we are called to respond. What are some possible responses?
4. Occasionally we are called to respond not knowing where God is leading us. I call it a risk factor. How can we learn to place more of our trust in God to guide us?
5. The people in Coastal Mississippi and Louisiana are still rebuilding and will be for years to come. What can your church do to help?

Notes:

_____

_____

_____

_____

_____

_____

_____

_____

_____

_____

_____

_____

_____

_____

_____

_____

LIVE THE LIGHT: The Lighthouse in Action

Mission Mississippi. Our church has been blessed through helping others, particularly in the hurricane-ravaged Gulf coast area of Biloxi, Miss. Rev. David Cumbest, pastor of Heritage United Methodist Church, near Biloxi, had this to say: "When the world we lived in was suddenly washed away, many cried out 'Why Me?' Many who lived on the edge of the chaos and were spared, quietly asked, 'Why not me?' For the people of God, the answer to the 'why not' should be easy: We are blessed so that we may be a blessing. From the promise of Abraham to the practical application of James, God reminds us that we are blessed by God's love, not just so we can feel loved but so that we can share love."

Rev. Cumbest continues to be the contact for anyone wishing to volunteer in the rebuilding efforts. "I don't have any special training for this. I'm just a United Methodist pastor." Cumbest was on-call 24-hours-a-day, meeting the needs of his community. Often he would go from the Sunday morning pulpit to a Bobcat, unloading 18-wheeler trucks of supplies for hurricane assistance. He reorganized the Heritage church building, turning it into a warehouse for supplies where more than 1,500 people were served daily. The sanctuary became a medical center by day and a dormitory by night.

Cumbest's ability to organize the disaster response in the community lead to the construction of a dormitory on church grounds to house volunteers. By December 2006, Heritage had hosted more than 3,500 volunteers, sometimes more than 200 in one week. The teams have helped more than 400 families return to their homes. Cumbest continues to be involved, directing crews for work and training volunteers to help. (Excerpt from the *Mississippi United Methodist Advocate*.)

If you or your church would like to help with the rebuilding effort, you may contact Rev. Cumbest at HeritageUMC@bellsouth.net

Your Action Ideas:
Throughout this book you have read our ideas. How is God leading you? How should you respond?

1. _____

2. _____

3. _____

Thank you for loving me! *by Sue Keen*

God does not want my commitment. The church may want your commitment to a program, committee or small group, but God wants more than a commitment. He wants my full surrender. Like the chorus of the famous hymn: *"I surrender all. I surrender all. All to Jesus, I surrender. I surrender all."*

How do I surrender all when I have been in charge for so long? I love the Lord with all my heart and I am searching and seeking and I am a committed Christian. Therein likes the problem. Committed, but not surrendered to His will. I pray "Thy will be done," but in the back of my mind I am thinking, "What can I do to make the outcome the way I want it to be?" How selfish are my prayers!

Lord Jesus, I need your help. I am but a sinner saved by grace. I don't want to be just a committed Christian. I want to fully surrender to you: my heart, my soul, my mind, my money, my job and my family. What will it take to make me realize you — and only you —can guide me in this life? All these things I have are only temporary. One day I will be going home to be with you.

Help me lead others to Christ. I can't save anyone; only You have given us that free gift of salvation; only You can save. How can I lead anyone to Jesus if I am only committed to you and not fully surrendered to you? I want to change — today, right now, this very minute. I need you now more than ever before. Jesus, do whatever you need to do to help me to surrender my will, my agenda and my life to your perfect will. I give everything to you this day, this minute.

Thank you, Lord, for loving me. Thank you, Lord, for your patience and goodness to me all the days of my life. I have been trying to come to you in my own strength and power and will — and I can't. I can't!

Thank you for loving me, Lord! I am so very unworthy of your love, but I know you love me still.

LIVE THE LIGHT

NOW WHAT?

Live the LIGHT

Love the Lord as we Invite, Grow and
Help others To live like Christ.

I wait quietly before God, for my salvation comes from him.
He alone is my rock and my salvation,
my fortress where I will never be shaken.
Psalm 62:1-2

For the last five weeks, more or less, you have dedicated yourself to read-ing this book. My prayer is that God inspired you in the midst of the process. You may have several action ideas to work on already. But the question you must ask is: "Now what?"

For years, I was too busy becoming a successful businessman. The long hours of work were stressful and required a high degree of passion and dedication. Unfortunately, during those years, I made many poor choices that put my whole life out of balance. Don't misunderstand me. I appreci-ate and value hard work, dedication and passion. I thrive on stress that requires the best of my talents and resourcefulness; but, as with so much in life, too much of a good thing is bad. I became too "successful," too busy for my family, for church and even for God. I was in trouble.

A Psalm writer and King named David struggled with similar issues: *"So many enemies against one man — all of them trying to kill me. To them I'm just a broken-down wall or a tottering fence. They plan to topple me from my high position. They delight in telling lies about me. They are friendly to my face but they curse me in their hearts." (Psalm 62:3-4)* I could feel David's pain.

Everything changed when I took a business trip to Dallas, Texas. The purpose of my trip was to learn how to teach "Born to Win," a motivational seminar designed by Zig Ziglar. While there, I read one of Ziglar's books, *Confessions of a Happy Christian*. Somehow, Ziglar's experiences touched my heart in a way that forever changed my life. I literally could not stop reading this special book.

The next morning, after staying up all night reading, crying, thinking and praying, I gave my heart and soul to Jesus Christ.

The rest of the trip is literally a blur as I soaked up the training, enjoyed the priceless experience of learning from Zig Ziglar, and imagined how excited everyone would be to hear about my newfound faith and how my life would dramatically change.

Change. *Change?* My life had to change! On the flight home, the reality of my decision began to sink in. I was managing a business, not teaching a Sunday school class. I had just made a commitment that would require radical changes in my business practices and how I treated my family, a greater commitment to my church, and improving my relationship with God. Ouch! Now what?

Now what? Maybe it was time to panic — or better yet, listen to David. *"Wait, quietly before God."*

Once again, in Psalm 62, David provides answers: *"I wait quietly before God, for my hope is in him. He alone is my rock and my salvation, my fortress where I will not be shaken. My salvation and my honor come from God alone. He is my refuge, a rock where no enemy can reach me. O my people, trust in him at all times. Pour out your heart to him, for God is our refuge."* (Psalm 62:5-8)

On the plane that evening I poured out my heart to God. And like David, I learned to put my hope and trust in my rock and my salvation, my fortress where I will not be shaken. I needed to drastically change my workaholic ways and and focus on my relationships with my family, my church and my God.

Now what? "God," I prayed, "help me trust in you at all times, for my salvation and honor come from You."

In many ways, everything changed after that flight home and, over time, I learned to put my life and my hectic schedule in God's steady hands. I also became a more devoted husband and father, and increased my church involvement and my one-on-one time with God. But the best part of all is that my business life actually improved as I learned to wait on and trust in God!

Since that time, my life has changed dramatically as I have moved from business leader to church pastor. My obligations are different, but the temptations and frustrations are much the same. More than ever, I rely on the lessons learned in Dallas those many years ago:

- Be willing to pour out your heart to God.
- Put your hope and trust in your rock and salvation.
- Be willing to change what needs to be changed.
- Keep your life in balance, always giving God top priority.

Maybe you, too, are feeling the pressure of a busy and often unfulfilling career. Is your life out of balance with too many commitments and too little time? Have you stretched the limits of your personal resources and come up short?

Maybe it's time to wait quietly before God, remembering that your hope is in Him. He is your rock and your salvation. Pour out your heart to Him — God is your refuge.

Since you are reading this book, I will assume that, at some point, you made a commitment to God. Maybe it was a long time ago. Perhaps it happened recently or even while you were reading this book. Now it's time to put your action plans to work and *Live the LIGHT:*

L   Love our Lord as we
I   Invite,
G   Grow and
H   Help others
T   To live like Christ.

But now what? Is anything holding you back? Remember:

- Be willing to pour out your heart to God.
- Put your hope and trust in your rock and salvation.
- Be willing to change what needs to be changed.
- Keep your life in balance, always giving God top priority.

The commitments you make to God right now could make a big difference to your co-workers, to your community, to your family and to you.

When I was a young boy, I lived in Camden, Arkansas. Any boy who lived in Camden played baseball. That was the tradition. One day, while walking home from baseball practice, I took a shortcut through a neighbor's back yard. There was a chicken coop nearby but I didn't think anything of it. Everyone knew chickens didn't hurt people, right? They just ran around the yard clucking or sat in the hen house laying eggs. I knew these things because, at the ripe old age of eight, boys are cocky and fearless — and dumb.

Everything was fine at first. As I approached, the chickens scattered in every direction. That is, except for one colorful rooster. He stood his ground as if daring me to enter his territory. Our paths crossed, I stopped, and we both stared at each other. At first, nothing happened.

Suddenly, the bird flew at my face. There was no time to think about the proper way to fend off a chicken attack, so I placed my baseball bat between the angry bird and me. The rooster hit the bat, dropped back to the ground and angrily stared at me again. (At least I think he was angry. Do chickens get mad?) Now I was afraid. What would this angry rooster do next?

The answer came soon enough. Once again, the crazed bird flew at my face and again I shoved him back with my baseball bat. Our staring contest lasted at least another three hours. (Well, it seemed like three hours.) For a third time, the rooster flew at my face and again, I pushed him away. He stared at me for a moment, seemed to shrug and walked away.

I cautiously moved away, then made a mad dash for home, crying and sobbing all the way … "Mommy!" Suddenly older and hopefully wiser, I vowed to God and my mother that I would avoid backyard chicken coups.

We all face scary situations. Some fears are rational. Some, as with my chickens, are laughable. But we must learn to cope with fear — whether it's losing a job or a trusted friend, facing sickness or even coping with death. The question is not whether we are afraid; the question is "how will we cope with our fears?"

In Psalm 27, David, the biblical poet king, found himself surrounded by the enemy. Yet, he was still able to write: *"The Lord is my light and my salvation — so why should I be afraid? The Lord protects me from danger — so why should I tremble? When evil people come to destroy me, when my enemies and foes attack me, they will stumble and fall. Though a mighty army surrounds me, my heart will know no fear."* (Psalm 27:1-3) What was David's secret for facing fear?

1. **Declare your reliance on God.** *"The one thing I ask of the Lord — the thing I seek most — is to live in the house of the Lord all the days of my life, delighting in the Lord's perfections and meditating in his Temple."* (Psalm 27:4) David put his faith and trust in God.
2. **Ask for help, boldly.** *"Listen to my pleading, O Lord. Be merciful and answer me. … Do not hide yourself from me. … Do not reject your servant. … Don't leave me now; don't abandon me."* (v. 7-9) You can almost hear David's anguish as he cries out for God.
3. **Trust the Source and timing of the answer.** *"Wait patiently for the Lord. Be brave and courageous. Yes, wait patiently for the Lord."* (v. 14) The Hebrew word we define as "wait" describes the twisting of strands for strength as a rope. Chuck Swindoll writes: "Wait, twist yourself around the strands of God's strength … wait."

Reading this book was challenge number one; but your response may be the toughest challenge of all. *Now what?*

1. Declare your reliance on God.
2. Ask for help boldly.
3. Trust the Source and timing of the answer.

Lisa Beamer lost her husband, Todd, in the terrorist attacks of September 11, 2001. Following this tragedy, Lisa wrote in her book, *Let's Roll: Finding Hope in the Midst of Crisis,* "In that dark moment, my soul cried out to God and He began to give me a sense of peace and a confidence that the children and I were going to be okay. But even that comfort didn't take away the wrenching pain or the awful sense of loss I felt."

Lisa's husband, Todd, also turned to God in the midst of his fiery trial. With a telephone operator, he prayed the Lord's Prayer and recited the Twenty-Third Psalm. He finally whispered "Help me Jesus" several times before calling his fellow passengers to action with the words we now honor: "Let's roll!"

Whatever your fears — chickens or terrorists, imagined or real — move forward, determined to *Live the LIGHT: Love our Lord as we invite, grow and help others to live like Christ.*

Now what? Declare your reliance on God. Ask for help boldly. Trust the Source and timing of the answer. Then, move forward confidently and Live the LIGHT. *Let's roll!*

SEE THE LIGHT

We all face scary situations. Some fears are rational. Some — like the chickens — are laughable. But we must learn to cope with fear — whether it's losing a job or a trusted friend, facing sickness or even dealing with death. Remember what we have learned:

- Be willing to pour out your heart to God.
- Put your hope and trust in your rock and salvation.
- Be willing to change what needs to be changed.
- Keep your life in balance, always giving God top priority.

then...

- Declare your reliance on God.
- Ask for help boldly.
- Trust the Source and timing of the answer.

The question is not whether we are afraid; the question is "how will we cope with our fears?" Will we put our faith and trust in God and move forward confidently, answering His call with a resounding "Yes!"? I pray that we will.

SHARE THE LIGHT

1. Maybe you, too, are feeling the pressure. Is your life out of balance? In what areas?
2. If you were to pour out your heart to God, what would you say?
3. What do you need to change to put your life in better balance?
4. In the midst of change we often face scary situations. How can God help you cope?
5. What steps can you take to put your trust and your life in God's hands?
6. Face your fear. Declare your reliance on God. Ask for help, and trust the Source and timing of the answer. Then, *let's roll!*

Notes:

LIVE THE LIGHT: The Lighthouse in Action

This is the end of the book, but it doesn't have to be the end of our connection. Please visit me at www.SowingSeedsofFaith.com. You will find hundreds of online devotions and helpful articles. You can also sign up for our weekly devotions so that you will continue receiving Bible study, Godly encouragement and helpful ideas for your ministry.

Also, be sure to sign up for our weekly prayer lists so you can be a part of our world-wide prayer team. Up to three times per week you can receive prayer needs from around the world. You can even respond with your own e-mails, offering encouragement and prayers.

My e-mail address is near the bottom of every Sowing Seeds web page. Please send me some of your thoughts and action ideas. You never know, they could appear in one of our weekly columns.

Your Action Ideas:
Now that we've decided to "roll," list the first three actions you can take to answer God's call in your life or the life of your church:

1. _____

2. _____

3. _____

"A few weeks ago I searched for a website of prayer and faith. I happened to see yours and decided to see what it was all about. I desperately needed prayer and my faith in God restored. I put in a prayer request for financial freedom and faith in God. I expected to receive an informal, computer-generated note. What I received instead was awesome. Within a few days I received prayer e-mail from around the world. I made new Christian friends. My faith in mankind was restored. I could hope again. The prayers were so personal. Every single person who responded actually took the time to read what I needed and prayed. ... They contacted me and personally ministered to me: no judgments, reprimands, insults [or] disgust. I received total understanding, Christian love and devotion to my prayer needs. I received advice, encouraging e-mail, understanding for my situation and love, love, love. Thank you for restoring our faith." —Jacqui

REFERENCES

Sowing Seeds Ministry (www.SowingSeedsofFaith.com) has many free, helpful materials, including information on divorce recovery. The Sowing Seeds Prayer Ministry is an excellent way to get involved in sending prayers of encouragement to people around the world. Visit the Sowing Seeds website and sign up today!

Books you may find helpful as you seek to Live the LIGHT:

Buford, Bob. 1997. *Halftime*. Zondervan.
Hybels, Bill. 2002. *Courageous Leadership*. Zondervan Press.
Lewis, Brad. 2006. *Pastoral Ministry in the 21st Century*. Group Publishing
Lucado, Max. 2006. *Cure for the Common Life*. W Publishing.
Nappa, Mike and Amy. 1995. *Bore No More*. Group Publishing
Sjogren, Steve. 2002. *101 Ways to Help People in Need*. NavPress.
Sjogren, Steve. 2001. *101 Ways to Reach Your Community*. NavPress.
Swindoll, Charles R. 2005. *So, You Want to Be Like Christ*. W Publishing.
Wilke, Richard. 1993. *Disciple: Becoming Disciples Through Bible Study*.
    Abingdon Press.
Wilkinson, Bruce. 2000. *The Prayer of Jabez: Breaking Through to the Blessed Life*.
    Multnomah Publishers.

Organizations mentioned in this work:

Gleaning For The World (www.gftw.org)
Heritage United Methodist Church, D'Iberville, Miss.
    Rev. David Cumbest (HeritageUMC@bellsouth.net)
Lamb's Wool Ministry (www.LambsWool.org)
Lighthouse Movement (www.LighthouseMovement.org)
MOPS / Mothers of Preschoolers (www.mops.org)
Parish Nurses (www.ipnrc.parishnurses.org)
Sowing Seeds Ministry (www.SowingSeedsofFaith.com)
Stop Hunger Now (www.stophungernow.org)